THE MYSTERY OF
Spring-Heeled Jack

"Probably no one in the world but John Matthews could have written this book. His scholarship is, as always, of the highest order yet joined to a deep love of stories. His unwillingness to make artificial separations between traditional folklore and popular culture allows Spring-Heeled Jack to come vigorously to life."

RACHEL POLLACK,
AUTHOR OF *THE CHILD EATER* AND
CO-CREATOR OF THE RAZIEL TAROT

"John Matthews intrigues, disturbs, and delights us with his detailed account of the legendary Spring-Heeled Jack who, whether real or not, terrified victims amid the shadows of Victorian London and beyond. Leaping into the fears of the unwary, such figures persist in the modern imagination, and Matthews gives us much to chew on with regard to our fascination with untamed, semi-animal, evil in superhuman guise. Victorian supernaturalism, ghost stories, Jack the Ripper, the Green Man, demonic lore, and much else illuminate the shifting image of 'Jack' in Matthews's crepuscular romp through the ginnels and repressions of fervid times, where unearthly clawing and ripping threatens to confront us with the archetypal fiend."

TOBIAS CHURTON, AUTHOR OF
ALEISTER CROWLEY: THE BEAST IN BERLIN

"Thoroughly researched, John Matthews's writing is effortlessly accessible for both newcomers and those familiar with London's original bogeyman. This book could and should become one of the definitive texts about Spring-Heeled Jack in the years to come."

JACK BOWMAN, COWRITER OF
THE SPRINGHEEL SAGA AUDIO DRAMAS

"For a fascinating guide to the history and mystery of England's most famous phantom attacker, look no further than John Matthews's remarkable book."

ROBERT VALENTINE, COWRITER OF
THE SPRINGHEEL SAGA AUDIO DRAMAS

THE MYSTERY OF
Spring-Heeled Jack

From Victorian Legend to Steampunk Hero

JOHN MATTHEWS

Destiny Books
Rochester, Vermont • Toronto, Canada

Destiny Books
One Park Street
Rochester, Vermont 05767
www.DestinyBooks.com

Destiny Books is a division of Inner Traditions International

Text stock is SFI certified

Library of Congress Cataloging-in-Publication Data

Names: Matthews, John, 1948- author.
Title: The mystery of Spring-Heeled Jack : from Victorian legend to Steampunk hero / John Matthews.
Description: Rochester, Vermont : Destiny Books, 2016. | Includes bibliographical references and index.
Identifiers: LCCN 2016011254 (print) | LCCN 2016023311 (e-book) | ISBN 9781620554968 (paperback) | ISBN 9781620554975 (e-book)
Subjects: LCSH: Spring-heeled Jack (Legendary character) | Urban folklore—England. | BISAC: BODY, MIND & SPIRIT / Supernatural. | SOCIAL SCIENCE / Folklore & Mythology. | HISTORY / Modern / 19th Century.
Classification: LCC GR141 .M37 2016 (print) | LCC GR141 (e-book) | DDC 398.20942—dc23
LC record available at https://lccn.loc.gov/2016011254

Printed and bound in the United States by Lake Book Manufacturing, Inc. The text stock is SFI certified. The Sustainable Forestry Initiative® program promotes sustainable forest management.

10 9 8 7 6 5 4 3 2 1

Text design by Virginia Scott Bowman and layout by Debbie Glogover
This book was typeset in Garamond Premier Pro with Legault, Cambria, Myriad Pro, and Kinesis Pro as display fonts

To send correspondence to the author of this book, mail a first-class letter to the author c/o Inner Traditions • Bear & Company, One Park Street, Rochester, VT 05767, and we will forward the communication, or contact the author directly at **www.hallowquest.org.uk.**

Push me down again, Dear Childe,
I'm safely hid away.
But I'm not gone; it won't be long
Till Jack comes out to play.

ROBERT WINTHROP, "JACK IN THE BOX,"
LONDONTOWN RHYMES FOR THE NURSERY, 1893

Contents

Acknowledgments

I have preferred to give the reports as far as possible in the words with which they were first described at the time rather than retelling them in my own. For this I am grateful to Mike Dash's astonishing collection of newspaper reports collected in the *Fortean Times;* to Stephen J. Ash of *The Complete Spring Heeled Jack Page;* to Anne Avery who generously took time out of her busy schedule to send me more cuttings; and to the staff of the Bodleian Library in Oxford for finding obscure book references. Thanks also, as ever, to Caitlín Matthews for reading several drafts and for making some inspired suggestions, and to Jack Bowman and Robert Valentine for sending me copies of their amazing audio series on Spring-Heeled Jack. The wonderful decoration at the head of each chapter throughout is from Wireless Theatre's *The Springheel Saga,* artwork by Jamie Egerton, used with gratitude and appreciation. Grateful thanks also to the amazing crew at Inner Traditions for making the journey from manuscript to book as easy as possible.

INTRODUCTION

The Unsolved Mystery

*Stories of the wildest and most extravagant nature got into
the newspapers and formed the staple of conversation.*
NEWS OF THE WORLD, NOVEMBER 17, 1872

On October 4, 1888, police investigating the notorious Ripper murders in London received a letter. It was one of several purporting to be from the killer, but this one was different. It was signed "Spring-Heeled Jack—The Whitechapel Murderer."

By 1888 fifty years had elapsed since the reported sightings of Spring-Heeled Jack, and that Jack, for the most part, did very little serious harm to anyone, unlike the Ripper, who was a merciless and horrific killer. Still, the association would not have been lost on Inspector Frederic Abbeline, the lead detective in the Ripper case, and his men. The exploits of the character known as Spring-Heeled Jack were far from forgotten in the time of the Ripper murders, and assuming the letter was not a forgery (which most researchers think unlikely), it is significant that the killer of prostitutes should choose to identify himself with the older, well-established figure of Spring-Heeled Jack.

This Jack, the subject of this book, made his first appearance in January 1838, and the last reported sighting—excluding, for the moment, modern appearances—occurred in 1904. He literally leapt to public attention, springing over hedges and walls, from dark lanes and dank graveyards to frighten and sometimes physically attack women.

1

Fig. I.1. The Whitechapel Murderer

He showed up first in the twilight world of Victorian London, only gradually moving farther out to towns such as Bradford and Sheffield. He moved through a world that, though well connected by roads and canals, was not yet fully served by the new railways; a world where the night was unillumined by gas or electricity and where messages took time to get from place to place.

The reports of the mysterious leaping man in both national and local newspapers fueled a hysterical response and lead to copycat attacks, ghostly tales, and extraordinary claims to his real identity—ramping up the paranoia and boosting Jack's appearance from a white bear to a fire-breathing man.

Spring-Heeled Jack has attracted writers as different as Philip Pullman, Mark Hodder, and Stephen King, as well as numerous references in popular culture from graphic novels to audio plays. Despite previous books and many articles and a catalog of appearances in fiction, TV, and film, Spring-Heeled Jack, though a familiar character from the archives of the strange and unexplained, is almost completely unknown.

People who claimed to have seen Spring-Heeled Jack described him as having a terrifying appearance, with bat-like wings, clawed hands, and eyes that resembled wheels of fire. Other reports claimed that, beneath his black cloak, he wore a huge helmet and a tight-fitting white garment apparently made of oilskin. Others said he was tall and thin, with the appearance of a gentleman. Several reports mentioned that he could breathe blue flames.

In more recent times various researchers have attempted to suggest who he might really have been, including an alien visitor from another planet, but none of these theories hold up to close scrutiny. Instead, we should look for the origins of Spring-Heeled Jack among much earlier mythical figures, conjured into being though hysterical newspaper reports and the Victorian obsession with strange phenomena and sinister figures.

A vast urban legend built itself around Spring-Heeled Jack—influencing and influenced by many aspects of Victorian life for decades—especially in London. His name became equated with the bogeyman, as a means of scaring children into behaving by telling them that if they were not good, Spring-Heeled Jack would leap up and peer in on them at night. Surprisingly, in our own times, new sightings have been reported, while the recent disturbing stories of the Slender Man can be seen to display notable similarities with those of the older Jack (see chapter 7 for more on the Slender Man).

It is these parallels, as well as the original reports, that tell us the real story of Spring-Heeled Jack. I have sought to retell it, as far as possible, in the words of the original newspaper reports and have retained the original spelling and at times aberrant punctuation of these. In accomplishing this, I have had the help of several colleagues, mentioned in the acknowledgments, but I should like to pay tribute here especially to the brilliant, pioneering work of Mike Dash, whose own book on Spring-Heeled Jack remains eagerly awaited. Without his tireless assemblage of contemporary reports, my own work would have been vastly extended.

PART ONE

◻

THE LEGEND

CHAPTER 1

The Birth of a Legend

I came from Pandemonium,
If they lay me I'll go back;
Meanwhile round the town I'll jump,
Spring-Heeled Jack.

ANONYMOUS,
THE PENNY SATIRIST, 1838

The story begins, quietly enough, on January 9, 1838. Several column inches of the London *Times* newspaper for that date contained a report, along with a letter, concerning some strange events that had apparently taken place in Peckham, a quiet suburb of the metropolis.

The Times

TUESDAY, JANUARY 9, 1838

MANSION HOUSE—Yesterday the Lord Mayor said, that he had received a letter upon a subject, the odd nature of which had induced him to withhold it from the public for some days, in the expectation that some statement might be made through a source of indisputable authority relative to the matter of which it treated.

The following is the letter:

**TO THE RIGHT HON.
THE LORD MAYOR**

My Lord,

The writer presumes that your Lordship will kindly overlook the liberty he has taken in addressing a few lines on a subject which within the last few weeks has caused much alarming sensation in the neighboring villages within three or four miles of London.

It appears that some individuals (of, as the writer believes, the higher ranks of life) have laid a wager with a mischievous and foolhardy companion (name as yet unknown), that he durst not take upon himself the task of visiting many of the villages near London in three disguises—a ghost, a bear and a devil; and, moreover, that he will not dare to enter gentlemen's gardens for the purpose of alarming the inmates of the house. The wager has however, been accepted, and the unmanly villain has succeeded in depriving seven ladies of their senses. At one house he rung the bell, and on the servant coming to open the door, this worse than brute stood in a no less dreadful figure than a spectre clad most perfectly. The consequence was that, the poor girl immediately swooned, and has never from that moment been in her senses, but, on seeing any man, screams out most violently: 'Take him away!' There are two ladies (which your lordship will regret to hear) who have husbands and children, and who are not expected to recover, but likely to become a burden on their families.

For fear that your Lordship might imagine that the writer exaggerates, he will refrain from mentioning other cases, if anything more melancholy than those he has already related.

This affair has now been going on for some time, and strange to say, the papers are still silent on the subject. The writer is very unwilling to be unjust to any man, but he has reason to believe that they have the history at their finger-ends, but, through interested motives, are induced to remain silent. It is, however, high time that such a detestable nuisance should be put a stop to and the writer feels sure that your Lordship, as the chief magistrate of London, will take great pleasure in exerting your power to bring the villain to justice.

Hoping you're Lordship will pardon the liberty I had taken in writing,

I remain your Lordship's most humble servant,

A RESIDENT OF PECKHAM

The lord mayor was clearly not impressed. The rest of the article made this clear:

In his opinion . . . if any trick had been practiced by fools, he had no doubt that the vigilance of the police might be depended upon to prevent annoyance. It appeared to him that the letter, which was written in a very beautiful hand, was the production of a lady, who might have been terrified by some burglars into this method of obtaining retribution at the hands of the Lord Mayor, but as the terrible vision had not entered the city, he could not take cognizance of its iniquities. A gentleman stated to his Lordship that the servant girls about Kensington, and Hammersmith, and Ealing, told dreadful stories of a ghost, or devil, who, on one occasion, was said to have beaten a blacksmith, and torn his flesh with iron claws, and in others to tear clothes from the backs of females. Not one of the injured people had been known to tell the story; perhaps they didn't like to tell it. The Lord Major believed that one of the ladies who had lost their seven senses was his correspondent. He hoped she would do him the favor of a call, and he would have the opportunity of getting from her such a description of the demon as would enable him to catch him, in spite of the paid press and public.

The year 1838 had been a dramatic one for Londoners. In January the Royal Exchange, center of British trade and commerce, burned to the ground; in June the young Princess Victoria ascended to the throne, ushering in the longest reign of a monarch in British history; in the winter months, during one of the coldest frosts in recorded history, the Thames froze over. Perhaps the events launched upon the country by the *Times* report might have passed unnoticed, but something about the story touched into more ancient, deeper fears, and in the following months an extraordinary range of reports appeared in the press. Many were, almost certainly, the invention of reporters or editors who saw the story as likely to increase their readership (which it undoubtedly did), but others, if examined carefully, show something else.

The following day, January 10, London's *Morning Chronicle* ran a lengthy story debunking the *Times* report, referring to it as evidence of ridiculous superstition and attacking the credulity of those who placed any credence in it. The article then took a closer look, revealing that this was not in fact the first of such reports and referring to an incident that had taken place on nearby Barnes Common some four months earlier. Here, it was alleged, a large white bull had attacked several people, "particularly females, many of whom had suffered most severely from the fright,"[1] to the point that "no respectable female had since left home after dark without a male companion."[2] The language used here was to occur in several of the reports that followed, each suggesting that "respectable" women (of course only women of another kind were expected to be out alone after dark) had been singled out for these attacks. The report added that in East Sheen, another rural suburb of London, a white bear had carried out similar "pranks."

The article stated:

The Morning Chronicle

WEDNESDAY, JANUARY 10, 1838

[I]n the course of a few days afterwards all Richmond teemed with tales of females being frightened to death and children torn to pieces by the supposed unearthly visitant, who was, in consequence, so closely searched after by the local police that he soon thought it prudent to quit the green lanes of that fashionable resort for the quiet and retired villages of Ham and Petersham, where in the image of an imp of the 'Evil One' he nightly reigned supreme, and neither man, woman, nor child durst venture beyond the threshold of their domiciles without a lantern and a thick club stick. From Petersham, Kingston was the next resort of the alleged supernatural visitant; but, as at Richmond, the police of that borough soon rendered his visit most dangerous to his own safety, and he in consequence crossed the water, when Hampton Wick, Hampton Court &c., soon rung with the mighty deeds of an unearthly warrior, clad in armor of polished brass, with spring shoes, and large claw gloves, who, whenever pursued after frightening not only children but those of an older growth, scaled the walls of Bushy Park, and instantly vanished.

Teddington, Twickenham, Whitton, and Hounslow were next in succession the scene of stories of a similar description, and many and fearful were the tales of injuries inflicted by him in the Duke of Northumberland's demesne of Sion Park, and other parts of the village of Isleworth. Among other things it was stated that a carpenter named Jones, residing in that village, while returning through 'Cut-throat-lane', on his way home, about 11 o'clock at night, was seized and most unmercifully belabored by the ghost, who was attired in polished steel armor, with red shoes, &c. Being a powerful man, Jones instantly grappled with his assailant, when two more ghosts came to the assistance of the first one, when Jones's clothes were torn into ribbons, and 'cast to the winds'. Heston, Drayton, Harlington, and the neighbourhood of the town of Uxbridge, were next the scenes of his tricks; when, returning by the Great Western Railway towards the metropolis, he in turn visited Hanwell, Brentford, Ealing, Acton, Hammersmith and Kensington. At Hanwell, Brentford, Ealing and Acton, he has been represented as clad in steel armor, and, in addition to frightening various persons, severely injured a blacksmith residing in the village of Ealing, who, it is stated, has ever since kept his bed in consequence of the fright he sustained. At Hammersmith an itinerant vendor of pies and muffins, it was reported, was attacked while returning home through Sounding-lane by 'the ghost', and his clothes torn from his back, and one female was stated to have been frightened to death at the idea of meeting him. Even the precincts of the Royal Palace of Kensington have not escaped, children having seen the unearthly being dancing by moonlight on the Palace-green, and ever and anon scaling the walls of the royal forcing gardens, in the direction of the churchyard in Church-street. In consequence of the above ridiculous stories, some parties adopted every means for obtaining information on the subject, and personally visited many of the places above mentioned. It was found that although the stories were in everybody's mouth, no person who had actually seen him could be ascertained. An amusing circumstance, in connection with the reports, is related. A few nights since, as one of the police was on duty in Little Ealing-lane, he heard some person running at full speed toward him, and in a few minutes afterward he met the son of a respectable inhabitant of Old Brentford, who, in a state of the greatest alarm, declared he had seen 'the ghost'. The police-man accordingly proceeded to the spot named by the booby, when he found the inspector on his white horse, awaiting the report of the sergeant of the section, totally unconscious of the alarm he had occasioned. The Hammersmith 'Sounding-lane' statement also turns out to be the invention of some wag; and although it has been stated by many respect-able persons at Brentford that his ghostship had been a few nights since seized by a policeman at Brompton, and, after being nearly killed by the populace, conveyed for examination at Kensington, yet neither the authorities at Kensington, nor persons resident at Brompton, have heard anything respecting him beyond the above reports; and we strongly suspect that the Peckham statement will, on investigation, have a similar result.

One aspect of the story that undoubtedly added fuel was the setting of these first events—rural districts that surrounded the city. Stretches of gorse-covered common land separated houses of size and importance, each standing in its own walled garden, with shuttered windows and high iron gates. These were the homes of wealthy merchant princes who had given up the custom of living over their business premises and had begun to build mansions in the bourgeois peacefulness of the suburbs.

Burglaries were not uncommon, and the fledgling police force, only then beginning to be established in the city, was hard-pressed to cope with these. Footpads (thieves) lurked in the quiet roads, and few people ventured forth at night without an armed escort.

But the stories that began to surface were different, somehow darker. According to the report in the *Morning Chronicle,* sightings of ghosts, an imp, and a devil were included. We can see the imagination of the populace working overtime to discover ways to explain the phe-nomenon of the attacks, searching amid the folklore and superstitions of the time for likely suspects.

We should also notice the word "pranks." At this point the press seemed determined to suggest that the attacks were nothing more than a foolish, lighthearted game played by some despicable, well-to-do young gentlemen who had, as stated in the letter to the mayor, "laid a wager with a mischievous and foolhardy companion" to adopt a series of frightening disguises intended to terrify women and upset others.

Later, when the reports took on a darker tone, this idea was to be repeated a number of times and led to the identification of the "prankster" as a member of the landed gentry (see chapter 5).

Though the article continued to ridicule the whole story and anyone foolish enough to believe it, the same report lists a bewildering array of recent "sightings" in a number of other outlying London boroughs. These included Richmond, Petersham, Kingston, Hampton Wick, Hampton Court, Teddington, Twickenham, Whitton, and Hounslow, among others (see fig. 1.1). In each instance, despite investigation, no

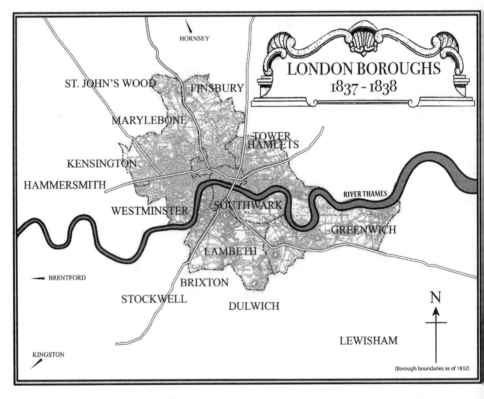

Fig. 1.1. The London boroughs between 1837 and 1838 when
the highest incidence of Spring-Heeled Jack sightings took place
(Map by Wil Kinghan after Richard Furlong)

one had come forward to be identified with the various attacks, frights, and hauntings reported.

A particular detail is worth noting here. In one of the reports, the attacker is described as "an unearthly warrior, clad in armor of polished brass, with spring shoes and large claw gloves." This is the first mention of the particular costume adopted by the "ghost"; in a matter of weeks, this attire would provide him with the name by which he has been known ever since—Spring-Heeled Jack.

Next day, January 11, 1838, a response to the original report was published in the *Times*. Once again the reporter's tone is jokey and frivolous, but the letters from a variety of people—some named, others anonymous—suggested that the original account was very far from being a solitary incident and that some took *these seriously.*

𝕿𝖍𝖊 𝕿𝖎𝖒𝖊𝖘

JANUARY 11, 1838

MANSION HOUSE—The Lord Mayor received the following communications in the course of yesterday . . . relative to the individual who is said to be occupied in winning a wager by appearing in various terrific characters at night in the villages around the metropolis.

My Lord Mayor—The public are much indebted to your Lordship for bringing forward the letter, as stated in yesterday's Mansion House report. Although there is yet no authenticity attached to that part of the letter in which it is stated that lamentable accidents have arisen from this wicked prank, . . . that it has been played [out] lately to a considerable extent in the neighbouring villages I can assure your Lordship to be a fact.

In the neighbourhood of Hornsey, where I have a residence, some scoundrel has been alarming the neighborhood in these disguises, and I heard yesterday . . . [that] the same thing has been played off near Kingston, and from a respectable neighbor in Cheapside that Hertfordshire has been similarly visited.

It is stated that some individual

('gentleman' he has been designated) drives about with a livery servant in a cab, and, throwing off a cloak, appears in these frightful forms, and is to win a wager by the joke—if it be a joke, one that is very likely to produce the catastrophe [of the kind] detailed in the letter, but which, till the writer comes forward and acknowledges it, cannot be considered as fact.

I should rather [be] inclined to think it was some determined thief who visits houses in the absence of the heads of families and who by this method of at once paralyzing the energies of the servants to obtain and escape with his booty on easy terms.

I shall shortly remove my family from my town residence to that stated, where if I catch Mr. Ghost on any part of my premises I shall administer that to his substantial parts that if he ever [re]appears it shall be only his aerial essence, or as a ghost in fact.

Other heads of families in my neighbourhood having expressed the same determination, I trust this ghost will soon be laid; meantime publicity to the matter would do good, and attract the notice of the authorities [around] the city.

I have the honour to be, my Lord,

Your Lordship's most obedient humble servant,

BOW LANE, JAN 10,

THOMAS LOTT

Again we have suggestions that these sightings are nothing more than a series of pranks, carried out either by a single person or a gang bent upon winning a wager. To this is added the notion of a burglar intent upon stealing from well-to-do householders.

A second letter included in this collection of responses is from a man who withholds his name but states that he is a magistrate and a barrister, writing from an address in Lincoln's-Inn-Fields—still the heart of London's legal profession. He seems to be trying to impress upon the mayor that for this reason he is less likely to be misled by the sensational nature of the reports. He also declares his intention of investigating further in the event that the police fail to uncover the miscreants "who are undoubtedly working real mischief, though under a childish and grotesque guise."[3]

Following this preamble the writer gets to the point.

THE TIMES, JANUARY 11, 1838

Some weeks ago, an old female domestic, who lived in my service many years, and who now resides in respectable circumstances, as the wife of a decent tradesman at Hammersmith, called on me, and in the course of conversation informed me that the females of Hammersmith and its vicinity feared to walk abroad after nightfall in consequence of the molestations of a ghost or monster to which they were exposed.

At first I, with your Lordship, thought this visitation in the 19th century, so near the metropolis, and with such a well-organized police as we have now, too absurd for belief; but on further enquiry I ascertained that several young women had been readily frightened into fits—dangerous fits, and some of them had been severely wounded by a sort of claws the miscreant wore on his hands. I expressed my surprise the attention of the police had not been called to the nuisance. My informant assured me that repeatedly their vigilance had been aroused on the subject, but the fellow or fellows have been adroit enough to avoid capture. I have such reliance on the witness I allude too, that I have no doubt she reports facts.

Now the mysterious attacker is called specifically a ghost or a monster, though again we have reference to his clawed hands. In fact it is really very unlikely that he was either of these things—though monster is not an unreasonable epithet and may refer to an older attacker dubbed "the London Monster" (see page 16). The ghost idea is easily excluded since the attacker is far too physical (ghosts do not normally scratch people or rip their clothing) and moves around—contrary to the way ghosts normally haunt a single place to which they are somehow bound.

What we also see here is that the report is based more solidly on evidence and upon the statement of a respectable source—an elderly servant clearly not given to inventing or dramatizing events.

Two other letters, dated January 9 and addressed to the lord mayor's clerk, variously named as Hobler or Holder, were of a more dramatic nature.

Fig. 1.2. The London Monster

THE TIMES, JANUARY 11, 1838

There have been rumors, in St John's Wood and its neighbourhood, for the last fortnight, of the appearance of the monster alluded to. . . . The bet is, however, understood to be one of an even more grave nature than that stated, and, if it be true, amounts to murder. As far as the writer has been informed, the bet is that the monster shall kill six women in some given time. . . . It is asserted that he has been seen in St John's Wood clad in mail, and as a bear.

Suddenly the story has become darker. Now the man (or men) in question (no one seems certain of the numbers at this stage) has taken a bet that he (or they) will kill six women. In addition we are now told that at least one person is dressed as a bear!

With a similar air of certainty, another correspondent adds:

THE TIMES, JANUARY 11, 1838

On reading the letter in the papers of this day received by your Lordship, I can see that you are not inclined to give credence to the account furnished by your correspondence.

The villain mentioned . . . as appearing in the guise of a ghost, bear, or devil, has been within the last week or two repeatedly seen at Lewisham and Blackheath. So much, indeed, has he frightened the inhabitants of those peaceful districts that women and children durst not stir out of their houses after dark.

There ought to be a stop put to this; but the police, I am afraid, are frightened of him also.

For the first time we learn that the police are disinclined to take action and may even be afraid of the creature. Despite this, the mayor seems to have remained unconvinced and continued to play down the whole affair. He gave, via his clerk, a statement to the effect that

it was evident that considerable terror had been excited by the appearance of some man or men, in the outlets of the metropolis, in disguise, and that a great deal of mischief might arise from the Pantomimic display at night in a retired and peaceful neighbourhood. But he thought from the first that the greatest exaggerations must have been made, and he believed it to be quite impossible that there could be any foundation for the report that the ghost had performed defeats of a devil on earth. He also withheld his credence from the statement that so many ladies [had] been frightened to death, although he had been given to understand, from an authority he could not question, that one of the female servants of a gentlemen who resides near his house at Forest Hill, was a short time since terrified and into fits by the sudden appearance of a figure clad in a bear's skin.

The Morning Chronicle

JANUARY 11, 1838

The bearskin, on being drawn aside exhibited a human body in a suit of mail, and with a long horn, the emblem of the King of Hell himself. Mr. Holder [the mayor's clerk] said he believed that there were stories about this ghost all around the metropolis, and that the matter would in all probability one day end in a good ducking. If anything serious had resulted from the tricks which were said to have been already played, the police no doubt, would have been apprised of it, and the newspaper, out of which it was almost impossible to keep anything likely to attract curiosity, would have been ready enough to take hold of it as a recompense for the want of parliamentary intelligence. That some mischievous fellows, who deserved to be well trounced, were at work, there existed no doubt. A gentleman, who stated that he had heard a great deal of conversation on the subject, mentioned that the ghost was said to have appeared armed cap-a-pie in Lord Holland's park [now Holland Park, between Kensington and Notting Hill Gate] to the terror of a few ladies and gentlemen, who were in the habit of meeting there by moonlight, and that since that period that park had very nearly recovered its reputation, as casual visitors of the description alluded to, considered that his business was to preserve the chastity of the place, and had not been seen since.

This is a reference to the somewhat dubious reputation attributed to the park, which was known as a trysting place for prostitutes and their clients. The suggestion that the "ghost" was somehow attempting to act as a moral guardian may seem ludicrous now, but at the time it would have been taken seriously. However, it seems most unlikely that the mysterious attacker was actually intent upon any such action—though it is just possible that a moral vigilante might have adopted the disguise of the attacker, as others appear to have done later on.

Two days later the *Greenwich, Woolwich and Deptford Gazette, West Kent Advertiser,* and *Milton and Gravesend Journal* ran extended pieces that summarized the lord mayor's correspondence and dismissed the various sightings as a great hoax that any sensible person would see through at once.

The next day the *Observer* ran its own version of the events, referencing the stories that must have caused great amusement among the readers of various newspapers.

The Observer

JANUARY 14, 1838

A GHOST STORY

The most exaggerated tales of the horrors resulting from this folly have been put forth, and on Thursday the commissioners of police directed their superintendents to order their men to make a special report upon the subject; but although it turns out that a tall figure in white had been seen in the neighbourhood of Brentford, and, among others, by the daughter of the Rev. Mr. Geary on her return from a party, and she was not at all alarmed even when it walked by her side, very few were unable to give any account of the occurrences which have been described except from rumor or mischievous invention. No doubt the ghost will soon be laid and the terrors of the superstitious set at rest by his being thus deposited in some stationhouse or convenient ditch.

At this point the whole idea was seen as both ridiculous and founded purely on superstition and mischief by "some fool who, under various disguises, has contrived to alarm the old and young of half the parishes around the town."[4]

Others, however, took it more seriously, even though still determining it was a hoax. On January 20 a letter was printed in the *Sun*—an evening paper of the time and nothing to do with the current publication—as well as in the *Morning Chronicle* and the *Morning Herald*. It was from no lesser a person than the lord mayor's clerk, Mr. Hobler. After mentioning the alarm caused by the actions of "some vagabonds, who have appeared . . . in the form and fashion of hobgoblins and ghosts."[5]

The Sun

JANUARY 20, 1838

A committee of gentlemen have spiritedly come forward for the purpose of raising a fund for securing these unfeeling wretches, alias 'ghosts', and visiting them with that severe punishment which they richly deserve. The Lord Mayor has kindly consented to receive subscriptions from ladies and gentlemen whose peace and comfort have been destroyed by these scamps, and his Lordship has already in his possession subscriptions amounting to £35 [around £2,800 in today's currency (4,116 in American dollars)] towards the expenses of the prosecution. The liberal donation of five Guineas has been forwarded to his lordship from Plutarch Dickinson Esquire, of Plumer Villa, Dulwich, whose daughter was nearly deprived of her senses, and is now lying in a very dangerous state, by the sudden appearance of one of these ruffians enveloped in a white sheet and blue fire, on her return home last week from a party of friends. A donation of £3 has also been received from Mr. Benjamin Marsh, of Hammersmith, whose son Timothy, a youth of nine years of age, was terribly frightened at the sight of a fellow dressed as a bear. The committee has been informed that some of the rascals are connected with high families, and that bets to the amount of £5000 are at stake upon the success or failure of their abominable proceedings. The committee can scarcely give credence to the following report which has reached their ears, that the object of the villains is to destroy the lives of not less than 30 human beings! viz eight old bachelors, ten old maids, and six lady's maids, and as many servant girls as they can, by depriving them of their reason, and otherwise exonerating their deaths.

The committee have already circulated placards about the suburbs of London offering a reward of £10 [or £800 in today's currency] for the apprehension of any of these heartless scoundrels and proceedings will be instituted against them immediately when they are captured.

There are a number of things to notice here. First, that the lord mayor's office took the matter seriously enough to set up a scheme to attempt to bring the perpetrator (or perpetrators) of the vile attacks to justice, and by extension that the police were already considered unable to deal with the situation. The second being that the reports that had been received (from where we are not told) of further attacks involving someone clad in white and with blue fire (the first recorded mention of what was to become a regular aspect of Spring-Heeled Jack's appearance) and that it was believed that a very precise number of people had been targeted. It's clear that the lord mayor's office either had access to sources that are no longer extant, or that someone had decided to project a very specific number of targets to draw attention to the seriousness of the situation. Once again, we notice, the victims are old women or men, children, and young girls.

On January 20, 1838, a longer article appeared in the *County Herald and Weekly Advertiser* (Middlesex), which began by printing an order issued by the commissioner of the Metropolitan Police Service to his officers.

Country Herald and Weekly Advertiser

JANUARY 20, 1838

The superintendent will cause the strictest enquiry to be made in their respective divisions (horse patrol included) whether any person has been injured or frightened in any manner by the figure which is said to be going about the outskirts of the town, resembling a ghost, bear, devil etc., for the purpose of alarming the inhabitants. A special report of everything connected with the case which can be satisfactorily accounted for will be made to the commissioner at orders tomorrow.

Though we do not learn what the reports had to say, the writer of the article, who must have been making his own enquiries, goes on to describe further assaults:

COUNTRY HERALD AND WEEKLY ADVISOR, JANUARY 20, 1838

We understand that in the neighbourhood of Brentford the only female who had been frightened by the supposed ghost had in fact been alarmed by a white faced heifer; and at Kensington, where it is alleged that his ghostship had been in the habit of prowling ... on the [Kensington] Palace Green, in the form a white bear ... three persons only stated to have seen him. ... On the police enquiring of them what they had seen, one of them (the wife of a musician in the Guards) stated that while returning, about 8 o'clock from a visit to the barracks at Kensington, she saw on the Palace Green 'a something'—but that was 16 years ago! The above female, it must be understood, was reported to be in a dying state from the fright she had received. The second, who is alleged to have kept to her bed ever since, was a respectable female, who states that she a few weeks ago also saw 'a something,' but what it was she cannot describe. She was not, however, much alarmed. The third, a boy 12 years of age, named Foster, living at Earls Court, states he saw the figure of 12 feet high in one of the lanes, but he also can give no description of it.

These descriptions are not only vague but also disparate, while the words of the lady who apparently saw "something" sixteen years previously and had been "dying" ever since can almost certainly be discounted.

THE OUTRAGE OF JANE ALSOP

After this, perhaps in the face of renewed efforts by the police, not to mention those of a group of gentlemen vigilantes, there are no more reports until February 22. However, when it did appear, the story was the first of those that not only had sufficient detail to substantiate it, but also contained a very full description of the character and appearance of the attacker who was also, for the first time, clearly named as Spring-Heeled Jack.

Once again it is the *Times* that sets off a sequence of explosive events.

The Times

FEBRUARY 22, 1838

OUTRAGE ON A YOUNG LADY

Many among the public have hitherto been incredulous after the truth of various representations made to the Lord Mayor of the gambols of 'Spring-heeled Jack', the suburban ghost, and believed, from there being no positive proof of the miscreant carrying his pranks beyond the mere act of alarming unprotected females, that those statements were more the effect of imagination than reality. The following authentic particulars, however, of a gross and violent outrage committed on a respectable young lady, and which might not only have caused her death, but that of both her sisters, by the unmanly brute, will remove all doubt [from] the subject.

Yesterday Mr. Alsop, a gentleman of considerable property residing at Bear-bind cottage, in Bear-bind-lane, a very lonely spot between the villages of Bow and Old Ford, accompanied by his three daughters, waited upon Mr. Hardwick at Lambeth-street Police-office, and gave the following particulars of an outrage committed on one of the latter:

Miss Jane Alsop, a young lady eighteen years of age, stated that at about a quarter to nine o'clock on the preceding night she heard a violent ringing at the gate at the front of the house, and on going to the door to see what was the matter, she saw a man standing outside, of whom she enquired what was the matter, and requested he would not ring so loud. The person instantly replied that he was a policeman, and said, 'For God's sake, bring me a light, for we have caught Spring-heeled Jack here in the lane'. She returned into the house and brought a candle, and handed it to the person, who appeared enveloped in a long cloak, and whom she at first really believed to be a policeman. The instant she had done so, however, *he threw off his outer garment, and applying the lighted candle to his breast, presented a most hideous and frightful appearance, and vomited forth a quantity of blue and white flames from his mouth, and his eyes resembled red balls of fire* [my italics].

From the hasty glance, which her fright enabled her to get this person, she observed that he wore a large helmet, and his dress, which appeared to fit him very tight, seemed to her to resemble white oilskin [my italics]. Without uttering a sentence, he darted at her, and catching her partly by her dress and the back part of her neck, placed her head under one of his arms, and commenced tearing her dress with his claws, which she was certain were of some metallic substance.

She screamed out as loud as she could for assistance, and by considerable exertion got away from him, and ran toward the house to get in. Her assailant, however, followed her, and caught her on the steps leading to the half-door, when he again used considerable violence, tore her neck and arms with this claws, as well as a quantity of hair from her head; but she was at length rescued from his grasp by one of her sisters. Miss Alsop added, that she had suffered considerably all night from the shock she had sustained, and was then in extreme pain, both from the injury done to her arm, and the wounds and scratches inflicted by the miscreant about her shoulders and neck with his claws or hands.

Miss Mary Alsop, a younger sister, said, that on hearing the screams of her sister Jane, she went to the door, and saw a figure as above described ill-using her sister. She was so alarmed at his appearance that she was afraid to approach or render any assistance.

Mrs. Harrison [from the context, an older sister] said, that hearing the screams of both her sisters, first of Jane, and then of Mary, she ran to the door, and found the person before described in the act of dragging her sister Jane down the stone steps from the door with considerable violence. She [Mrs. Harrison] got hold of her sister, and by some means or other, which she could scarcely describe, succeeded in getting her [Jane] inside the door, and closing it. At this time her sister's dress was nearly torn off her, both her combs dragged out of her head, as well as a quantity of her hair torn away. The fellow, notwithstanding the outrage committed, knocked loudly two or three times at the door, and it was only on their calling loudly for the police from the upper windows that he left the place.

Mr. Alsop, who appears very feeble, said that he and Mrs. Alsop have been laid up for several weeks with a rheumatic affection, so as to be scarcely able to get out of bed, but such was the alarm on the night before, that they both got out of bed, and he managed to get downstairs, and found his daughter [name misprinted as Susan] with her clothes torn, and having all appearance of receiving the most serious personal violence. Mr. Alsop also said, it was perfectly clear that there was more than one ruffian connected with the outrage, as the fellow who committed the violence did not return for his cloak, but scampered across the fields, so that there must have been some person with him to pick it up. In conclusion, Mr. Alsop said, he would most willingly give a reward of 10 guineas [£12,000] for the apprehension of the miscreant.

Mr. Hardwick expressed his surprise and abhorrence of the outrage, and said that no pains should be spared to bring its miscreant perpetrators to justice.

Here we have the description of a full-blown and intense attack. Its sheer brutality marks it out from the previous accounts, and here also we have, for the first time, a full-on description of Spring-Heeled Jack, complete with glowing red eyes, blue fire erupting from his mouth, tight-fitting suit, and steel claws. What is interesting about this is the apparent randomness of the attack. Since we have no further details, we may assume that his victim did not know her assailant and that he had, perhaps, chosen the house because of its remoteness and the sickness of Mr. and Mrs. Alsop. The fact that all three Alsop daughters supported the story and that presumably the scratches inflicted upon Jane were visible makes this believable.

If it were not for the strange appearance of the figure, one might assume it was a simple rape attempt, but the fact that no other harm was inflicted upon the young woman, as well as her assailant's claim that he was a policeman and that he had caught Spring-Heeled Jack, point to something more. It suggests immediately that it was expected that Jane Alsop would know who was being referred to and would not question the idea that he might have been caught outside her front door. We assume it was dark outside and that she was unable to see the supposed policeman until she brought a candle, at which point he threw off his cloak and revealed himself in all his terrifying glory.

The cloak itself is something of a mystery. Mr. Alsop's later remarks to the police that the assailant must have had an accomplice who returned to get the cloak suggests that it had disappeared. More important than any of this, the event makes it abundantly clear that this is no ghost.

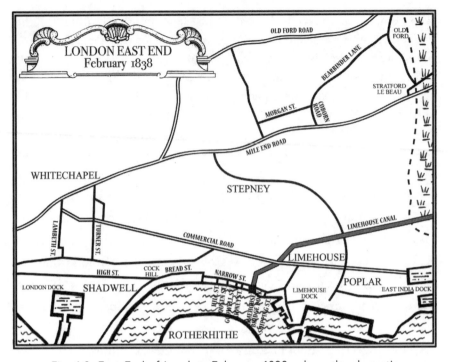

Fig. 1.3. East End of London, February 1838, where the dramatic events around Bear-bind Lane took place and where other early sightings of Spring-Heeled Jack were reported in Limehouse (Map by Wil Kinghan after Richard Furlong)

The report once again sent what was soon to be referred to as "Spring-Heeled Jack mania" into overdrive. A flurry of reports followed, including this one from the *Morning Herald,* which having repeated the story from the *Times,* went on to describe the results of an investigation carried out by two independent detectives, both former Bow Street Runners, into the events at Old Ford.

The Morning Herald

FEBRUARY 23, 1838

From what they had learned he had no doubt that the person by whom the outrage had been committed had been in the neighbourhood for nearly a month past, frightening men as well as women, and had, on one occasion, narrowly escaped apprehension. A person, answering precisely his size and figure, had been frequently observed walking about the lanes and lonely places, enveloped in a large Spanish cloak, and was sometimes in the habit of carrying a small lantern about with him. On one occasion he partially exhibited his masquerade in Bow-fair fields, and was closely pursued by a number of men in the employ-ment of Mr. Giles, a coach-master at Bow, but, by the most extraor-dinary agility and apparently a thorough knowledge of the locality of the place, he got clear off. The officer added he was perfectly sat-isfied of the truth of the statement of Miss Alsop as to the violence inflicted upon her by the person she described; indeed the whole family, all of whom had seen him, agreed precisely in his description; but he differed in opinion with Mr. Alsop that there was more than one per-son concerned in the outrage. The situation of Mr. Alsop's house being at a considerable distance from any other, and in a very lonely spot, afforded ample opportunity for the ghost, as he was called, to play off his pranks with impunity; but besides this, it was quite evident that the family were not strangers to him, as he was well acquainted with the name of Mr. Alsop. After the outrage was committed, it appeared, the family threw up the windows, and called out loudly for the police and assistance, and their cries being heard at the John Bull public house, some distance off, three persons set out from thence in the direction of Mr. Alsop's and on their way thither they met a tall person wrapped up in a large cloak, who said as they came up that a policeman was wanted at Mr. Alsop's, and they took no fur-ther notice of him. This person, he felt convinced, was no other than the perpetrator of the outrage himself.

Interestingly, we are again given to believe that the appearances of the figure now called Spring-Heeled Jack had been happening for some time before this. Were they simply retrospectively identified or had there indeed been a series of such activities in the area, which had previously gone unreported?

The local magistrate, a Mr. Norton, who had called for the investigation, was apparently surprised that the miscreant "could so long pursue his abominable practices with impunity."[6] The detective replied that in his view "in consequence of the notoriety which the gambles of Spring-Heeled Jack had gained, the character was now assumed by many thoughtless young men, who considered it a good lark."[7]

This, as we shall see, was to become a leading view within the constabulary.

The next report, dated February 23 but possibly recorded several days earlier, not only resolutely returned to the idea of a supernatural entity at the heart of the appearances, but also shifted the location away from London to Essex, giving us a rather romantic addition to the story:

Chelmsford Chronicle

FEBRUARY 23, 1838

We were told a great deal a few days ago, about a most ungentlemanly hobgoblin, who roamed up-and-down the byways, and even the highways of London . . . now it appears he is making the tour of Essex—probably for the benefit of his health—as a butcher, at Upminster, testified. . . . On Tuesday last, our butcher, a strong, and apparently as fearless as the Oaks of the forest, was returning from Corbets Tye [a local public house], to his dwelling, about the verge of midnight of course.

Here, apparently unable to find the words to describe the scene, the reporter breaks into verse, quoting a few lines of a long narrative poem by Robert Bloomfield called "The Farmer's Boy":

CHELMSFORD CHRONICLE, FEBRUARY 23, 1838

In thought still half absorbed, and chill'd with cold;
When lo! An object frightful to behold,—
A grizzly Spectre, clothed in silver grey.
Around whose feet the wavering shadows play,
Stands in his path!—

The reporter then completes his rather colorful description of the dreadful "hobgoblin":

CHELMSFORD CHRONICLE, FEBRUARY 23, 1838

Stands too, as huge and hideous as if all the ghosts of all the bullocks, sheep, pigs, and poultry he had slaughtered had been rolled into one, and now shrieked out, like Shakespeare's sprites—

'The Butcher is come
The fierce the cruel butcher,
Who stabbed us in the shop at Upminster.'

It was impossible that flesh and blood—at least such flesh and blood as walk about the soil of Essex—could stand against this; the butcher made a resolute plunge, but Mr. Ghost was not to be baulked of his fun in this way . . . and at every dodge the butcher found himself confronted by the gentleman with the cocked tail and saucer eyes, till at last, wound[ed] to desperation, he fled, looking neither behind not the right hand or to the left, till he reached the sanctuary of human habitation.

Finally, the reporter asks the all-important question, one that was being asked everywhere by this time, but to which he, perhaps unsurprisingly, had no answer:

CHELMSFORD CHRONICLE, FEBRUARY 23, 1838

'And of what was the hobgoblin made after all?' says the reader. Really we cannot tell. Whether it was composed of the 'thin air' of the good things which hospitality deal out at Cobbet's Tye [alcohol], or whether it was formed of a substance which could have been most effectively laid with an oaken cudgel, we must leave to those who are deeper read in the science of ghostology to determine.

Now the figure has become a hobgoblin or a ghost—though it is clear that the reporter had his tongue very firmly in his cheek and considered the most likely cause of the fracas to be inspired by the local brew.

By February 27, the reporting was once again suggesting a gang, more precisely "the Spring-Heeled Jack gang," one of whose number appeared at the house of a Mr. Ashworth, of 2 Turner Street, Commercial Road, at around 8:00 p.m., asking for the master of the house. Before the boy who had answered the door could respond, "Jack had thrown off his cloak and presented a most hideous appearance. The screams of the poor lad having alerted the family, the villain, unable to accomplish any further mischief, succeeded in [e]ffecting his escape."[8]

Next day the *Morning Chronicle* carried a further report of the ongoing police investigation. This time three officers: Mr. Young and Mr. Guard, respectively superintendent and inspector of the K division, and Mr. Lea, an ex-Bow Street Runner, were involved— reflecting the seriousness with which the Spring-Heeled Jack attacks were being considered. Reporting to the magistrate, J. Hardwick, the officers referred back to the Alsop case and declared their opinion that in her fear Miss Alsop might have exaggerated the description of her attacker. They were also convinced that within the next few days, that "they would be able to prove to the entire satisfaction of his worship [the Mayor] and the public, that the occurrence was merely the result of a drunken frolic, and not the act of an individual who has started to make his appearance in different outlets of the metropolis in so many different shapes."[9]

Three young men who lived in the area were already under suspicion. There was also an unnamed man, who lived not far from the Alsop house, who claimed to be able to "produce the parties concerned"[10] in the next day or so.

Hardwick, the magistrate, declared that he could conceive of no possible reason why Miss Alsop should invent details of her terrifying ordeal and insisted that the investigation must continue to be of a "most strict and searching"[11] kind. He then quoted a letter received from no lesser a person than Sir Edward Codrington, MP, one of the most widely admired leaders of his time and the victor of the Battle of Navarino (1827) in which he defeated a combined Egyptian and Turkish fleet in a conclusive battle of the Greek War of Independence. Dated February 23, from an address in Mayfair, it reads as follows:

The Morning Chronicle

FEBRUARY 28, 1838

Sir—There is something so very dastardly, so diabolical, in the conduct of the monster referred to in the accompanying account of representation made to you, that I think we are all bound to do our utmost to effect discovery of the parties. As the monster evidently has accomplices, it appears to me that the offer of a considerable reward would lead to detection. I, therefore, take the liberty of troubling you with the offer, on my part, to transmit to you £5, to be added to the reward offered by Mr. Alsop; and if you think my suggestion likely to be useful, I will send the five pounds to you by letter, or through Messes Drummond [bankers], or in any other way in which you may be pleased to point out. Begging your pardon for the liberty I have taken in thus troubling you, I remain, your very obedient servant,

EDWARD CODRINGTON,
ADMIRAL

Whether or not it was as a result of the "considerable reward" (£5 at the time was the equivalent of approximately £400 or $588 in today's currency), the *Morning Herald* announced the capture of one James Priest, a blacksmith of Islington, who, though he is not named as Spring-Heeled Jack, is clearly a similar type of rogue. The report reads as follows:

The Morning Herald

MARCH 1, 1838

For some time past numerous complaints have been made to the police of Islington, by respectable individuals, of a fellow of frightful appearance attacking their daughters, and taking indecent liberties with them; and in several instances some young ladies had been exceedingly terrified. Description was taken of this person, but the wretch escaped the vigilance of the police until Tuesday night last, when he followed a Miss Simmons and several other young women in a by-thoroughfare in the above neighborhood, and acted toward them in the most disgusting manner. They ran away greatly alarmed, but the miscreant pursued them, and dogged them about until their screams alerted [Constable] Wray, of N division, who pursued him, and eventually overtook him, when he made a violent resistance, but he was secured and taken to a stationhouse, where he gave his name as James Priest, a blacksmith. His countenance is most disturbing and his appearance generally deformed, and calculated to excite fear in females. Yesterday morning he was brought to this office, and examined before Mr. Rogers [another magistrate], when he was recognized as having been several times before in custody for similar conduct, and was committed to the House of Correction and hard labor for three months.

Mr. Rogers expressed his indignation at the prisoner's conduct, and regretted that the law did not empower him to send him for 12 months, or that the pillory was done away with, as he deserved severe punishment. He now committed him for three months and hard labor to the House of Correction.

The prisoner was hooted on his way to the lock-up place.

Here we finally have an actual human being, behaving in a way similar to Spring-Heeled Jack, held in captivity. But this is a poor substitute at best for the strange prowler. But though James Priest's "disturbing" countenance and "deformed" body make him sound like a monster, in reality he was probably no more than a lonely, disturbed man with a penchant for exposing himself to women (in the "most disgusting manner"). In any case, almost as if the idea that the mysterious attacker had at last been captured required a response, there appeared, the following day, and from the same newspaper, news of a further incident, this time in Lincoln's Inn Fields.

Headed "Spring-Heeled Jack" the report reads:

The Morning Herald

MARCH 2, 1838

The notoriety this miscreant has obtained seems to have the effect of making many silly young men take upon themselves to enact the ruffian in a small way, considering it something clever to frighten women and children out of their wits, under the belief that Spring-Heeled Jack was attacking them. Only a few nights since a respectable married woman living in Cary Street . . . was passing along the south side of Lincoln's Inn Fields, when a fellow in a huge cloak suddenly appeared from behind one of the gates of the College of Surgeons, and clasping her around the waist, enveloped her in the folds of his cloak. The woman was greatly terrified and struggled to get away, when the ruffian said, 'It's of no use struggling, I am Spring-Heeled Jack'. She screamed loudly, and the fellow ran away after giving her a tremendous blow on her mouth with his clenched fist. Last night (says a correspondent) between 10 and 11 o'clock, a genteelly dressed man went into the White Lion public house on the corner of Vere Street, Clare Market, and called for a glass of rum. Mr. Carne, the landlord, was [away] from home at the time, and his sister, Mrs. Hiam[s], was within the bar, and served it; she perceived something strange in the manner of the man, who averted his face and held pocket-handkerchief up to it. On a sudden he said, "Young woman, you don't know who I am I suppose— I am Spring-Heeled Jack," and drawing forth a self-protector [a thick stick or bludgeon] from his coat pocket, aimed a desperate blow at Mrs. Hiams, who fortunately avoided it, and called loudly for assistance—the man then started out of the house and escaped.

The reporter is very definite in thinking this is a copycat Spring-Heeled Jack, and in all likelihood he is correct. Certainly by admitting to being the terror, and showing none of the usual aspects of Spring-Heeled Jack other than his violent behavior, it seems more than likely that this man was indeed a fake. In any case, and despite the capture of James Priest, the police continued their investigation into the mystery of the Alsop attack, and on the same day that the above report appeared, the *Times* led with a full account of further enthralling events.

THE CASE OF THE MISSING CLOAK

The magistrate, Mr. Hardwick, again oversaw the case, assisted by two others, Mr. Norton and Mr. Stock, who is listed as a "county magistrate." Two suspects were arraigned—one a bricklayer named Payne or Paynes (the newspaper prints both) and a second man, a carpenter named Millbank. Also present were Mr. Alsop and his son and three daughters. We are fortunate to have a full account of the following enquiry.

The Times

MARCH 2, 1838

The first witness called was a James Smith, a coach wheelwright of 9 Prospect Place, Old Ford Road. He described how he had been proceeding along New Road between eight and nine on the night of the attack, and as he drew near the Alsop house, heard a violent ringing at the door and saw what appeared to be an attack on the young women who opened the door.

Smith at once hastened to give aid, but as he was carrying a wheel on his shoulder at the time, pre-sumably having repaired it, he was slowed down. As he went he met another man, a Mr. Richardson, a shoemaker, and together they hurried toward the scene of the attack. On the way they met two other men, hastening away from the scene, one of who wore a kind of shooting jacket and was several paces ahead of his companion.

At this point Hardwick asked the witness if he could identify the two men, and he answered that he was certain they were the men in the dock.

Continuing his testimony Smith described asking the men what was the matter, but they did not reply. He and Richardson continued on to the Alsop house where they heard what had just taken place. The report continues.

THE TIMES, MARCH 2, 1838

While doing so, Mr. Paynes, who we had just met before in the lane, returned, and went up to where we were, and said to Mr. Alsop Jr, 'You know me'. Mr. Alsop replied, 'Yes, you are Mr. Paynes'. Mr. Paynes then stated, that as he came by the house he heard some person say, 'Give Spring-Heeled Jack a light', and then went away.

Smith then described how, soon after, he went on towards Coborn Road, adjacent to New Road, still carrying the wheel on his shoulder and there saw the same two men.

They were in conversation, and Paynes said to the other, 'It was rascally; I would not have done it upon any account', or words to that effect. I was carrying my work upon my shoulder at the time, and they recognized me, and the man in the shooting jacket said, 'There is the [blank] who was in the lane'. He then came up to me, and caught hold of the wheel I was carrying, and pulled it off my shoulder, saying at the same time, 'What have you to say to Spring Jack?' I desired him to leave my wheel alone, and then Paynes came and took him [the other man] away.

Clearly in need of a drink after these disturbing events Smith went into the nearby Morgan's Arms public house, only to see the two men follow him in. They went into the taproom or parlor and Smith asked the landlord if he knew who the man in the shooting jacket was. He was told it was Millbank, and that he lived just across the road from the landlord's own house. Smith concluded that he had no doubt at all that it was this Millbank who had attacked Miss Alsop, but denied that either he or Richardson had seen any blue lights.

Hardwick then enquired of Payne if he had heard the ringing at the door, to which he answered that he had only heard the screams and that this had brought him back to the scene. The following exchange then took place:

MR. HARDWICK: Had you been in the company of Millbank on the Tuesday?

PAYNE: Yes; we had been together, but we parted at the White Hart, and I did not again see or speak to him until I met him at the Morgan's arms.

MR. HARDWICK: Then you mean to say that you did not meet Smith in the lane at all, and that what he states about you being in company with Millbank, and your remarks to that person, is

| all false and the mere invention of the witness? | **PAYNE (AFTER SOME HESITATION):** I do say so. |

There is a lot of confusion here. First, it sounds as if Payne (as reported by Smith the wheelwright) is saying to his friend that the attack was rascally and he should not have done it, which could be taken to mean that it was his friend who had carried out the attack. Equally, Payne's return to the scene of the crime could have been a ploy intended to throw suspicion away from him. The behavior of both men toward Smith paints them as a pair of rogues, but this is still not enough to say they were guilty. Payne's strange remark—"What have you to say to Spring Jack?"—can be read in several ways. He might have been ironically assuming that Smith believed in the whole story of the strange attacker, or he could be saying that he was Spring-Heeled Jack, or that his accomplice was.

Next into the witness box was the landlord of the White Hart, Mr. Nicholson, who related that both Payne and Millbank had been at the public house on the evening in question and that they had both been out shooting. What they had been shooting at is not detailed, but we can assume they had been out in the open countryside trying to bag a rabbit or two for the pot, or taking pot shots at local bird life. In any case, Nicholson said that Millbank had been so drunk that he was required to leave his gun behind when he left the premises.

Mr. Burden, landlord of the Morgan Arms, where the reported fracas had taken place, corroborated Payne's evidence and added that Millbank, who had been dressed in a white jacket and hat, was so drunk that he probably had no memory of the incident.

This now seemed to be Millbank's only defense—that he had no memory of anything that had occurred that night. However, two of the investigating officers, Lea and an Inspector Juard, declared that Millbank had "purchased a brown great-coat with a large collar, after leaving the White Hart, and that he had purchased a candle at a chandlers shop between the White Hart and the Residence of Mr. Alsop."

In the face of this damning evidence, Millbank again claimed to have no knowledge of it. The Misses Alsop and their sister Mrs. Harrison again stated what they had seen on the night in question and insisted that their attacker had not been drunk.

The three magistrates admitted themselves baffled as to the motive for the attack and to its apparently supernatural element. It is clear they thought that the Alsops had made up this part of the account, probably to get more sympathy, but none of them could account for Millbank and Paynes's behavior. Why had Millbank said: "What do you think of Spring-Heeled Jack now?" or words to that effect, to Smith, and why was he carrying the remains of a candle when he was taken into custody? Mr. Hardwick declared that

---

THE TIMES, MARCH 2, 1838

it was evident, from what had taken place, that the two persons suspected knew more about the affair than they wished to acknowledge, or, if they were innocent, it certainly was most extraordinary that so many concurrent circumstances should be adduced to fix upon them certainly the strongest possible suspicion. He could not conceive what motive the witness Smith could have in making the statement if it was groundless and without foundation, while he could at once find a motive in its denial by the accused. Besides, the fact that Mr. Payne had not mentioned the circumstance to any person in the parlor of a public house on the night in question was, in his mind, a circumstance pregnant with suspicion.

Finally, the magistrate requested that a more thorough investigation be carried out and that an appeal be made for witnesses to present themselves at a further hearing on the following Friday. He especially asked "the person who was present with the cloak on, on the night in question, to attend on that day."[12]

The results of this further investigation appeared in the *Times* on

March 3, 1838. Richardson, the shoemaker, repeated the evidence he had given earlier, adding some details, the most important of these being that as he approached the scene of the attack, he had met

The Times

MARCH 3, 1838

a young man in a large cloak and a boy, and the former said something about Spring-Heeled Jack being in the lane. This he said in a rather joking or laughing manner. Witness instantly called out 'Police' and Mr. Smith, coming up at the time, asked him if he would not come on. He replied that he would, and as they were hurrying towards Mr. Alsop's he observed a man dressed in a white fustian [heavy cotton twill cloth] shooting-jacket, standing in the lane, nearly opposite to Mr. Alsop's, whom he asked what was the matter. Mr. Alsop Jr. and his sister were calling for the police from the front windows, and on observing them [Richardson and Smith] they came down and related what had happened, and described the appearance of the person by whom the outrage had been committed, but not in such a manner as to impress him with the idea that it [had] been so serious as he subsequently saw it described in the newspapers.

This is a curious statement. It suggests that Smith, at least, felt the affair had been overdramatized, and as Mike Dash notes (*Fortean Times*), if the attack had been as serious as that described, Smith could hardly have failed to see it.

It would seem that the magistrate, Mr. Hardwick, was also beginning to wonder, as he now recalled Millbank "who was dressed differently from the day before"[13] and asked Richardson if he was certain this was the man he had described as standing in the lane on the night of the attack.

THE TIMES, MARCH 3, 1838

Richardson, after looking at him, replied that he did not think he was, as the person he observed was, in his opinion, much younger, taller and thinner.

Smith, the other witness, however said that he was positive he was the individual, as he had not only an opportunity of seeing him when he forced the wheel off his shoulder, but also at the Morgan Arms public house.

MR. HARDWICK (TO RICHARDSON): You have stated that you distinctly saw a lighted candle brought from the home of Mr. Alsop immediately after you heard the violent ringing of a bell and before you heard the screams of the female.

RICHARDSON: I did, sir.

MR. HARDWICK: Now, from the position you were in at the time, can you take it on you to say that if a greater light than that produced by candle had been exhibited in the garden of Mr. Alsop you must have seen it?

RICHARDSON: I certainly must.

MR. HARDWICK (TO SMITH): Are you of the same opinion?

SMITH: I am sir; I saw no light but that of a candle.

MR. HARDWICK (TO RICHARDSON): About this young man in the cloak, can you say what became of him?

RICHARDSON: I cannot, sir.

At this point, "a gentleman, residing in the neighborhood of Old Ford" stepped forward. He declared that he had been so fascinated by the enquiry that he had taken it upon himself to make his own enquiries "to allay, if possible, the terror which had spread over the neighbourhood."[14]

Then came an astounding statement. The "gentleman" had traced, after a good deal of searching, a man named Fox, who was prevented from attending by a serious illness but whose sworn statement he had taken down. With Mr. Hardwick's permission, he then read the words of his mysterious informant.

THE TIMES, MARCH 3, 1838

I hereby declare I was the person with the boy, spoken of by one of the witnesses respecting the outrage committed at Mr. Alsop's house; but I had no cloak on, nor did I see anyone with a cloak. I stopped at the gates, when I was told that they had seen 'Spring-Heeled Jack'. I thought it was all a game and left them. The boy came there with me, but I do not know him. —J. Fox.

What are we to make of this? Mr. Fox (seemingly well named) is never mentioned again, nor, as far as we know, was his statement questioned or further explored. He clearly implies that the cloaked individual was a figment of the Alsops' imagination. Either that or the mysterious Mr. Fox, who was too ill to attend, is lying to the unnamed "gentleman"—who may himself have been recruited by Millbank or Payne to refute their involvement in the attack. Once again, we see that there was considerable doubt on the veracity of the matter, though the long suffering Mr. Hardwick seems unwilling to give up, as he then inquired of Millbank whether his memory of the night had been at all refreshed. Millbank stated that "he was still unconscious of anything that occurred from before leaving the White Hart at Old Ford, until the following morning, and how he got home or to bed, he was unable to say."[15]

At this point another "witness" came forward. Again unnamed, he is described as a "respectable tradesman" who lived in the area. Apparently he was well known for "larking" (enjoying himself by behaving playfully), and this had led to several people accusing him of being the perpetrator of the attack. He had come forward now, he said, to refute any such suggestions or insinuations that could cast a cloud on his good name. He then added: "the outrage, as it was called, was most injurious to him, as some tenants of his in the neighborhood talk about quitting their tenements, in consequence of their fears to go out after dark."[16] He concluded, in what the reporter described as "a very theatrical manner, and with a peculiar flourish, that he believed the greater part of the statements as to the appearance of the individual committing the outrage was a mere fudge, and that a burning candle, through the fright of the parties, no doubt, had been magnified into the blue and white lights they had heard so much about."[17]

Hardwick's reply showed that he was feeling hard-pressed. He declared that while there might be a little exaggeration, it was impossible for him to ignore the statements, made under oath, of the respectable Alsops.

He then referred to two earlier witness statements, neither of which we have heard of before and which do not seem to have been recorded anywhere else, of "a very intelligent girl, in whose probity her mother and mistress had placed the utmost reliance, [who] had on the last examination given an accurate and detailed description of a person dressed in a pantomimic costume, that she had seen, not very far from this neighborhood, and who appeared to vomit forth similar lights to those spoken of."[18]

Another woman, not present, had apparently witnessed a similar phenomenon not far from the Alsop residence. This implied, continued Mr. Hardwick, that the case of the Misses Alsop "was not a solitary instance of such practices."[19]

There was, however, one matter that continued to give him concern, and which he found "incongruous and staggering"[20]: neither Richardson nor Smith claimed to have observed the blue light.

In an effort to better understand this matter, he now called an expert witness, a Mr. Farrell, proprietor of the Pavilion Theatre, whom "he questioned as to the chemical substances necessary to produce such a light as that described, and that gentleman said that the dropping of certain strong acids on a sponge charged with spirits of wine would produce such appearances as those described, and that the color of the flame admitted would depend on the peculiar quality or description of acid."[21]

At this point Millbank apparently made an impassioned and bitter statement that he had been greatly wronged by being accused of the matter and that the affair was bound to cause irreparable damage to both his character and business. Mr. Hardwick's response seems to suggest that, while he still believed they had not reached any kind of satisfactory conclusion, he was convinced that neither Millbank nor Payne were guilty. Indeed, he seems to have been convinced that both men were of good character, despite the rowdy behavior at the public house. He concluded with the hope that Millbank's character would not suffer as a result of the inquiry and added that

THE TIMES, MARCH 3, 1838

the outrage committed was of a serious description, and one which the magistrates are bound to enquire strictly into. The officers were in possession of some information, which should be promptly followed up and acted upon, as no efforts would be spared to bring the party or parties concerned in these disgraceful and mischievous proceedings to justice. The further enquiry, therefore, should stand for the present.

Millbank and Payne were released and are heard from no longer. The *Examiner* carried a brief statement the following day to the effect that "after lengthy examination . . . the evidence did not suffice, however, to fix more than a strong suspicion, and the case was held over for further enquiry."

The legend was beginning to spread. Further inquiries would quickly show the extent of Spring-Heeled Jack's activities.

CHAPTER 2

The Legend Spreads

Some say he was black and some say he was white,
Some said he was short and some said he was tall,
But many amongst them saw nothing at all.
"PRANKS OF THE GHOST," CIRCA 1884

Mr. Hardwick did not have to wait very long for further evidence of Spring-Heeled Jack's latest activities to reach him. Two days later, reported in the *Morning Post* on the seventh, came another vivid and detailed account.

The Morning Post

MARCH 7, 1838

THE GHOST, ALIAS 'SPRING-HEELED JACK'

Yesterday Mr. Scales, a respectable butcher, residing in Narrow-Street, Limehouse, accompanied by his sister, [Lucy] a young woman 18 years of age, attended before Mr. Hardwick, and made the following statement relative to the further gambols of 'Spring-Heeled Jack'. Miss Scales stated that on the evening of Wednesday last, at about half past eight o'clock, as she and her sister were returning from the house of their brother, and while passing along Green Dragon-alley, they observed some person standing in an angle in the passage. [Lucy Scales] was in advance of her sister at the time, and just as she came up to the person, who was enveloped in a

43

large cloak, he spurted a quantity of blue flame right in her face, which deprived her of her sight, and so alarmed her that she instantly dropped to the ground, and was enveloped with violent fits, which continued for several hours.

Mr. Hardwick immediately questioned the witness, and in reply, Miss Scales said that on approaching the individual she [first] thought it was a woman, from the headdress being apparently a bonnet or something of that description, but she was afterward satisfied it was a man. He appeared to her to be tall and thin, but her sister, who was with her, could give a more accurate description of his person, as she had a better opportunity of noticing him; but she was not at home when the officer called, or else she would have attended.[1]

Mr. Scales now spoke up, adding

THE MORNING POST, MARCH 7, 1838

On the evening in question, a few minutes after his sisters had left his house, he had heard the loud screams of one of them, and on running up Green Dragon-Alley he found his sister Lucy, who had just given her statement, on the ground in a strong fit, and his other sister endeavoring to hold and support her. She was removed home, and he then learned from his other sister what had happened. She described the person to be of tall, thin, and gentlemanly appearance, enveloped in a large cloak, [who] . . . carried in front of his person a large lamp, or bulls eye, similar to those in the possession of the police. On her sister, who was a little before her, coming up to the person, he threw open his cloak, exhibited the lamp, and puffed a quantity of flame from his mouth into the face of her sister. She also stated that the individual did not utter a word, nor did he attempt to lay a hand on them but walked away in an instant.

Mr. Scales then drew attention to the fact that one of his sisters had been reading an account of the recent inquiry just a few minutes before they left the house. He himself "had remarked that it was not likely that this personage would come to this neighborhood from the fact that there were so many butchers residing in it, and the account so far from alarming his sister seems to have had a different effect."[2]

This almost seems to suggest that Mr. Scales himself believed that his sisters might have been influenced by what they had been reading and that this might have caused them to exaggerate the affair. However, he then produced a statement from one Dr. Chaz Pritchel, surgeon, of 18 Cock Hill, a certificate of attendance on Lucy Scales. Strangely, this contains two conflicting dates. The certificate is dated March 6, which appears to be the actual day of the attack, but says that Dr. Pritchel visited Lucy Scales on Wednesday, March 28, but this must be a mistake, perhaps by the reporter. It read: "This is to certify that, on Wednesday, the 28th ult., I visited Lucy Scales, of Week's-place, Limehouse, who was suffering from hysterics and great agitation, in all probability the result of fright."[3]

This established that in the view of the physician, Lucy was hysterical—a state widely attributed at the time to any woman who appeared disturbed in any way. Another witness, described as "a respectable female, [who] said she was attracted to the spot by the shriek of Miss Scales, corroborated her statement as to her being on the ground in a strong fit."[4]

Lea, the ex-Bow Street officer who was apparently still working on the case, made a curious statement to the effect that "no place could be better adopted for such an act as the spot selected, as persons could be seen at a considerable distance approaching it on both sides."[5] This seems an odd remark to make, unless Lea is trying to suggest that the attacker appeared suddenly and unexpectedly out of nowhere. However, he also gave further evidence of a more scientific approach in that he had been, that very morning, at the London Hospital, observing experiments that proved, to his satisfaction that "lights like those described could be produced by blowing through a tube in which spirits of wine, sulphur, and another ingredient were deposited and ignited."[6]

Mr. Hardwick noted that all the evidence pointed to this being the actions of the same perpetrator as the attack on Miss Alsop.

The dating of Scales's account, which apparently took place on the previous Wednesday, March 6, would seem to exonerate Millbank and Payne, since both were being questioned at the time. The setting for the attack in Limehouse also placed the sighting at some distance from Old Ford. The description of the attacker, who carried a lamp hidden beneath a cloak, gave rise to a later belief that he was wearing some kind of gas tank strapped to his chest. This, as we shall see, fueled later claims that Spring-Heeled Jack was an alien (see chapter 7).

Scales's rather odd remark to the effect that it was unlikely that any such person would be seen in the Limehouse area due to the number of butchers that lived there seems strange. Was he suggesting that butchers were somehow too fearsome, perhaps armed with cleavers, thus making Limehouse an unsafe place for a would-be attacker to approach with impunity? Not to mention that any butcher, who spends most of the day carving up large haunches of meat, would be liberally splashed with blood.

There is no doubting the similarity of the two accounts. Both speak of a garish figure. The use of the word "pantomimic" by one of the witnesses is interesting as it recalls the demons that regularly popped up from a trapdoor under the stage with a bang and a whiff of sulfur. But there is something genuinely strange and deliberate about these attacks. Assuming, as I think one must from the evidence, that we believe they were not the product of the young woman's imagination, perhaps brought on by earlier reports such as those being read by the Scales sisters shortly before setting out, we are seeing here a very specific, targeted series of assaults—for such we must call them even when no physical damage was done—that bear the hallmarks of a deranged mind.

A COLLECTION OF JACKS

Over the next few weeks, sightings of Jack die away somewhat, with only a few reports appearing in the newspapers. Following the attack upon Lucy Scales, almost a week went by before the *Morning Post* for March 13 reported how a thirteen-year-old boy, in the employment of Mr. Priest, poulterer, while driving his master's cart along Westmoreland Mews, Great Marylebone, saw two tall figures, enveloped in cloaks, standing before him: "their arms were raised to the fullest extent, and their faces smeared with red ochre or brick dust."[7] The boy was so horrified by what he perceived as members of the Spring-Heeled Jack family that he screamed loudly and fell to the earth in a faint. He was quickly picked up by passersby and taken home, where he apparently had not recovered by the next day.

This was very evidently a prank, though the suggestion that the two men might belong to the Spring-Heeled Jack family is interesting, suggesting what the news reports begin to bear out at this point—that a number of copycat actions were taking place. A report on April 4 in the *Morning Post* even carried the headline "Capture of Spring-Heeled Jack," though this again proved false.

The story leading up to this capture took place between March 25 and April 20, 1838, when both the *Morning Post* and the *Examiner* carried stories concerning a new pretender to the throne of Spring-Heeled Jack.

The Examiner

MARCH 25, 1838

POLICE—MARYLEBONE

On Monday a tall, ill-favored young man, who gave his name as Charles Grenville, was charged with having frightened a number of women and children nearly into fits, by imitating the silly and dangerous pranks of Spring-Heeled Jack. Police constable 24S stated that he was on duty in Kentish Town on Saturday evening, when he was informed that Spring-Heeled Jack had just made his appearance, and that his frightful leaps and hideous appearance had scared a number of women and children into fits. He accordingly lay in wait for the monster, determined on capturing him and putting an end to his career. He had not been long watching before he saw the prisoner suddenly dart out of a dark lane and make towards some children, who ran away screaming at his approach. He (the constable) found little difficulty in capturing the monster who had created so much alarm, who turned out to be the prisoner [Charles Grenville]. He lived in the neighbourhood and was considered of weak mind, but perfectly harmless. His face was enveloped in [a] huge mask (painted blue and bright at the lips!) now produced, and had occasioned the consternation.

The magistrate, a Mr. Rawlinson, seems to have taken the view that this was nothing to get excited about. He asked the prisoner if he had anything to say "To which the prisoner, with a vacant smile, replied: 'Why it was only a bit of fun, that's all; I meant no harm.'"[8] Mr. Rawlinson seems to have agreed and discharged the prisoner with the stern warning: "don't do it again."[9]

This was the first of a spate of Spring-Heeled Jack imitators, and not the last to appear before Mr. Rawlinson. Less than a month later, after a relatively long silence, the *Examiner* reported the arrest of an eighteen-year-old youth named James Painter, who was charged with having terrified the peaceful inhabitants of Kilburn Village by dressing up as a ghost. (Despite this, we notice that the report is headed "Spring-Heeled Jack.") The report continues with the evidence given by Mrs. Anne Ansinck, of Kilburn.

THE EXAMINER, MARCH 25, 1838

About 8 o'clock on Saturday evening, she was walking along Waterloo Place, contiguous to Mrs. Chater's residence, accompanied by a female friend, when suddenly she found herself seized by a ghostly figure, habited in a white sheet, and wearing a hideous mask, from which depended a long beard. The figure, on clasping her, exclaimed: 'Who the devil are you?' And her friend, having recognized the voice of the 'ghost' replied very promptly, 'We'll let you know who we are, and that we are not to be frightened by you.' The ghost then beat a retreat, followed by the complainant and her friend, and, seeing it to vanish over a wall surrounding Mrs. Chater's premises, they were pretty well convinced that the defendant was the ghost.

The story continues, with some barely concealed wit, in a more extended version in the *Morning Post*.

The Morning Post

APRIL 4, 1838

To make sure of the matter, they asked a water carrier named Snell, who had a good view of the ghost, and who assured them it was the defendant. Miss Charlotte Hagerstone, the companion of the complainant, after corroborating her statement, said that she knew the defendant well. He had for a considerable period been playing his mischievous tricks upon females, some of whom he had frightened in a very serious manner. She recognized his voice the moment he spoke, and he had attempted upon several previous occasions to frighten her. . . .

The defendant denied the offence, and called Charles Laxton, Mr. Chater's coachman, for the purpose of providing an alibi, in which he failed. He then proceeded to state that Mrs. Ansinck had been to his mistress' house in a great passion, and, seizing him in the hall, had bestowed summary punishment in the shape of sundry hard smacks on the face . . .

Mrs. Ansinck said it was true she had called at Mrs. Chater's house to remonstrate respecting the defendant's conduct, when the defendant behaved in the most insolent manner, said he would never serve her out, and actually called to a dog to [be] set on her. Finding that she was not likely to obtain redress at the house, she was determined upon seeking it at this office, and accordingly obtained the warrant against the defendant. She denied striking him.

The magistrate made it very clear he was not amused, declaring to Painter,

THE MORNING POST, APRIL 4, 1838

[T]his is a very aggravated assault, made worse by the defense set up, and I have not the least doubt of your being the real offender. If fellows like you think they can frighten respectable females with impunity by imitating the scandalous pranks of Spring-Heeled Jack, they will be convinced of their mistake by finding themselves within the walls of Newgate. It is a very serious offence and might, under the particular circumstances, have caused death or other lamentable circumstances, and the public, especially the female portion of it, are much indebted to Mrs. Ansinck for the spirit and courage she has displayed bringing such an offender to justice. You are fined £4, and it is to be hoped you will learn better for the time to come.

With this tale the reports begin to change direction. Although this is very far from the last sighting of Spring-Heeled Jack, the reports begin to move away from London at this point. Perhaps the city became too hot for him—or them; if indeed we have a multiplicity of Jacks. Before we move on to consider these outlying occurrences, we need to look at two authors whose work has, in its way, contributed to a deeper misunderstanding of Spring-Heeled Jack by adding stories for which there is little or no supporting evidence.

THE LEAPING MENACE

Elizabeth Villiers (the pseudonym of Isobel Mary Thorne) in her 1928 book about highwaymen, *Stand and Deliver,* includes a chapter on Jack. She describes several actions of the infamous leaping menace that unfortunately seem to be invented, since no trace of them has come to light so far. This may seem odd, given that the accounts of the highwaymen in the book, though sensationalized, are nonetheless generally accurate. However, Villiers is not the only writer to have apparently made up stories about Jack, as we shall see. These are included here not only because, while they have yet to be confirmed, they are also not definitely *unconfirmed* and because they demonstrate how the legend of Spring-Heeled Jack has continued to grow into our own time.

In the first of her accounts, apparently set in 1838, Villiers paints a vivid picture of the scene:

> By one side of Clapham Common runs Lavender Hill, surely the most pretty named of any London streets . . . In 1838 walled gardens and thickset hedges . . . shut in Lavender Hill on the south, while the north was open ground with scattered farmlands and the lavender gardens, giving the place its name, covered the steep hill, which lost itself in the Battersea marshes, the haunt of wild duck beside the river.[10]

Here, according to Villiers, lived a young woman named Mary Stephens, probably in service either at Lavender Sweep, a handsome town house later owned by the editor of *Punch* magazine, or at one of the mansions that stood at the corner of Lavender Hill where it joined Falcon Lane. On this day Mary Stephens had been visiting her family and finding that she was late decided to take the shortcut along the charmingly named Pig Lane (now Latchmere Road), which would bring her out on top of Lavender Hill not far from the opening of the less pleasantly named Cut-Throat Lane, which was gated by a stile.

As she reached this spot, rain began to fall. The night was dark, and Mary hurried toward the entrance of the dark lane. At this moment, according to Villiers, Spring-Heeled Jack pounced.

> To her unspeakable horror a tall figure left from the darkness of the lane. It cleared the stile with a single bound and reached her side. In terror she would have sunk to the ground, but strong arms caught and held her prisoner. She felt a man's lips on her face, deliberately he kissed her, then with a loud laugh let her go, and leaping extraordinarily high, vanished into the night as mysteriously as he had come.

Scream after scream broke from her, and falling she lay in a paroxysm of terror across the entrance to the haunted lane. Her cries reached the ears of a man passing along the road at some distance. He gave the alarm, with the result that half a dozen strong fellows who are gathered at The Falcon [public house] set off up the hill, confident fresh devilry was afoot in Cut-Throat Lane.

They found a girl in the throes of hysteria, but searched as they would no trace of any assailant could be discovered. After some delay they took her to her master's house and gathered in the kitchen to hear her strange story.[11]

Villiers gives quite a lot of precise detail here, perhaps to add color to her story, but she leaves us in no doubt that the customers of the Falcon were not convinced.

All were ready to agree there was 'something queer about it', yet looked at sanely, no very great weight was attached to her recital. The girl had been alone, there were no witnesses to prove whether she had exaggerated what had occurred or told the simple truth, but she confessed she was nervous of the dark and was particularly afraid of Cut-Throat Lane, so what more probable than that some mischievous lad should have hidden among the shadows and sprung out to frighten her? The story of his having leapt clean over the stile could be dismissed; it was the highly colored version of the simple incident, which an hysterical woman might be expected to give.[12]

However, though the story was made light of, "it had to be confessed Mary Stevens was a perfectly sensible, highly respectable girl, not likely to suffer from hallucinations."[13]

As if to substantiate Mary Stevens's account, according to Villiers, a further dramatic incident occurred the next night. A carriage returning home from London was damaged when its horses bolted along Streatham High Road, just across the common land from Lavender

Hill. Both the coachman and the footman were injured, and though the former had no idea what had frightened the horses, the footman declared that a "huge creature, whether man or bird or beast he could not say, leapt from the shadows on one side of the way and springing clean across the road, which was of considerable width, and vanished over a high wall."[14]

At first, Villiers tells us, everyone thought the footman was deranged, but when Mary Stevens's story came out, and several others came forward with similar stories, the residents of the area, which included Clapham, Wandsworth, Tooting, and Streatham, began to think otherwise.

One of those who came forward was an elderly lady who recalled visiting a friend in Clapham Village, after which she set out to walk home, only a short distance away, accompanied by her two sons. Villiers continues,

She had reached the railings which shut in Clapham Churchyard at the corner of the common when she remembered she had left her tambour frame [an embroidery frame], or some such adjunct of her fancywork, behind and both the boys volunteered to return for it. As the boys hurried back along the way they had come, in the village High Street they met a solitary pedestrian whom they described afterwards as being a tall young man, very slimly made and wearing dark clothes with cape coat as was the fashion. His hat was pulled down over his eyes so they could not see his face.

Walking rapidly he went past them towards the church where their mother awaited. The scream came to them from the distance. They recognized her voice.

Back they rushed, to find her clinging to the railings, while in the speechlessness of terror she pointed with her other hand into the darkness where the white gravestones glimmered dimly. Nothing else could be seen.

When she had somewhat recovered, in broken words she told how a black object had leapt past her, clearing the railings in a bound to disappear into the shadows.[15]

The alarm was given, and a number of local people came out with lanterns to join in the search. What they found is interesting, if it is to be believed, as it fits with other Spring-Heeled Jack sightings. Villiers describes it as "two deep footprints, as those of a man who had alighted heavily from a height. Also the footmarks were a curious shape, lending color to the belief that 'Jack'—so he was already called for lack of another name—had 'machines' or springs attached to his shoes. Unfortunately no care was given to these marks and soon they were blotted out."[16]

There is much here that possesses a ring of truth—though it seems unlikely (if not impossible) that no report of this event found its way to the local newspapers. No such account has, to date, been located. The detail that the two boys had met a man in a cloak with a hat pulled down over his face is reminiscent of the affair at the Alsop house, but it may be no more than a coincidence. It is possible that Villiers is simply drawing upon the whole range of Spring-Heeled Jack stories to make one of her own. Certainly her description of what follows sounds very like the actual train of events during Jack's reign of terror.

Several young women came forward with similar stories to those of Mary Stevens. Other crimes, which would normally have been seen as random and unconnected incidents, were attributed to Jack. An old lady was found strangled in an upper room with the door locked. Had Jack leapt from the garden through the window? A younger woman was found dead on a lonely footpath, apparently as the result of a heart attack. But was it the sight of the spring-heeled terror that had brought on the attack?

Villiers continues:

Plenty of people definitely swore they had seen him leap right over the roofs of large houses, that cottages and hayricks were as nothing to him, but mail coaches and post chaises and family barouches were taken in his stride. Then, rather unaccountably, public opinion veered from thinking him a new form of highwayman and declared he was an inventor experimenting with a form of flying machine, while others maintained he was not flesh and blood but a haunting spirit born of the evil associations of Cut-Throat Lane, since from that lane he never went far and seemed to use it as his headquarters.[17]

Villiers then rejects the ghostly theory on account of the "sworn statements of the women who said they had been kissed," though she adds: "the kisses might have existed in their imagination!"[18]

Finally, she trumps the pack by adding a story, which she claims she herself heard from the lips of an old lady of her acquaintance who, though old, was "a clear-headed, intellectual woman whose word could be taken, whose memory was clear."[19]

Her home . . . was on Tooting Bec common, and not far away was a gypsy encampment in whose people she was interested. . . . Most of the people near the common looked askance at the Gypsies, but this particular lady had sympathy and gave them help. Fever broke out in their camp, and daring the infection she visited them with food and medicine. . . . On a particular day she visited the camp, carrying food to a woman who, lay very ill, and when she came away from the sufferer's tent—into which she had had to crawl on her hands and knees, as she would recall with amusement—a mist had sprung up and the evening was closing in.

Naturally she was anxious to reach home, so was the woman servant who had accompanied her, but the distance was not great and half a dozen of the Gypsy men formed themselves into a volunteer escort to see her safely back.

She and her maid were nearly home, the camp was some distance behind, when . . . out of the mist he leaped, making straight toward the two women with bounds so wide and high his identity was unmistakable. In answer to her scream the gypsy guard came up at the double, and seeing them the figure paused midway, then wheeling round went leaping off in the other direction.

Standing to watch, the lady saw him clearly in spite of the mist, as he went across the open common, jumping over good-sized furze bushes and clumps of gorse with no apparent effort, though she came to the conclusion that any greater leap would have been impossible. He was doing far more than an ordinary man could have accomplished without mechanical aid, but nothing resembling the exploits to which he was credited by rumor . . .

According to her he was not a tall man, at least she was sure his height was less than her own, though as she was exceptionally tall for a woman that does not prove much. He wore dark clothes and seemed to have a cloak swathed around him, and she thought he was bareheaded.[20]

Again, this story has a ring of veracity to it, and given the circumstances of her contact with the gypsy encampment—then, as now, travelers were regarded with suspicion—it is possible to believe that the lady had kept silent about her encounter. Her description is remarkably levelheaded and perhaps more believable than many of those given in other reports—certainly those in the newspapers. In the end we cannot be sure, but even if we dismiss the stories of Mary Stevens and the footman from the coach, I am inclined to believe this last account.

THE MURDEROUS FIEND

If Elizabeth Villiers did make up some of the stories in her book, she was not the only person to do so. The journalist and researcher Peter Haining (1940–2007) who until recently was the only person to write a full-length book about Jack—*The Legend and Bizarre Crimes of Spring-Heeled Jack,* published in 1997—appears to have invented at least two of the most dramatic appearances. Once again, we cannot be certain, but the lack of any record, either in the newspapers or police records, suggests they are at best doubtful. Mike Dash, who wrote to Haining in 1996 requesting further information about his sources, reported that the writer claimed to have lent his papers to a scriptwriter planning a film about Jack but had subsequently failed to retrieve them.[21] Haining's death in 2007 makes it unlikely that we shall ever know the truth. However, in the interests of completeness, his additions to the body of legend are included here so that readers may make up their own minds. Haining's book opens with a very detailed, but clearly fictionalized account of an encounter involving one Polly Adams, a seventeen-year-old serving girl at the Green Man Hotel and Tavern in Blackheath. This hostelry, founded before 1629, was an important staging post on the Dover Road, one of the major routes into London, and is certainly real.[22]

On this evening, October 11, 1837, Polly Adams was on her way to visit the great "hog and pleasure fair" held every year on this date

Fig. 2.1. The Green Man Hotel, Blackheath

on Blackheath itself. People of all classes went there, and the event was noisy, riotous, and wild. Adams had persuaded her employer to allow her two hours off to visit the fair, and she was excited to be going there. Haining spends a good deal of time describing her journey, in particular her passage near the gallows on Shooters Hill and then her passage around the noisy, colorful, and thrilling fair. Adams's pleasure in all of this was cut short when a man, whom she recognized as a nobleman from his attire, grabbed her and pressed a drunken kiss on her mouth. Terrified, Adams fled, hearing behind her a peculiar ringing laugh. Later, she was to recall the man's bulging eyes, which protruded enough for her to see the whites all around the pupil.

Her enjoyment gone, along with her best shawl, Adams decided to return to the safety of the Green Man and set off along Shooters Hill. She was almost home when the second incident took place. As she was passing a "strange dark hillock on the heath known as Whitefield's Mount," once the site of military activity but now abandoned, a terrifying figure emerged from the dark copse of trees that crowned the hillock. Haining describes the scene:

> The figure, appearing gigantic in the shadows, bounded towards her on legs that covered such distances with each stride that they scarcely seemed human. Behind it swirled a cloak, which billowed and flapped noisily. But above this cloak, it was the face which caught and held Polly's attention: a face with eyes that glowed like coals and a mouth which spat flashes of blue fire; a face from the very depths of hell. . . .
>
> A moment more and the figure was upon her. With a final leap that carried the creature almost over her and indeed blotted out everything except his frightful shape, he confronted her. There was the smell of sulphur and the warmth of fire on Polly's face and in her nostrils. . . . The eyes which glared at her seemed to swim in flame, and when the creature breathed, blue fire flashed from between his lips.[23]

As Adams screamed, the figure gripped her shoulders with cold, metallic fingers and laughed in her face. There was something strangely familiar about the laugh, and as she looked into the face of her attacker, she saw that its eyes bulged in a horrible way. About to faint, Adams would have fallen had not the "creature" held her. It now began to tear at her clothes, ripping her bodice from her breasts and leaving her exposed to the cold night air. With this Adams fell back, feeling darkness descend upon her, but the strange figure was already turning away, and as she fell in a swoon, it bounded once more into the night.

Such is Haining's luridly written account, worthy indeed of the penny dreadful literature that was soon to adopt Spring-Heeled Jack as its own. (Penny dreadfuls, pamphlets no more than eight pages in length, were nineteenth-century forerunners of the comics of the 1950s and the pulp fiction of early science fiction. These stories were hammered out by mostly talentless and anonymous authors and mass-produced to sell on street corners for the price of a single penny.) Some of the details are certainly accurate. Whitefield's Mount is real, once the site of gatherings to hear the eighteenth-century itinerant preacher George Whitfield, and as we have seen, the Green Man Tavern also existed. But beyond this, is there any evidence at all to support Haining's story? The time is certainly right, as this event occurred when sightings of Spring-Heeled Jack were at their height, but nothing has come to light so far, either in newspaper reports or police records. It therefore seems likely that the author adapted several Jack stories to his own ends. In particular, Adams's description of the man who molested her at the fair is clearly intended to suggest the Marquis of Waterford, noted for his loud laugh and staring eyes (see chapter 6). Haining likely inserted this description into the story in preparation for his attempt to prove that the "real" Spring-Heeled Jack was in fact the marquis. As we shall see Haining was not the first to do so.

But Haining was not yet done with his overblown account. He now added a story that, if it were true, would make Spring-Heeled Jack not only an attacker of defenseless women but also a murderer.

THE MURDER OF MARIA DAVIS

The story told by Haining takes place some years later, when the appearances of Spring-Heeled Jack were beginning to die out. He sets it in one of the most infamous sites in the whole of Victorian London—Jacob's Island, bordered by Mill Street, Bermondsey West Wall, George Row, and Wolseley Street. In his book *Oliver Twist,* novelist Charles Dickens immortalized this area, where the villain Bill Sikes dies. Dickens's description bears all the hallmarks of his vivid narrative powers.

> [C]razy wooden galleries common to the backs of half a dozen houses, with holes from which to look upon the slime beneath; windows, broken and patched, with poles thrust out, on which to dry the linen that is never there; rooms so small, so filthy, so confined, that the air would seem to be too tainted even for the dirt and squalor which they shelter; wooden chambers thrusting themselves out above the mud and threatening to fall into it—as some have done; dirt-besmeared walls and decaying foundations, every repulsive lineament of poverty, every loathsome indication of filth, rot, and garbage.[24]

It was to this den of iniquity, a place that was home to watermen, thieves, and prostitutes, that Spring-Heeled Jack made an appearance, according to Haining, on November 12, 1845. During the night he was apparently seen, leaping from rotting gallery to rotting gallery, his cloak flying out behind him and fire issuing from his mouth. The sight of this demonic figure caused such fear among the gin-sodden dwellers of the island that they fled before him. Haining describes what happened.

> But as he leapt from one side of the island to another, Jack paused on the bridge across the appropriately named Folly Ditch, cornering a bedraggled young prostitute of thirteen years old named Mariah Davis, who was about to set out to earn a few pence.

The ragged, wretched girl . . . stood rooted to the spot as Jack bounded up. He took one look at her, grasped her by the shoulders, and breathed fire into her face.

Huddled behind their windows, the few eyewitnesses said Jack picked the terrified girl up in his arms and with one jerk hurled her into the fowl, muddy waters below. With a laugh, he then bounded over the bridge and was lost in the maze of buildings."[25]

Despite her cries no one came to help the girl, who sank beneath the mud of the ditch in much the same way as Dickens had described the death of Bill Sikes. The "facts" were then reported to the police, and the ditch was dragged to recover the girl's body. An inquest was made and found her the victim of "death by misadventure." Nothing further was ever discovered.

This story seems even more unlikely than Haining's previous tale. Not only has no record of this murder and subsequent inquest ever come to light, but it also seems completely out of character with the rest of the accounts of Spring-Heeled Jack's activities. As Haining points out, there were other murders attributed to him, but none of them were ever proven, and in most cases the real culprit was caught and executed.

Of course it is possible that among the countless murders that took place in Victorian London, most especially in the area described, this incident could have gone unrecorded. Certainly the death of a thirteen-year-old prostitute would not get much attention from the police, but it seems unlikely that no record of any kind can be found. Finally, Haining included a contemporary illustration captioned "Recovering the body of the prostitute Maria Davis from Folly Ditch."[26] This shows a boat with two men, apparently hauling something from the ooze. However, further investigation by Mike Dash proved that the picture had nothing to do with this story but actually showed two men filling a water container from the filthy water of the ditch.

Haining's final story, for which, again, there is no external evidence, is perhaps one that one most wishes were true. Haining notes that Admiral Codrington, who put up a reward for the capture of Spring-Heeled Jack (see page 31), was not the only famous military figure to become entangled in the story. No lesser a person than Arthur Wellesley, the Duke of Wellington (1769–1852) and victor of Waterloo, was, according to Haining, driven to come out of retirement to lead the hunt for Spring-Heeled Jack. We are told that in January 1838, incensed by the reports of Jack's attacks, the Iron Duke, then nearly seventy, vowed to catch the villain himself. Apparently, every night "the Duke set out . . . on horseback from his London home to patrol Spring-Heeled Jack's likely locations. Even he, though, was not prepared to underestimate his opponent, and, to his saddlebow, he attached holsters in which he carried his most trusty pistols."[27]

Haining adds, with a flourish, that

> the sight of this marvelous and much revered old man setting off in the dusk each evening was said to have been watched by many London citizens and, according to one report, 'so cheered those who saw him that they felt able to sleep easy in their beds that night'. Fortunately, however, they heard the noise, and returned to her assistance, whereupon the ruffian ran off, thus escaping the chastisement he richly deserved. The woman was injured by the fright, but is recovering.
>
> It was a spirited gesture—but also destined to come to nothing. For even the man who had taken on and defeated some of the world's most feared armies and their commanders could not deter the leaping terror of Southern London."[28]

The effect of this is to make the saga seem even more extensive and dramatic, but in fact, a careful search of several biographies, diaries, and letters from this period, as well as newspapers from the time, brings no sign of any such attempt on the part of the great duke to single-handedly capture Jack. Such an omission is extremely unlikely, since any action by the duke became the center of reportage.

DELICATE LITTLE THINGS

Looking back over the reports gathered here, we might feel astonishment at the sheer extent of the newspaper reports about Spring-Heeled Jack. But these suggest that there must have been a substantial oral reportage going on at the same time. It seems more than likely that stories of Jack's appearances were passed from mouth to mouth and ear to ear in public houses, gambling clubs, and any other place where the citizens of London gathered.

By March 1838, Jack was being referred to as "the celebrated Spring-Heeled Jack."[29] Within three months of the first accounts, he had gone

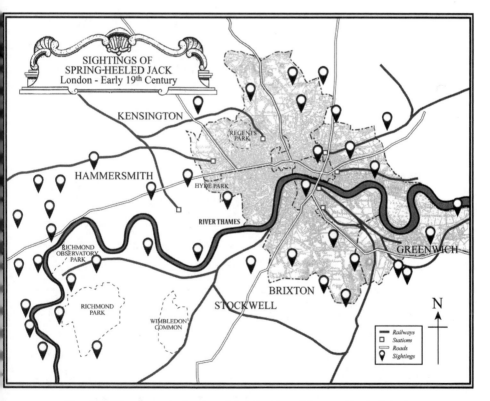

Fig. 2.2. The spread of principle sightings of Spring-Heeled Jack around London between 1838 and 1872. These are by no means all of the reported appearances, but they show a pattern reported in the press during this period. (Map by Wil Kinghan)

from being seen as part of a gang of annoying and mischievous youths to a famous personage! One thing is clear, and that is the almost constant state of excitement generated among the general populace of London. One must also remember that the streets of the metropolis, especially in the more outlying areas where the sightings mostly occurred, were without streetlights, which did not extend beyond the city center until the 1890s.

It may seem almost too obvious to note that Jack's appearances almost always took place at night and that this added considerably to the fear generated by the attacks. We cannot help wondering whether these attacks would have been as widely believed or caused such widespread panic if they had taken place in broad daylight.

The story of the Alsop girls illustrates this clearly: If Jane Alsop hadn't brought the candle to the door, little would have been seen beyond shadowy figures. Depending on the fullness of the moon, the outside world was for the most part pitch black. The appearance of a cloaked figure, with a bright lantern or even a candle, would have been shocking, while the glaring eyes and blue fire were calculated to bring anyone to a state of shock.

The exact nature of Spring-Heeled Jack's attacks remains difficult to pin down due to the vagueness of the reporting. Terms such as "outrage" and "assault" were sometimes used as an indication of a sexual attack, but because such were considered too awful to describe, we cannot be certain whether Jack's attacks were of this kind or not. If he was indeed a predator who sought out young women (one as young as fourteen), then he seems never to have actually done much harm. Claims that his appearances were all a prank perpetrated by several young men in disguise evolved to a story that he planned to murder six women over a specific period of time. That these murders never happened is indicative of the sensationalism that boosted Jack's story to new levels of terror.

It is worth noting also that most of the attacks were aimed at women. In the Victorian era, women were perceived as delicate creatures likely to faint at the drop of a handkerchief. Spring-Heeled Jack may have harbored this stereotypical view of women, which prompted him to choose women as victims, but it's virtually impossible to ascertain the true nature of his intentions. Was he simply out to frighten women (and some men), or were his actions driven by something altogether more serious, and perhaps not recognized given the mores of the time? At least one anecdote in *The Penny Satirist* for March 10, 1838, suggests that some commentators—or possibly those who sought to use the stories of Spring-Heeled Jack for their own (often misogynistic) ends—put words in the mouth of this particular attacker to make a point about feminine behavior. The illustration attached to the article shows an apparently naked figure (other than cloak, boots, and helmet) reaching out for two fleeing women. While the latter cry "murder," this Jack utters the following:

> I have seen your wickedness! I know all your naughty doings . . . I have heard all your gossiping tales and slanderous anecdotes! Now is the day of retribution! I am the spirit of judgment! . . . I come to hold the reins of sin, and check the course of immorality. It is the sinner only that fears! The good I harm not! The innocent will kiss my hands, and play with my talons; but the wicked heart I will tear out."[30]

The intention may be satirical, pointing a finger at the moralists whose vociferous rantings were to be heard on so many street corners, but the underlying note of sexism is very much to be heard. *Equally, it could be argued that in accordance with the thinking of the time, gossiping women might be subject to punishment and that such was being meted out by Jack.*

The phrase "overexcited female imagination" is certainly bandied about in many of the reports and says much about the attitude of both the press and the authorities. Thus the implication in the Lucy Scales case (pages 43–47) is that the whole thing was the product of an overactive imagination brought on by having read a previous account of Spring-Heeled Jack's activities before leaving the house.

It may be hard for us, living in the twenty-first century, to understand this kind of thinking, but the truth is that girls were brought up in such constrained circumstances, and their lives so fenced around by stereotypical rules, that only the few who possessed the tenacity to break free of their appointed roles in society could ever hope to live full lives.

In the countryside beyond the metropolis, things were very little different, but whatever caused Jack to move his area of activity there, he was to find a tougher and more determined response to his activities.

CHAPTER 3

Jack Takes a Holiday

For I done the deed and my name is Spring-Heel Jack.
Catch me if you can.

JACKSON'S OXFORD JOURNAL, 1861

After the capture and arraignment of James Painter in April 1838, reports of Spring-Heeled Jack's activities around London begin to dry up. It seems as though he had decided to take a holiday from the grim metropolis and head for more open climes. There is a report from the *County Herald and Weekly Advertiser* for April 24, 1838, which places him at Southend, followed immediately by two attacks in Yarmouth and another in Plymouth.

The Southend appearance reported "a gross attack . . . made on the wife of one of the preventative men [customs officials],"[1] who was returning home from the local chapel, when she was seized by the heels, thrown to the ground, her clothes torn, and grass stuffed into her mouth to prevent her from calling for help. No more details are given other than that the attacker was dressed as a gentlemen and fled the scene when she managed to alert her friends.

This is very likely a common sexual attack and not only bears no resemblance to the previous accounts, but is also very different from all others. The only thing that connects it is the heading "Spring-Heeled Jack at Southend," suggesting that by this time, any attack on a woman was automatically attributed to Jack.

A further report links Jack with Rose Hill, also in Sussex, though he appears this time again in the form of a bear.

The Times

APRIL 14, 1838

Spring-Heeled Jack has, it seems, found his way to the Sussex coast. On Friday evening, between 9 and 10 o'clock, he appeared, as we are informed, to a gardener near Rose-Hill in the shape of a bear or some other four-footed animal, and having first attracted attention by a growl, then mounted the garden wall, covered as it was with broken glass, and ran along it upon all fours to the great terror and consternation of the gardener, who began to think it time to escape. He was accordingly about to leave the garden, when Spring-Heeled Jack leapt from the wall, and chased him for some time; the dog was called, but slunk away, apparently as much terrified as its master. Having amused himself sometime with the trembling gardener, Spring-Heeled Jack scaled the wall and made his exit. The fellow may probably amuse himself in this way once too often.

The *Leeds Mercury* for May 19 of the same year followed up with a story of what we might call a typical Spring-Heeled Jack attack on a woman. Again, the form taken is that of a bear, but this time the scene has moved to Whitby, a considerable distance away, farther around the coastline of Britain.

The Leeds Mercury

MAY 19, 1838

Spring heeled Jack is playing his pranks at Whitby. One female has been grossly insulted by him in the shape of a bear. Her clothes were torn from her back, and her face much injured and disfigured, by the scratches from his claws—firmly fixed to his hands. The woman was almost frightened out of her senses. Let the police of Yorkshire

look after this mysterious vagabond, and accomplished that which
the London police officers were
unable to do—cage him.

Again, this sounds like a sexual assault, and despite the references
to the bear, it is clear that both these reports consider the person to be
a human perpetrator somehow disguised as an animal.

At this point sightings become sparse. One of interest is reported in
1840, and finds Jack briefly back in the familiar territory of Camden
Town, London. The attack is, once again, fairly typical, though there
is an element of sexual assault, which was not so much present in the
previous reports.

The Examiner

MAY 11, 1840

During the past week much alarm
has pervaded the neighbourhood
of Kings Road, Camden Town,
and caused as much terror in the
minds of the female population of
the inhabitants as did the pranks
and gambles of Spring-Heeled
Jack, on his first appearance about
three years since; indeed they are
afraid to leave their houses after
nightfall. The cause of all this failure on the part of the females is
a tall man, or brute, enclosed in
a large blue cloak, the glasses of
a dark color over his eyes, which
give him the most 'awful' appearance. As soon as night comes on he
patrols the above road, but, on the
appearance of any male, he darts
into a doorway, and hides until
his disturber has passed! Here he
will remain until he sees a female,
when he suddenly jumps from his
hiding place, and assaults his helpless victim in the most shameful
manner.

Here we notice that Jack's normally black cloak is now blue and that
he appears to be wearing dark glasses. The British weekly newspaper the
Era for the same day gives a much more detailed account of this sighting. Having repeated the earlier story more or less verbatim, it continues:

𝕿𝖍𝖊 𝕰𝖗𝖆

MAY 11, 1840

The spot generally selected by this vagabond for his assaults is College Grove, a dark and badly paved turning leading from the above road to Camden High Street. This turning, in parts, is very narrow, and without a light all the way down, although the inhabitants are heavily taxed by the paving commissioners for that commodity. The way in which the females are frightened and insulted in this place is as follows: the miscreant jumps from his hiding place, and stretching out his arms under his cloak, makes that article of clothing have the appearance of a huge pair of black wings, which completely blocks up the thoroughfare. He then envelops the frightened female in the folds of his cloak and commits the most disgusting assaults upon her. A few evenings back a lady, proceeding to her residence in Kentish Town, was met by this fellow, a few paces from St. Pancras workhouse, who commenced taking the most indecent liberties with her. She made great resistance, and, disengaging herself from her assailant's grasp, retraced her steps and entered the Elephant and Castle public house in the most agitated state, and after detailing the brutal way in which she had been treated, one of the inmates proffered his services to see her home, which was gladly accepted. A sharp lookout was kept by the man, but no traces of the miscreant could be seen. Since the above a young girl, named Coke, residing in College Grove, has been so maltreated and frightened by the same fellow that she is now in a very bad state of health. Information of the above and several other outrages on females in the above locality has been given to the police, who have their eyes on the delinquent; and he has not only to try and avoid their vigilance, but that of the husbands of several females he has assaulted, who will take the law into their hands, and call his brutal propensities by ducking him in the canal which is very near the spot.

The report of this attack, which seems far more serious than many others and received more column inches, vanished from sight, with no further coverage.

The next sighting of which we have any detailed information is reported in the *Bristol Mercury*. It takes a different tack by suggesting the effect one of Jack's appearances could have on an individual. The victim in question was a fourteen-year-old girl named Ellen Hurd, described as "exceedingly delicate" with a somewhat vacant expression on her face. Hurd was accused of stealing from a local grocer and brought up before the magistrates. Her defense is possibly unique in the history of Spring-Heeled Jack. Her brother-in-law told how she was transformed from a normal girl with exemplary character into the miscreant before the judges.

The Bristol Mercury

AUGUST 7, 1840

Up to the period referred to in the present charge, she had born[e] the most exemplary character, and as lately as December last was in full possession of her intellectual powers. In the course of that month, some miscreant who, we are sorry to say, has escaped detection, and who has been frightening persons in various parts of the city, under the assumed character of Spring-Heeled Jack, attacked her in Park Street, as she was going on an errand, and cut of[f] all her front hair. She was so dreadfully terrified by the outcome as to become deranged, and after remaining at home for some time in a state of much danger, she was admitted an inmate of the lunatic ward of St Peter's Hospital. After a while, she, under the care of the medical attendance of that institution, became so far recovered as suggested by her discharge, and she was returned to her friends. . . . Although not in a state to warrant her detention in hospital, she has never recovered full possession of her mental facilities; and having fallen in with a designing girl, who lives at the house of notorious character in Gloucester Lane, she was by her persuaded to leave her friends, and, subsequently, to take up goods . . . from Mr. Strickland and others.

This is a very different kind of story. Was it, perhaps, made up by the girl's brother-in-law to help her avoid charges? If so, it was successful, as Hurd was released into the care of her friends. However, the description of the attack, including the cutting of her hair, seems to be real. It was reported in the same newspaper, dated August 7, 1840, and describes the attack upon Ellen Hurd by a tall man dressed in a rough greatcoat who cut off the hair from the back of her head. Apart from the disagreement regarding the front or back hair, the attack seems real enough. Once again, this seems atypical of previous Spring-Heeled Jack attacks, and the reporter notes that this was almost certainly the work of someone who assumed the character of Spring-Heeled Jack.

The Hurd case illustrates once again the way in which women were considered unstable and prone to "fits." Here the suggestion is that Spring-Heeled Jack's attack had driven the girl mad. Since she reputedly ended up in a mental institution following the alleged assault, this is certainly the conclusion we are meant to draw. However, we cannot help wondering if the real reason for Hurd's incarceration was the failure of her family to understand or believe in the nature of the incident. If she indeed stuck to her story, she may well have found herself treated with ridicule, and this could well be the real reason for her incarceration.

THE BULL-MAN OF YARMOUTH

Virtual silence on the matter of Spring-Heeled Jack falls over the next five years—though there were random sightings in Edinburgh—which seem to be unsubstantiated or to be simply copycat activities.

The next two reports of interest come to us from Yarmouth, in the county of Norfolk, and date from fully five years later. They concern the death of a fifty-year-old man named Purdy. The *Illustrated London News* drew attention to the case on September 27, 1845, describing it as most unusual because the elderly man had apparently met his fate "in an affray with a young man of the name of Noble, while [im]personating the mysterious Spring-Heeled Jack."[2]

In fact it was Mr. Purdy himself who was mistakenly identified as Jack, rather than the young man. The report continues:

The Illustrated London News

SEPTEMBER 27, 1845

From the evidence it appeared that the deceased, had, for several days prior to his demise, been suffering from pleurisy and inflammation of the lungs. On Saturday night, his wife, who had been sitting up with him, fell asleep from extreme fatigue, and during her slumber the poor man, in a state of delirium, got up, left the house with only his shirt on, and imagining that his donkey had got loose, was feeling about the shutters of the neighboring house . . . when he was perceived by a female occupant of the dwelling, who . . . screamed for assistance.

It was the young man, one Henry Noble, who came to her aid. Apparently, seeing the nightshirt-clad Purdy, he assumed "it was the spree of a certain Spring-Heeled Jack, [and] proceeded to inflict severe punishment upon the deceased, who died on the following day."[3]

Fortunately for the young man, the coroner, who made a postmortem examination of the body, pronounced the cause of death to be natural causes, stating that the blows had no effect on Purdy's demise and had not even accelerated it. Henry Noble was released.

Such stories only go to demonstrate that by this time incidents of this kind were routinely ascribed to Spring-Heeled Jack—not intended to actually identify the attacker but as a way of describing or characterizing the assault, though the incident bore no resemblance to Jack at all.

However, two years after this, in the spring of 1847, a further outbreak of Jack "sightings" took place in Teignmouth, Devon. This time the event was reported at some length and bore several marks of similarity to the original London accounts.

The first note was in *Woolmer's Exeter and Plymouth Gazette* and is dated March 13, 1847, though apparently referring to events that had taken place several weeks earlier. The reporter makes it clear that the event had severely shaken the peaceful residents of the town.

Woolmer's Exeter and Plymouth Gazette

MARCH 13, 1847

Great sensation has been created in our somewhat peaceable town within the last few weeks by the appearance of a goblin-like form enveloped in a bullock's hide, and otherwise hideously arrayed, to the great terror of the timid inhabitants who may chance to cross his path. Some weeks since, a respectable young woman, whilst wending her way amidst the shades of night towards her home, situated along a by-road, encountered the hideous form, and became greatly alarmed. Her shrieks soon brought the assistance of friends, who arrived in time to witness the flight of this monster in human form over a high wall; the girl has ever since been confined to her bed.

We may note here the description of the attacker "enveloped in a bullock's hide," which seems to hark back to the earliest appearances of Jack in London in 1838. A similar story, recorded by the poet Kathleen Raine, will be examined in chapter 5. Indeed, throughout the series of stories that follow from this point, Jack is more often referred to as a ghost, as had been the case at the beginning of the scare.

Following an investigation, the police remanded a Major Kelson, whose only apparent crime seemed to be the possession of a large white moustache, which, in the eyes of the newspaper reporter, was clearly seen as giving him a fiendish appearance!

A few days later, on March 27, the same newspaper reported the appearance of another military man, a Captain Finch, before the magistrates, accused of an attack on a servant girl named Louisa Herd, bearing all the hallmarks of Spring-Heeled Jack. The case was apparently widely known within the local community, and the courthouse was packed on the day of the trial.

After some legal shuffling, with the complainant's attorney asking for an adjournment and the defendant insisting on continuing, the trial got under way with the appearance of Louisa Herd who gave evidence that Captain Finch had

Woolmer's Exeter and Plymouth Gazette

MARCH 27, 1847

accosted her in Fore Street, in open day, using the insinuating terms of 'My pretty little dear', that he did also, several times, assault her in a private road leading to her mistress's house, situate[d] in McFarlane's Row, at which time he was disguised in a dress resembling a Bullock's Hide; that he also took hold of her and used her very roughly. The sudden fright and alarm had thrown her into hysterical fits, and caused such material injuries, as she may never recover. The complainant said she had seen the defendant in a mackintosh, which, at her appearance, he had thrown open and disclosed the identical disguise [presumably the Bull's hide] tied around his person.

Louisa Herd then identified the defendant as the person who had assaulted her and though cross-examined "at some length" by Mr. Jordan, Finch's attorney, remained unshakable in her assertion. A further witness, one Walter Palmer, then disclosed that he had seen the defendant "standing on the Teignmouth Bridge about seven o'clock on the same night, in a disguise similar to that described by the complainant."[4]

Next to appear, on behalf of the defendant, was a Dr. Withers, who had attended Captain Finch for the last three to four months and had at times found him very ill. He was, apparently, suffering from "an internal disease, and any excitement or bodily exertion might cause instantaneous death."[5] Dr. Withers added that he had never known his patient to be out after four o'clock. This was backed up by three other military men, Major McDougall, Captain Hall, and Major Stevenson, all of whom were intimates with Captain Finch. Major Stevenson gave evidence that he had visited Captain Finch on January 13, the date of one of the alleged attacks, and found him at home. A variety of other witnesses then appeared, including the captain's domestic servants, each one swearing that Finch virtually never left home after four.

Despite the testimonies the case went against Captain Finch. The magistrate summed up that it was his painful duty, despite the apparently general good character of the defendant, to dismiss his alibi and to fine him seventeen shillings[14] for each offense, as well as costs of a further five pounds.[6]

Following the report, the newspaper then printed two letters, the first signed by the witnesses of good character and the second by Captain Finch himself.

WOOLMER'S EXETER AND PLYMOUTH GAZETTE, MARCH 27, 1847

Shaldon, 23rd March, 1847

Dear Sir,—greatly commiserating the unfortunate position you are placed in by the conviction of Monday last before the bench at Teignmouth, we, your neighbors and friends, wish to assure you that we are convinced you are entirely incapable of acting the way described by the witness against you. Since your residency here, the very retired life you have uniformly led, your honorable and gentlemanly bearing, to say nothing of the distressing malady with which you are afflicted (Aneurism of the heart), as incapacitating you, according to your medical adviser's disposition, lead us to form a decided opinion that you cannot be, and are not, that violator of decency and honor you were convicted of being.

Assuring you of the continuance of our highest esteem, and our deep regret that we feel called upon to address you upon this unfortunate occasion,

We are, dear sir,

Yours very sincerely,

JAY MCDOUGALL,
LATE MAJOR, K.C.B.
WILLIAM ROW
N. A. BARTLETT
ROBERT BOWDEN
J. REES
J. TOOGOOD COWARD
CHARLES HALL
JOHN S. CLAPP
DR. WITHERS

Finch's response, dated March 25, 1847, reads as follows:

WOOLMER'S EXETER AND PLYMOUTH GAZETTE, MARCH 27, 1847

GENTLEMEN,—I thank you for your letter; this is not the first time that I have been the victim of conspiracy; I regret it the more that it should have fallen upon me in the shattered state of my health to defend myself. I trust time will unravel this affair and that you will have no reason to regret the view you have taken of my case. Let me assure you, I will not rest under the disgrace of this accusation, for I consider, were I to do so, no man's life or honor would be safe from the attacks of dis- honest and unprincipled persons. With many thanks for your kind communication, especially as I am almost a stranger among you.

I remain, gentlemen, yours very truly,

EDWARD FINCH

Leaving aside the curious names of some of the signatories to the letter (J. Toogood Coward! John S. Clapp!) what are we to make of this—indeed of the whole trial? It is very clear that the evidence given by Louisa Herd was taken as absolute truth and that she did not give way under cross-examination. But it seems surprising that the evidence of the doctor and the officers was so easily set aside. For the most likely explanation, we must turn to a further report, this time in the *North Devon Journal*.

North Devon Journal

APRIL 1, 1847

EXTRAORDINARY CASE—'SPRING-HEELED JACK'

Teignmouth was greatly excited on Monday in consequence of a 'Spring-Heeled Jack' investigation before the magistrates. A delinquent of the genus occupied himself during the winter in frightening and annoying defenseless women, some of who were rather roughly handled. The police having been on the alert for some time, suspicion fell on Capt. Finch, of Shaldon—a man of alleged ill health—and apparently 60 years of age, about the last person who could have been suspected. He was summoned before the magistrates. Mr. Tacker [appearing for the plaintiff] in opening the case for the complainant, said it was not only difficult, but most painful to him; his client belonged to the humblest rank, and the defendant, Capt. Finch, had been considered highly respectable. Should he not succeed in establishing the charge, the effect of the girl's evidence might prejudice her through life; should he succeed, the model character of one who had hitherto moved as a gentleman would be blasted. He had two charges of assault to prefer. His client, [Louisa Hyde] the servant of Miss Morgan, already living in McFarlane's Row, Bitton Road, had been twice assaulted in January, between nine and ten at night, by a man disguised in a skin coat having the appearance of the bullock's side, skullcap, horns, and mask, and the alarm had produced serious fits. Evidence having been given in support of the charges, the Bench expressed pain at finding an old soldier guilty of such an assault, but there was no material refutation to the complainant's evidence.

Two days later a brief statement appeared in *Woolmer's Exeter and Plymouth Gazette* for April 3, 1847: "Teignmouth.—Spring-Heeled Jack's case is not yet over—strange rumors are still afoot that the guilty party is not yet brought to justice; a private investigation has been going on this week, which is all to come out at the next magistrates meeting, when perhaps the long talked-of mystery will be solved."[7]

No evidence of any such "private investigation" has so far come to light, and nothing further is heard of Captain Finch or Miss Herd.

On the face of it, it seems unlikely that a sixty-year-old man, suffering from a heart complaint, could really have been guilty of several attacks—each one on the same girl and involving leaps over a wall—over a period of months. Yet, despite the good character references offered by Finch's neighbors, the girl remained convinced of her attacker's identity and the magistrates opted to find him guilty. The "disguise" described in the *North Devon Journal's* account is so like that of Spring-Heeled Jack's first appearances ten years earlier as to suggest they were borrowing from earlier accounts in order to spice up the case. If so, this is almost certainly the latest of several such accounts of random attacks on young women (mostly of the servant class), which appear to have been added to and dramatized by the addition of Jack's name and appearance.

This calls into doubt many of the earlier records we have explored here. If, as seems increasingly likely, Spring-Heeled Jack was at least partly an invention of overexcited minds, mixed with ancient folklore and superstition, many of the attacks laid at his door may have been either complete fabrications or overblown reportage based on insufficient facts. In the matter of Captain Finch, the mystery remains unresolved. Perhaps the captain was indeed a serial flasher, as seems so likely from the description of him opening his mackintosh, or maybe he had, at some point, addressed himself flirtatiously to the servant girl Louisa Herd, prompting her to invent the whole matter in order to teach him a lesson. Of these two options, the former seems more likely, with the dressing of the story in the costume of Spring-Heeled Jack being the work of the newspapers.

Following on from this, there are almost no reported sightings until October 1861, but the story is interesting. A petty session case brought before the magistrates at Bicester, Oxfordshire, on October 4 of that year, concerned three people accused of setting fire to a hayrick belonging to a Reverend H. J. De Salis at his farm in Fringford. William, Mary, and Charles Robinson, who worked for De Salis, were accused of arson; it was assumed with intent to protest against working conditions and the pitiful wages offered by their master. Following threats from an anonymous source, a police constable had been given the task of protecting the hayrick. On the night in question, the Robinsons had invited him into their home and plied him with refreshments, during which time both William and Mary left the house. Shortly after this, the fire started, and on the evidence of the constable, all three family members were arrested.

At this point the Reverend De Salis received a handwritten, ungrammatical, and badly spelled note, which reads:

> Don't Blame your Foreman [William Robinson] no longer for he is Inocent as A child unborn, For I done the deeds and my name is Spring Heel Jack. Catch me if you can. Don't Blame him no more for if you do you Blame the wrong man I am sure and I fear none of your Police finding me out you see that.[8]

Unfortunately for the Robinsons, a search of their house revealed some writing paper of the same type as that used in the message and a prayer book and some accounts with handwriting that matched the letter. All three were found guilty of starting the fire.

What is interesting here is the use of the name Spring-Heeled Jack as the perpetrator of the offense. This was, we remember, some years after the original stories, from which we may presume that, at least in the countryside, his name and deeds lingered on. Professor Karl Bell, in his study of Jack's presence in Victorian history and culture, suggests that the firing of the hayrick may be related to the so-called Swing Riots, which took place in the 1830s. These were in response to the introduction of new farm machinery, which meant less work for farm hands across the country and resulted in the destruction of threshing machines and the burning of barns and hayricks. At the time these were blamed on two mythical figures, Captain Swing and General Ludd (from which we get the word Luddites), whose activities, while they bear no resemblance to those of Spring-Heeled Jack, can be compared to his lawless practices and the fact that he was never captured. Perhaps the Robinsons saw a likeness to the heroes of the Swing Riots and thought they would convince the authorities that Jack had retuned and was on their side.

After this there is a further long gap before the next sightings of Spring-Heeled Jack once again caught the attention of the public—or at least of the newspapers.

The next series of sightings occur between November and December 1872 (twenty-five years on from the Teignmouth case and eleven years after the Bicester arson trial) with a return to Peckham and Camberwell, both places the setting for the first reports of the leaping man. Since these constitute one of the most protracted stories in which Jack is continually referred to as a "ghost," we shall explore them in greater detail in chapter 3.

JACK TAKES ON THE ARMY

The saga of Spring-Heeled Jack was beginning to come to end, at least for the Victorian period. He would reappear several times after this, as we shall see, right into our own time, but his last great trick—if we can call it that—dates from 1877, four years after his last reported sighting in Sheffield. This time he took on no lesser an organization than the army.

Just like the first reports of Jack back in 1838, almost forty years earlier, the first rumor of a visitation—reported in *Sheldrake's Aldershot and Sandhurst Military Gazette* for March 17, 1877—was low key. Even the reporter seemed determined to play down the whole matter. Headed "Questionable Larks," which set the tone for the piece, it read:

Sheldrake's Aldershot and Sandhurst Military Gazette

MARCH 17, 1877

QUESTIONABLE LARKS

Someone or other appears to have made up his mind to play some rather questionable pranks with the sentries at this camp while on night duty. About a week ago it appears, but we do not vouch for the correctness of the story, a sentry was on duty at the North camp, and at about midnight someone came towards him who refused to answer the usual challenge of 'who comes there', and after dodging about the sentry box in a fantastic fashion for some little time, made off with astonishing swiftness, not however until the sentry had loaded his rifle and fired, but without any effect. Spring-Heeled Jack, as he has been termed in Camp, then paid a similar visit to the sentry on duty near the cemetery, who also fired, but alas without hitting the object at which he aimed. What or who the individual who is thus amusing himself might be we do not know, but such little bits of fun might be carried just too far; and enjoyment of this kind had better be discontinued before one of the nocturnal pranks leads to an unpleasant result.

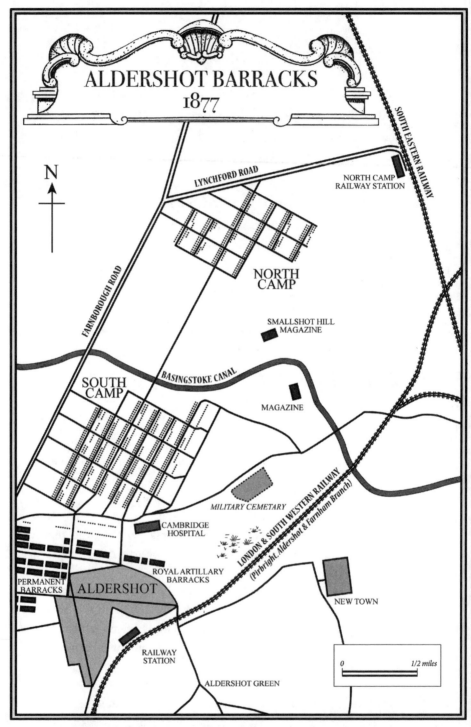

Fig. 3.1. Map of Aldershot Barracks in 1877, scene of attacks by a mysterious leaping figure. (Map by Wil Kinghan after Richard Furlong)

Fig. 3.2. The wooden barracks of North Camp, Aldershot, 1866.

These events took place at the Aldershot Barracks, then as now one of the largest installations of the British army. Established in 1854, on land purchased by the War Department to set up a permanent training camp, over time it grew into a military town and continues to be used by the army as such to the present day.

Before Aldershot, the army had no permanent camp for training troops on a large scale. The idea for such a site came from no lesser a person than the Duke of Wellington, who felt that a permanent base would enable the army to conduct military exercises more effectively. Beginning as a simple tented camp, the barracks grew into a permanent base with the outbreak of the Crimean War. Between 1854 and 1858, over twelve hundred wooden huts were built along either side of the Basingstoke Canal, dividing the site into North and South camps.

Queen Victoria and Prince Albert enjoyed reviewing the soldiery there and had their own Royal Pavilion built in 1874, in which they would stay through the visit.

Possibly because they considered it of no particular importance, or to simply play down the event, the next mention of the apparition was brief. On March 31, 1877, a reporter known simply as "Cove" notes in *Sheldrake's Aldershot and Sandhurst Military Gazette* that

Sheldrake's Aldershot and Sandhurst Military Gazette

MARCH 31, 1877

Spring-Heeled Jack has not been heard of, I believe, since the little affair with the sentries. Perhaps he has seen the error of his ways, or objects to the smell of powder. Whoever the silly mortal might be, he ought to be thankful that so far he has escaped [what] he richly deserves—a sound thrashing.

But a few days later, on April 11, a magazine known as *The World* included a much fuller account of the sighting (later reprinted in the *Illustrated Police News*), which added details that may or may not be true.

The World

APRIL 11, 1877

GHOSTS AT ALDERSHOT

A curious story comes from Aldershot. For sometime past the sentries on two outlying posts have been frightened to death by the appearance at night of two spectral-looking figures. The figures, glowing with phosphorus and otherwise alarming to the superstitious, are in the habit of suddenly manifesting themselves, taking tremendous springs of ten or twelve yards at a time, and upsetting the wretched sentry before he has had time to collect himself sufficiently to oppose earthly arms to his ghostly visitors. The latter do him no bodily injury, contenting themselves with upsetting the poor man, after which they mysteriously disappear. So great has been the panic it has been found necessary to double the sentries, and these have lately taken to loading with ball [shot]. Whether the rifles have been fired or not, I do not know; but I learn that the posts are still haunted. Neither have such precautions as sending out pickets [scouts] to explore the neighborhood been of any avail. It is supposed that the alarm has been caused by two practical jokers provided with powerful springs on the heels of their boots.

Here, the single leaper has become two, both described as ghostly apparitions, perceived, once again, as practical jokers. Cove clearly objected
to the sensational nature of the story and made a couple of brief, slight-
ing references to "Mr. Spring-Heeled Jack" and "Our Aldershot Ghost,"
adding that someone had apparently informed "a gentleman" that "his
object was to frighten the British Army." On April 28 Cove once again
held forth in response to a lurid picture included with the original
report in *Illustrated Police News*.

Illustrated Police News

APRIL 28, 1877

[T]o be favored by a sketch of one-
self in the pages of the beautifully
illustrated journal . . . is to have
arrived at the highest pinnacle of
notoriety. Such a mark of honor has
been conferred this week upon our
esteemed and popular 'Aldershot
Ghost'. The artist has displayed
great talent in the splendid work
of art, and no picture connoisseur
should think his collection complete without being in possession
of it. The moonlight nights have
rather interfered with the spectre's perambulations, and it is a
somewhat curious fact, to which
science has scarcely yet done justice, that ghosts seldom are particularly fond of the moon. Very
likely this one is now suffering
under lunar influences. There are
plenty of people anxiously awaiting his next coming forth, and so
little afraid have the weaker sex
become of him that I heard a young
lady declare the other evening, that
she sat up at her window all night
in hopes that she might catch sight
of the nimble goblin. But after all
is there anything strange about a
single Aldershot ghost, considering that every year there are whole
hosts of skeleton enemies annoying
and harassing our gallant soldiers.

The ironic tone of Cove's writing was not taken up by the *Times*,
which finally caught up with the stories of what had seemingly become
"nightly" appearances. The story was much amplified, and we learn that
the "gentleman" mentioned previously was in fact one of the guards.

The Times

MAY 15, 1877

For the past month the camp at Aldershot has been almost nightly visited by what is intended to represent a ghost. The author of these practical jokes has up to the present time escaped detection, and his doings have become the prevailing topic throughout the Camp. The object made its appearance about four weeks ago to a private in the 19th Regiment, who was on at guard at the North camp. It was midnight, and the sentry, perceiving something advancing towards him gave the usual challenge, to which no reply was made. The challenge was repeated, whereupon the would-be ghost went direct to the sentry box, slapped the soldier several times in the face, and before he could recover from his confusion, made off across the common with astonishing bounds. The soldier, in his excitement, loaded his rifle and fired, but missed his aim. From here the ghost went towards the military cemetery and in a similar manner attempted to frighten a private in the 100th Regiment, who was on guard by a powder magazine; and was again fired at, but without being hit. Nothing was heard of the ghost's movements after the above adventures until about a fortnight since, when he suddenly pounced upon a private in the Third Battalion 60th rifles, [standing] sentry by a powder magazine near the Basingstoke Canal. It appears that the ghostly visitor sprang on him from behind, and endeavored to snatch away his rifle. A sharp struggle ensued, which ended by the soldier receiving a pair of black eyes and losing his shako [a tall cap with a plume], which was found next morning in the canal. A few nights later a sentry by the Female Hospital [of the] South Camp, was discovered by a file of the guard on his post in [a] state of horror-stricken alarm, and on being asked what was the matter, pointed towards a retreating figure, which appeared to be a tall man dressed in a tightly fitting white coat. This was understood to be the supposed ghost and a chase ensued, but the object [out] distanced all its pursuers and was eventually lost to sight in some bushes. One sentry states that he was accosted the other night in the camp by someone with a mask, who informed him that he was the much-dreaded ghost and his object was to show the Nation how easily he could frighten the soldiers of the present day. At first there was great excitement in the Camp, but this [has] cooled down. Not the slightest clue has been obtained as to who or what the dancing individual is, but it might be mentioned that a few nights ago a tall gentlemen, carrying a carpetbag, was met by some provosts [army police] about 10 o'clock going into the Camp. He was stopped, but on stating he was an officer they allowed him to proceed. It is hardly probable, however, that the officer would be walking into the camp at that hour, there being no late train, or that he would have been having a carpet bag. It is therefore not reasonable to suppose that had the provosts followed the person in question the Aldershot ghost mystery would have been solved.

Here we learn that the activities of the "ghost" were "almost nightly over the past month" and that the attacks were far more physical than one would expect from a ghost. The slapping of the guard's face seems to be a kind of equivalent to the clawing actions of Spring-Heeled Jack forty years earlier, but here it is men who are the object of the attacks. Certainly the rather indifferent security of the place, which allowed the mysterious carpetbag man to enter simply because he said he was an officer, suggests that the ghost was right in his belief that it was easy "to frighten the soldiers of the present day."[9]

After this we again hear nothing further of the matter until five months later, on September 8, 1877, when the *Illustrated Police News* published the following report:

Illustrated Police News

SEPTEMBER 8, 1877

Not long ago speculation of every sort was at its height as to the so-called ghost, or as the soldiers irreverently styled him, 'Spring-Heeled Jack'. Suspicion finally settled on one particular corps, for the reason that the ghost had hitherto been seen where this regiment was stationed. The corps in question, however, has now left Aldershot, and the authorities were much astonished when they learned that 'Spring-Heeled Jack' has returned. His method of proceeding seems to be to approach unobserved some post, then climb the sentry box, and pass his hand (which is arranged to feel cold and clammy as that of a corpse) over the face of the sentinel. The sentries had lately been ordered to fire on the ghost, and were loaded with ball [shot], but this precaution had lately been given up. Jack pursued his old tactics on Friday last [August 31, 1877]. He managed to reach the powder magazine in the North camp. Here, having nearly frightened the sentry out of his wits, by slapping his face with his deathlike hand, he disappeared, hopping and bounding into the mist. The sentry recovered his presence of mind too late, and fired a round of blank ammunition, but without getting assistance in time to pursue the disturber of the peace. The reappearance of the ghost has caused the great sensation, principally one of indignation, and the authorities are determined this time to exhaust every means towards discovering the culprit.

Despite their presumed efforts, the authorities once again failed to capture the leaping ghost. As Mike Dash notes, the fact that the ghost reappeared only after the sentries had stopped loading their rifles with live ammunition suggests someone with knowledge of the camp.[10] Then there is the mysterious carpetbag man, who was allowed to pass unhindered into the camp but of whom nothing further is heard.

In June 1907 a Colonel Alfred C. E. Welby wrote to the journal *Notes and Queries,* a regular miscellany of curious and out-of-the-way information, with a suggestion of his own. Having summarized the events of thirty years previous with some variations (he makes the ghost sit on the sentry's shoulders and successfully steal his rifle), he concludes: "The pranks were popularly attributed to a lively officer of Rifles; he certainly was not convicted of them, and I do not know that he ever acknowledged himself to be Spring-Heeled Jack."[11]

We may assume that Colonel Welby had inside information, and the redoubtable Mike Dash searched the army records for such a person and found that he did exist. He also found a memoir by Lord Ernest Hamilton (1858–1939), soldier, MP, and novelist, whose book amazingly bears out Welby's account. The memoir, *40 Years On*, mentions that Spring-Heeled Jack had appeared at Colchester Barracks in 1878. This date, and the one that Hamilton gives to the activities at Aldershot, pushes the sightings forward by a year. This may be due to faulty memory. However, reports from several newspapers for 1878 strengthen Hamilton's account.

Reynolds's Newspaper

NOVEMBER 10, 1878

With the removal of the third Battalion 60th rifles from Aldershot to Colchester Spring-Heel Jack, whose vagaries at the former place excited considerable attention, seems also to have changed his quarters, and the garrison at Colchester is now in a state of excitement over his escapades. The principal scene of his operations is the Abbey Field, where he has visited several lonely sentries, all of whom he has frightened, and two so seriously that they are now under treatment in the garrison hospital, it being feared that the mind of one is completely unhinged. It is stated that the sentries [are] to be doubled.

Hamilton's memory is concerned more with the dullness of life at Colchester and how

REYNOLDS'S NEWSPAPER, NOVEMBER 10, 1878

in the winter of 1878, the monotony was pleasantly relieved by the appearance on the scene of an illusive midnight reveler known as 'Spring-heeled Jack'. This mysterious being was responsible for a series of visitations, which shook the nerves of the entire military camp to their foundations. Night after night sentries would be bonneted, cuffed and thrown down by an invisible assailant. Cavalry, infantry and artillery were all alike impartially victimized. In our own Cavalry barracks, the story told next day by the nerve-shattered wrecks who had been on sentry-duty the night before was that

Spring-Heeled Jack came flying 'without any preliminary warning' over the top of the stable buildings, dropped on their shoulders, knocked them down and was gone before they could recover their feet. Other reports were to the effect that a snow-white figure suddenly appeared from nowhere, hurled the sentries about with Superhuman strength and vanished into thin air. All accounts agreed that Spring-Heeled Jack's movements were absolutely noiseless.

The whole population of Colchester, both military and civil, was deeply stirred. Sentries were everywhere doubled and, even then, went on their rounds with shaking knees and perspiring brows.

At this point Hamilton adds several details that bear out the remarks of Colonel Welby in *Notes and Queries,* and at the same time leaves us with a fascinating glimpse of one of Spring-Heeled Jack's most striking pretenders. While the soldiers at the camp were apparently convinced the visitant was the devil,

REYNOLDS'S NEWSPAPER, NOVEMBER 10, 1878

[w]e, in the officers' mess, were just as firmly convinced that it was Lieut. Alfrey of the 60th Rifles. Probably both were wrong. Alfrey was a very big and powerful man, but extraordinarily active. He used to come out with the Essex and Suffolk hounds on a grey polo-pony of about fourteen hands, and it was the prettiest sight in the world to see the two in combination. On approaching a five-barred gate, Alfrey would vault off his pony's back whilst in full career. He and the pony would then jump the gate side by side, after which he would vault back into the saddle and continue the chase until the next gate was reached, when the performance would be repeated.

Hamilton's suspicions were strengthened when his battalion moved to Aldershot in the winter of 1879.

REYNOLDS'S NEWSPAPER, NOVEMBER 10, 1878

The 60th moved to Aldershot about the same time, and, at once, Spring-heeled Jack made his appearance in the new camp and commenced his old pranks on the night sentries. At Aldershot, the general panic became so great that eventually Spring-Heeled Jack was officially proclaimed in General Orders; ball cartridge was handed out to the sentries, and these were ordered to shoot the night terror on sight. These measures proved effective, and Spring-Heeled Jack was seen no more. Whether it really was Alfrey or not I have never learnt, and it would be interesting to have some pronouncement on the subject from his own lips or from his own pen. His equipment was supposed to consist of rubber-soled shoes and a sheet which was white on one side and black on the other.

If Alfrey was the culprit, he never came forward and is probably best consigned to the ranks of the other contenders for the crown of Spring-Heeled Jack. However, it seems safe to say that this particular manifestation was a practical joke played by someone in the camp. This does not, of course, explain the huge bounds apparently accomplished by the "ghost," or the fact that he was several times shot at with no apparent effect (we can assume this was most likely poor marksmanship), but these are probably no more than the association that accompanied the name Spring-Heeled Jack.

This is not quite the end of the Aldershot and Colchester story. On December 21 the London *Evening Standard* posted a report, reprinted in the *Ipswich Gazette,* which triumphantly claimed that this "Military Spring-Heeled Jack" had been brought to book.

The Evening Standard

DECEMBER 21, 1879

An officer of the third Battalion of the 60th rifles, one of the gallant gentlemen who have been accustomed to amuse themselves by frightening women and children after the fashion of Spring-Heeled Jack, has, we are extremely glad to hear, been laid up at Colchester, in consequence of a bayonet wound in the leg, inflicted by the sentry who captured him. Some of these humorous officers have been very successful in following and injuring residents of the districts which had the honour of holding them, and a writer in a military paper observes that in the pursuit of amusement the officers in question have brought about, unfortunately, a series of evils for which a bayonet wound in the leg is not adequate punishment. It may be that this supreme joke in frightening women in delicate health into fits, and causing results of which we do not care to speak, had emboldened the military Spring-Heel Jacks, and that the particular members of the body who is now lying at Colchester thought he could have an equal fun with the sentry. But for once he made a mistake; and we trust it may be assumed that the military authorities will not suffer the matter to rest, and consider that the offender has been sufficiently punished by his wound. What sort of discipline can be expected from soldiers during their leisure hours when officers thus misconduct themselves? The wounded young gentleman seems to have been caught *in flagrante delicto,* and residents in the neighbourhood of garrison towns will hear with great satisfaction that a court-martial relating to enquire into the matter as soon as this too-jocular rifleman is ready to appear before it.

Despite the wishes of the reporter, no such trial, if it took place, was ever recorded. It may well be that the story was put about by the military itself, in an attempt to silence the alarmists and restore the honor of the regiment. We notice also that here the miscreants are more than one in number, suggesting a more widespread attempt to impersonate Spring-Heeled Jack on the part of several officers. It seems likely that we shall never know the whole story, which was probably hushed up by the authorities.

It should be noted here that the description of Jack during his appearances at Aldershot had a profound influence on more recent identifications of Jack with an alien visitor.

There is only one further reference to Jack in the nineteenth century. On November 3, 1877, a few weeks after the attacks at Aldershot ceased, the *Illustrated Police News* carried the following report, accompanied with yet another dramatic picture. The event is quite startling and seems appropriate for what was to be the last reported sighting of Spring-Heeled Jack until 1904.

𝔍𝔩𝔩𝔲𝔰𝔱𝔯𝔞𝔱𝔢𝔡 𝔓𝔬𝔩𝔦𝔠𝔢 𝔑𝔢𝔴𝔰

NOVEMBER 3, 1877

A correspondent sends us the following account, together with a sketch, of a scene at Newport:— "For some time past," says our contributor, "the neighborhood of Newport, near Lincoln, has been disturbed each night by a man dressed in a sheepskin, or something of the kind, with a long white tail to it. The man who is playing this mystery has springs to his boots, and can jump to a height of 15 or 20 feet. The other night he jumped upon a colleague, and got into a window on the roof, and so frightened the ladies that one has not yet recovered from the shock. Some other people were so much frightened by the subject that every night a large mob of men, armed with sticks and stones, assemble and attempt to catch him, but to no avail. The nuisance became so great that two men got guns out and chased him. The picture represents him jumping up the Newport Arch, a very old Roman building built in 45 A.D. As he was jumping up he was shot at, but so tough is the hide he wears, that the shot did not penetrate, and running over the house-tops on the other side he escaped, but soon appeared in another part of the town. He was again chased, and as he was running on the wall of the new barracks was shot at by a publican, but the shot did not appear to take effect. He has also done other tricks . . . which we think worthy of a picture in the POLICE NEWS.

This report is strange and may well be spurious. We are not told who the "correspondent" is, and no other reports have come to light, which we would expect if the activity had been continuing for several months in the area as claimed. The description is in many ways similar to several earlier accounts of sightings, though as Mike Dash notes the claimed fifteen- to twenty-foot leaps are the highest attributed to Jack. This may simply be exaggeration, as is the description of the shots fired at the figure. The sheepskin (with tail) resembles older descriptions, right back to the bull's hide of 1838 and elsewhere, but is possibly an invention. It would seem to be a coincidence that Jack is shot at by a publican near to a barracks—but these details could well have been borrowed by the correspondent to dress his story with authentic-seeming details.

This constitutes most of the known history of Spring-Heeled Jack discoverable from contemporary documents of the nineteenth century. We have seen Jack appear and disappear, leaping far and fast; we have seen him attack women, instilling fear and anger in ordinary citizens; we have seen him called a ghost, a goblin, a demon, and a prankster. Toward the end of the century, he is more often seen in this light, as the advancement of science (and street lighting) makes it harder to identify him as anything supernatural.

Later sightings exist, right up to the recent past, and these will be explored more fully in chapter 7. Suffice it to say that Jack has never been far away, living always on the edge of human imagination, reappearing in novels, TV shows, films, and graphic novels, as well as the flora and fauna of urban legend. In our own times, perhaps not surprisingly, he has been seen as an alien, and these sightings will be explored later. But beyond this, when we look back over the landscape of Jack's Victorian appearances, we can see that there is a mix of rumor, fantasy, misdirection, and impersonation along with a very thin scattering of actual events. When we ask the all-important question—Who was Spring-Heeled Jack?—the answers we get back come from several different directions, some of them unexpected. We should take a look at these next before exploring the actual people identified over the years as the one and only Jack.

PART 2

THE MYTH

CHAPTER 4

The Urban Ghost

In thought still half absorbed, and chill'd with cold;
When lo! An object frightful to behold,—
A grizzly Spectre, clothed in silver grey.
Around whose feet the wavering shadows play,
Stands in his path!—

RICHARD BLOOMFIELD (1766–1823),
FROM "THE FARMER'S BOY: WINTER"

The nineteenth century was a period when belief in the supernatural, the survival of the human spirit after death, and a desire to make contact with loved ones who had passed on was rife. Never before (or possibly since) have so many mediums traded upon a desire of the bereaved to talk to the dead. Many were proved to be fakes and were prosecuted under the Fraudulent Mediums Act, which was not repealed in Britain until as recently as 1951.

Many of the earliest sightings of Spring-Heeled Jack described him as a ghost, though this was soon revised to suggest a very human menace, only turning again, toward the end of his initial appearances, back into a ghost again. But Jack was far too solid, scratching his victims and tearing their clothing, to be an unsubstantial spirit; nor was his behavior ghostly, and the number and variety of places where he was sighted differs from the normal behavior of ghosts, which tend to haunt one place only. Despite this, however, there is no doubt that the character and appearance of Spring-Heeled Jack borrows from the intense fascination with the supernatural during the Victorian era.

This was an era filled with ghost stories, spiritualism, and tales of supernatural experiences. Charles Dickens's bestselling novella *A Christmas Carol,* published in 1843, gave birth to an entire genre, with collections of stories by such luminaries as M. R. James, Sheridan le Fanu, and Wilkie Collins, fostering a belief in ghosts that had never been far from the surface of human imagination and became, in an age of scientific exploration, the subject of countless books and reports.

Dickens himself became a practitioner of mesmerism, in which subjects were put into a hypnotic trance during which they were "charged" or healed of a variety of ailments by unknown forces. Mesmerism was originally theorized by the physician Franz Anton Mesmer (1735–1815), who believed that a natural transfer of energy happened between both animate and inanimate objects. He called this "animal magnetism," but it soon became widely known as mesmerism. The theory became an overnight craze among the Victorian population between 1780 and 1850, with hundreds of people paying to be mesmerized by mostly charlatans seeking to make a quick buck.

At the same time, Christmas Eve became a time when families would gather by the fireside and tell each other stories of dark and dreadful events. Newspapers reported the strange and terrifying apparitions that made their presence felt around the country at séances. Though these séances mostly achieved their special effects through trickery, they were widely believed by people, who flocked to see "demonstrations" of supernatural contact or attend private séances in houses all over the land.

This séance craze began in 1848, several years before the first recorded appearances of Spring-Heeled Jack, when the Fox sisters—Leah (1814–1890), Margaret (1833–1893), and Kate (1837–1892)—claimed to have encountered the spirit of a murdered man in their house. This disembodied entity communicated with them by loud knocks on a wooden floor—a form of communication that became known later as

Fig. 4.1. The Fox sisters

"table rapping." Though the Fox sisters later admitted to having faked their encounter, their story spread like wildfire and became the origin of an entire spiritualist movement, beginning in America and rapidly spreading through Europe and into Britain.

Spiritualist masters, such as Daniel Dunglas Home (1833–1886), were the superstars of their day, traveling the world and demonstrating to packed audiences eager to believe in life after death and seeking to challenge the accepted teachings of the church. Bereaved relatives received comforting messages from their deceased loved ones, while others came to hear stories of a better world beyond, where all were equal and the happy dead played together in a realm of permanent summer.

So great was the interest in spiritualism and related phenomena that a Society for Psychical Research was formed in London in 1882 by William Barrett and Edmund Dawson Rogers. Their avowed aim was to investigate the claims of mesmerism, spiritualism, and ghostly apparitions using scientific methods. A host of notable people became members in the first year, including then prime minister Arthur Balfour, philosophers such as Henry Sidgwick (the society's first president and professor of moral philosophy at Cambridge University), and famous writers such as Henry James, Robert Louis Stevenson, and Algernon Blackwood.

It was into this world that Spring-Heeled Jack appeared: a place where belief in the supernatural, occasionally cloaked under scientific language, was widely accepted. If we look at the reports from this time, we see an audience eager for the stories to be true, willing to suspend disbelief, but still responding to them with a healthy regard for the facts and a tongue-in-cheek attitude.

THE CAMBERWELL GHOST

If Jack is any kind of ghost, he is an urban one. The areas where he appears are almost without exception in areas of conurbation, though he is often found at the edges of cities where houses and streets merge with country lanes and open fields. Yet his behavior is never really ghostlike, despite the large number of reports that describe him as such. Ghosts tend to appear at specific places and seldom move from there, whereas Jack, though often localized to a particular area, seldom appears in the same exact place more than once or twice.

Among the huge collection of newspaper articles covering Spring-Heeled Jack, some stand out in their view that the leaping marauder was supernatural.

The first of these, from the *Camberwell and Peckham Times,* is dated October 19, 1872, and refers simply to a "rascally nightbird" and "unutterable blackguard" who had frightened several people by "stepping out from the hedge on stilts, and in a sheet." The area of Honor Oak and Friern Manor, both lying close to a graveyard, was the center of these activities, but even a number of plainclothes policemen, patrolling the streets, failed to make an arrest.

Despite the reference to a man on stilts and dressed in a sheet, there is actually no attempt to associate these events with Spring-Heeled Jack, with the exception of a brief note in the *News of the World* (then, as now, much given to sensationalizing its reports), which headed its account "The Peckham Ghost," but made a very distinct identification with Spring-Heeled Jack.

For this reason it might be thought that the story falls outside the remit of this account, but it is included here for the insights it offers into the mind-set of those involved, as well as a further example of the kind of activities that served to extend the whole range of Spring-Heeled Jack stories into the realm of the supernatural.

Once again on October 26 the *Camberwell and Peckham Times* carried a story that listed several sightings by various people from the area around Lordship Lane and Wood Vale. In particular we hear of one Sarah Anne Foster, who lived opposite the Crystal Palace Tavern and charred (cleaned and did laundry) for a Mr. Smith of Lordship Lane.

Camberwell and Peckham Times

OCTOBER 26, 1872

THE LOCAL GHOST'S REAPPEARANCE

It appears that she had been to fetch the supper beer, and on her return she was required to go on another errand, when she complained to her mistress that there was a tall man waiting in the road. Mrs. Smith remonstrated with her on the folly of been frightened, and Mr. Smith said he would watch her from the window. She started on her errands, but had not left the front garden when a figure in white rose from behind the fence. She screamed loudly, and rushed towards the doorway, and was clasped in the arms of her master, he having seen the apparition from the window, and in rushing out caught his foot in something which threw him forward, and instead of catching the ghost caught the girl in his arms, who, thinking it was the unearthly spirit had got hold of her, went into a fit, in which she remained two hours, and is now seriously ill. The description given by Mr. Smith and the girl is as follows: about six foot high, dressed in long overcoat (having a white lining, which when thrown open, aided by a white waistcoat and out-stretched arms, give the desired effect) a dark felt hat, and a plume of black feathers, with which he hides his ignominious features.

From enquiries, we find that he has made his appearance in the vicinity of Nunhead and at the moment of going to press we have been acquainted that he has visited Champion Hill.

The almost comedic quality of this description may make us smile, but we should notice, as pointed out by Mike Dash, that there are several similarities to this description of the "ghostly" attacker and the "disguise" worn by the carpenter, Millbank, in the attack on Jane Alsop in February 1838.

A week later, on November 2, the *Camberwell and Peckham Times* listed a whole plethora of sightings, more indeed than was ever the case of the earlier Spring-Heeled Jack stories nearly forty years earlier. The story begins by calling the ghost a "scrubby mortal" and a "spurious spectre" and mentioning encounters with a postman and the landlord of a local hostelry. It then proceeds to a more drawn-out affair.

Camberwell and Peckham Times

NOVEMBER 2, 1872

On Sunday last, as the Misses Carver, daughters of the Rev A. J. Carver, DD, Headmaster of Dulwich College, were stepping out of the vestibule of their father's residence—the south block of the collegiate buildings—on their way to the college chapel, escorted by their resident governess, the bruit [brute] appeared some ten places in front of the door. They evidently had turned off the gas in the lamp post outside the premises, for it was not a gusty night by any means, and the lamp had been duly kindled. The young ladies and their friend alike describes the man as shrouded in white, and wearing 'a something over his face'. The trespasser vanished, leaving his footmarks (not cloven) along the edge of Dr. Carver's garden. The doctor (to whom the alarm was instantly given) tersely says that if he only had been a second sooner in emerging from his library, he would have 'run any distance after the cur'. We regret to add, that the health of the youngest of the ladies has, during this week, caused anxiety to her parents.

The account continues with the response of the local denizens of Camberwell and Peckham, who gathered together in vigilante groups well armed with life preservers (a kind of makeshift club studded with nails) and other weapons in search of the ghost. Apparently, some of the younger male residents of the area went so far

CAMBERWELL AND PECKHAM TIMES, NOVEMBER 2, 1872

as to dress up in feminine attire with a hope of being accosted by the spectre. The result being a hint on the part of the police to go home and change or things would be worse for them. The lanes and roads about Dulwich, Honor Oak, Nunhead, and Brockley, have swarmed overnight with the gregarious lads during the week, all bent upon laying their ghostly enemy. Excitement reigns supreme. The police have an impression that the Dulwich College boys are 'doing it'. The young gentlemen deny the soft impeachment.

This very tongue-in-cheek report is followed by a series of letters and contributions from people who all claim to have seen and experienced the activities of the ghost. One "eyewitness" account was from an itinerant musician named George, who arrived, covered in mud, at the Edinburgh Castle public house. Once he had imbibed several glasses of "potent liquor," he told a startling story.

CAMBERWELL AND PECKHAM TIMES, NOVEMBER 2, 1872

I had been playing at Browns, near the Nunhead station, and was quietly making my way across the brickfield, humming a tune, when I felt a pat on the shoulder. I turned around, when, oh! horrors. I saw a thing about seven feet high, all white, with its face ablaze. I was off in [an] instant, but the figure followed me. I ran my hardest, and in my fright I thought it was gaining on me. Faster I tried to run, but in vain. At last I reached the end of the field, but having missed the gate, I jumped over the hedge, and found myself up to my middle stuck fast in mud. I struggled, for I thought the ghost would have me every moment, and at last I succeeded in getting out and did not stop running until I arrived on Nunhead Green . . .

'Why did you not round on him?' asked a tough working man. To which 'George' replied, 'I bet you'd run if you saw the blazing face that I did'.

One cannot help wondering how much alcohol George had imbibed before his encounter. Nevertheless there is a ring of truth about it, and based on the reported comments, the people in the hostelry were inclined to believe him because of the mud in which he was covered.

The same story adds two more sightings, which share many points of similarity with older sightings of Spring-Heeled Jack and seem to agree on his appearance. The first concerns the ghost tapping on the window of the Linden tavern, just across the road from the Nunhead Cemetery. The bar was filled at the time with navies, tough working-men currently building a new reservoir.

CAMBERWELL AND PECKHAM TIMES, NOVEMBER 2, 1872

When they saw Mr. Ghost standing at the corner of the path. . . . They immediately gave chase, headed by the landlord, and one of them was not a couple of yards off the ghostly representative, when with a leap he went over the six-foot fence onto the reservoir works, and before his pursuers could get over was lost in the darkness. He is described by them as dressed in white with a white plume of feathers over his face.

This seems to have taken place on November 3, though the report is indefinite. Next day a servant girl in Linden Grove was going on an errand for her mistress, "when suddenly there appeared in front of her a tall figure in white, she screamed and rushed to the nearest house, where she fainted. The people of the house came out upon hearing the screams, and the girl was kindly taken in and remained until she was sufficiently recovered to return home."[1]

Relief was briefly given to the frightened householders of the area in a report that followed, headed "Reported Death of the Ghost." However, this proved to be a false alarm, brought about by an accident that happened to a servant girl, who fell to her death while cleaning a window in Lordship Lane. Some local boys, seeing the body carried under a sheet to the local hospital, assumed it was the ghost and spread the word. The reporter, confirming it was untrue, did not forget to add that the ghost had since been seen in Norwood, Bennett's Field, Queen's Road, Grove Lane, Camberwell, and Peckham Rye, all places in the immediate area—though no further details are included.

As if in response the *Camberwell and Peckham Times* included a roundup of ghostly incidents, along with two letters, one from someone defending the youths of Dulwich College from accusations of being the perpetrators of the events—which the writer felt they would have carried out far better than the "Nunhead Cemetery Idiot." The second letter is from a man who reported that his wife had been "accosted by the so-designated ghost" on her way home from a concert but gives no further information.

A better and more sober account comes in the following letter from G. H. R. Davidson of 36, Clifton Road, Peckham (but apparently in Dulwich, see below).

Camberwell and Peckham Times
NOVEMBER 9, 1872

November 7th, 1872

Sir,—while returning from a friend's house at Brixton Hill last evening, (via Herne Hill) I was accosted by that malapropre fellow of the ghost. I had just arrived at the point in Herne Hill Road where the footpath runs from the side of St Paul's into Half Moon Lane, when the figure came forth from beside the stile. I confess I was momentarily frightened, but speedy recovering my presence of mind, was on the point of making an onslaught with my umbrella, when the object turned sharp around, and clearing the low railings at a bound, made off across the country. Being now over 40, it was useless thinking of pursuit, but I, however, satisfied myself that he was wearing a black suit, which, by some means, he transposes into white when needful. He also has spring-heeled or india-rubber soled boots, for no man living could leap so lightly, and, I might say, fly across the ground in a manner he did last night. The perpetrator of this foolish joke, if joke it be, must have found the neighborhood of Nunhead and Peckham too hot for him, and my advice is, to Dulwichians, to take every opportunity of saluting him with brickbats, etc., and he will speedily seek other pastures.

Two further letters follow; in one we hear of a man dressing up as the ghost, in white clothing with white makeup on his face and his eyes reddened with ochre, and being dragged along the streets to loud cries of "They've got Spring 'eel Jack, hooray!" A good deal of laughter accompanied this, making it clear that it was a gag carried out in all likelihood by the students of Dulwich College. We may note in passing that, here at least, the identification of the ghost with Jack was clearly intended.

A further report of a sighting in Herne Hill followed and then—to the evident delight of the editor—a note from the ghost itself! Written on a diamond-shaped card and bearing the postmark for the South Eastern District of London, it read: "If you don't stay the publication of information concerning the ghost, you shall be visited by the Peckham ghosts—you and your wretches."[2]

An attempt had been made to draw a skull beneath these words, but it was evidently ill drawn, since the report remarked that their "weird correspondent" had sketched only "a fleshless head sporting whiskers on the left jawbone." To which the editor responded, "We certainly feel gratified with the prospect of so evidently an intended visit from the spurious Diavolo [devil] and promise him a hearty reception in the shape of a choice variety of revolvers."[3]

All of these letters and the responses from the newspaper suggest that few people took the ghost seriously—perhaps because it did not seem to actually do anything other than frighten people. On a more serious note, a letter from someone signing himself or herself "an indignant parent" described an encounter while returning home with his or her ten-year-old daughter. The parent remarked on what appeared to be bloodstains, where a hand might have gripped the sheet with which the "ghost" was attired—but again nothing more is heard of this.

Stories of a marauding figure from years previous had not faded entirely, though they were perhaps remembered unclearly, as a letter from "a South Londoner" indicated.

CAMBERWELL AND PECKHAM TIMES, NOVEMBER 9, 1872

SIR, those readers of yours who take an interest in the ghost mystery may be glad to know that there is a precedent for the proceedings of the insane idiot who, during the last week or two, has been making himself notorious in this neighborhood. Some years since it is said that a certain nobleman made a bet that he would—in the conventional garb of Mephistopheles—parade the streets in and about Lincoln's-Inn-Fields for so many nights without being arrested. Night after night he wandered forth, and night after night managed to scare those with whom he came into contact. More than once he was arrested by the police; but managed to overcome their scruples by liberal bribes. He kept up this little game for some time, and ultimately after having scared four old women to death, besides frightening many others, won the wager. Whether our local ghost is simply a nuisance or whether his peregrinations are attributable to a bet—as in the above instance—is, of course, doubtful, but is almost certain to be one of the other—For surely no man would behave as this one is doing, merely for his own amusement.

The writer is clearly remembering the stories of Spring-Heeled Jack from twenty-four years earlier and the theory, current at the time, that he was really the Marquis of Waterford. In the process he added several details, such as the death of four old ladies and his winning of the wager. As we shall see in chapter 6, the identification with the marquis has its own attendant problems, and nowhere has information come to light that the supposed wager took place or was, indeed, claimed.

Another correspondent, signing himself simply "H. E.," not only described a brief encounter with the ghost, but actually followed him to Victoria Road, where the gaslights revealed enough to provide not only a surprisingly detailed description, but also a possibly partial identity. "Tall, about 5 feet 9 inches or perhaps a little more, wearing a felt hat, long thin brown overcoat and lightish trousers. He is fair, with slight whiskers, which I particularly noted to be very fair, a pale complexion and carried a light stick."[4]

The writer then adds, "I have a faint recollection of having seen him in a billiard room at one of the houses on the Rye [Peckham Rye] on more than one occasion. . . . I fancy he must have entered a house near the railway station."[5]

This clue, if such it was, seems to have been ignored. But the same correspondent, H. E., appears to have had an interest in ghosts that went beyond the everyday. In a letter dated November 9, 1872, he launches into a lengthy discussion of what, exactly, the ghost might be. He seems to have forgotten his earlier suggestion of having seen the person in question in a billiard hall in favor of a more scientific explanation.

CAMBERWELL AND PECKHAM TIMES, NOVEMBER 9, 1872

The question then arises—what is he? That he is of the earth and earthy may be assumed. It by no means follows, however, that he is corporeal. . . . In this instance we are told (and there seems no reason to doubt the statement) the ghost is agile beyond all precedent. Though clad in white drapery, which would be an encumbrance to most beings, he clears six foot walls with the greatest ease.

He jumps without difficulty the broader ditches in the muddiest districts and the darkest nights. He travels across fields with a velocity, which no man can attain, and vanishes suddenly nobody knows where. To account for the strange phenomena it is suggested that he is in possession of some strange device in the way of India-rubber or spring-heeled boots, arrangements which—though capable of doing good service in the circus with the aid of a well fitted springboard—would, I submit, be rather an obstruction than otherwise in a cross-country run after dark through muddy districts.

In the face of all this I think that we must go further for solution of the mystery. The idea which I would throw out—and I put it forward as a suggestion only—is that this ghost is incorporeal and not of a corporeal nature. It seems to have been taken for granted that the figure which appears from time to time is a man dressed up in white. The evidence, I think, points to another conclusion. With Peppers ghosts we are all familiar [see below]. They were long exhibited at the Polytechnic. Mr. Pepper used to cut off their heads and make them talk after their bodies disappeared. To anyone acquainted with practical optics the creation of these figures is extremely easy. By a simple combination of lenses and reflectors the smallest model of a figure in white or any other corporeal object is made to appear in mid-air. The size may be increased or diminished at pleasure, and by a slight turn of the instrument the fabricated spectre can be made to jump over any obstacle, run with any rapidity, and vanish into space as required. Elementary scientific knowledge has been much abused of late, and it seems to me by no means improbable that the so-called Ghost is an optical image of this nature exhibited from time to time by some malevolent person.

I have thrown out the suggestion because I think it highly desirable that the nuisance should be stopped and the culprit caught. Those who run after it are simply running away from the object they seek to find. The creature may be cut in two, shot through and through, and stabbed all over, without the slightest injury, whilst the individual who has caused all the evil is walking down the road in his ordinary costume entirely unsuspected.

Of all the suggested explanations for the appearance of the ghost, this is the most sensible. The writer was obviously familiar with the provision of optical illusions. The famous John Henry Pepper (1821–1900) mentioned in his letter was well known for providing ghostly beings for a variety of theatrical performances. Indeed, this kind of effect is still used today.

The image was simply produced by placing a mirror at a forty-five-degree angle to the audience, thus producing the appearance of a ghostly being, actually an actor offstage, before their eyes. But it requires the use of subtle lighting as well. Just how the supposed perpetrator of the ghostly happening is supposed to have hidden a mirror large enough to throw the likeness of the ghost into the street, or across fields, as well as arranging for it to be lit, is less easy to explain, though it is not impossible. The originator of the effect was in fact a sixteenth-century scientist named Giambattista della Porta, famed for the creation of the first camera obscura. Della Porter's own description, from a seventeenth-century English translation, makes it difficult to imagine how this could be arranged to work outside.

> Let there be a chamber whereinto no other light cometh, unless by the door or window where the spectator looks in; let the whole window or part of it be of glass, as we used so to do to keep out the cold; but let one part be polished, that there may be a looking-glass on both sides, whence the spectator must look in; for the rest do nothing. Let pictures be set over against this window, marble statues and suchlike; for what is without will seem within, and what is behind the spectator's back, he will think to be in the middle of the house, as far from the glass inward as they stand from it outwardly, and so clearly and certainly that he would think he sees nothing but truth.[6]

What is really important about this is not whether it would work or not, but the desire on the part of H. E. to demonstrate that the ghost was not of supernatural origin, but a simple trick.

Printed in the same assemblage of letters was another, from a correspondent signing himself G. T., who had clearly reached the same conclusions as H. E. This gentleman describes a walk with his brother, which took them along a street known as Meeting House Lane, once again close by the cemetery that had previously featured in the appearances of the ghost.

CAMBERWELL AND PECKHAM TIMES, NOVEMBER 9, 1872

On reaching the top of the hill, in the aforesaid lane, we were suddenly brought to standstill by the appearance on the dead wall of a pale object. For a moment we were taken aback, but the recollection of the Ghost immediately came to mind, and instead of taking to our heels, which we might have done under other circumstances, we stood and surveyed the object, strong in each other's companionship. We quickly perceived that the light on the wall did not obscure the brick line, and was of the nature of limelight, which speedily changed color to green. Instantly the spectre vanished in the twinkling of an eye but we both perceived it in its upward course as it passed over the railings which crown the cemetery walls. No sound was heard, and after a short pause we resumed our walk.

The mention of limelight is worth noting. This was a type of stage lighting created by mixing hydrogen and quicklime, which produced an intense luminescence and was widely used in theaters at the time. G. T. seems to be hinting at a theatrical trick, but not wishing to "cast any doubt on the testimony of others,"[7] he offered an alternative explanation—"shadows cast on into space by the aid of magnifying power. A bulls-eye [lantern] furnished with a magnifier, magnetic wire and color discs would serve the purpose of the rogue who thought fit to further us with a fright last night. The operator was doubtless concealed in the earthworks facing the cemetery wall."[8]

On the one hand, it is possible that the kind of primitive effect suggested by G. T. could have created the impression of a ghostly presence, but the descriptions of the ghost are all far too solid for this to be tenable. Even if the sighting observed by G. T. and his brother was indeed a projection, this does not account for the other appearances, several of which appear to have had no place where the supposed perpetrator could have hidden. Nor was the light from a bull's-eye lantern, an oil-fired light with a powerful magnifying lens, strong enough to throw a shadow of such distinct shape and appearance onto anything less than a painted backdrop or a wall of mist.

Other correspondents to the newspapers tended to agree that the whole thing was a joke perpetrated by local youths upon those of a sensitive disposition (i.e., women) for a bet or personal amusement. But the stories of Spring-Heeled Jack from forty years earlier had not been forgotten. The *News of the World,* then, as now, tending to dramatize its stories for an avidly shock-hungry readership, made the connection no one else had precisely made in a leader for its November 17, 1872, issue, drawing on the stories collected in the *Camberwell and Peckham Times.*

The News of the World

NOVEMBER 17, 1872

The exploits of Spring-Heeled Jack are still remembered as having frightened London half out of its wits. The miscreant made night hideous by his tricks—leaping over hedges to the terror of lonely pedestrians, waylaying females, scaring children, and even rendering the drivers in charge of the mails helpless with terror. The suburbs of London were in a far different state forty years ago, when all this happened, to what they now are, and it can easily be imagined how great was the consternation thus occasioned among those residing in them. People were afraid to venture out after nightfall. Stories of the wildest and most extravagant nature got into the newspapers and formed the stable of conversation. Spring-Heeled Jack was believed by many to be a veritable demon; others declared him to be a nobleman in disguise who took delight in his cruel sport; while the majority were in favor of his being a vulgar footpad, who first terrified those whom he subsequently plundered.

Interestingly, this implies that Spring-Heeled Jack was little more than a common thief—though in fact none of the earlier accounts suggest anything of the kind. The writer goes on to compare the difference between the dark and lonely streets of forty years previous to the present well-lit, patrolled streets of his time and to outline the divided thinking around the origins of the mysterious leaping figure.

THE NEWS OF THE WORLD, NOVEMBER 17, 1872

Thus, while some credited him with horns and eyes of flame, an opposite set of eyewitnesses were in favor of the mask and the whitened face; and society was divided between believers in hoofs and those who asserted, with hardly less folly, that the extraordinary leaps in which he indulged we[re] effected by means of springs in his boots, powerful enough, some said to carry him over houses! Seeing the altered state of things in these days, it might have been thought that any successful revival of such a piece of folly or wickedness was impossible. Our suburbs are not only lit, but watched, and in place of fields and lanes, consist, for the most part, of broader thoroughfares with dwellings in all directions. In spite of this South London is even now in a state of commotion due to what is known as the Peckham Ghost . . . a mysterious figure, quite as alarming in manners and appearance as that which terrified the past generation.

The writer makes no secret of his own views in the matter, dismissing the stories brusquely and, incidentally, coming perhaps as close to the truth as it was possible to get at the time:

THE NEWS OF THE WORLD, NOVEMBER 17, 1872

As in all such cases much has to be set down to popular exaggeration, and the tendency of stories of the wild and wonderful to growing in the telling. This we can hardly be expected to credit, that the figure in question is eight feet in height, springs over stonewalls, lofty hedges, and on snaring a victim changes suddenly from grim blackness to luminous white.

The article continues with summaries of the appearances of the ghost in Lordship Lane and the experience of Dr. Carver's daughters outside Dulwich College. In the process it adds an interesting detail, which is absent from the earlier reports.

THE NEWS OF THE WORLD, NOVEMBER 17, 1872

On the following morning distinct traces were discovered, in the crushed and downtrodden grass, of someone having stationed himself behind a small shrubbery on the front lawn, from which he would command a full view of the doorway [to the college] without being seen. The effects of the apparition were at the time, as may be supposed, somewhat distressing; but it was attended by no serious consequences.

Again, the suggestion is that the perpetrator was a man, who had leapt out from hiding in order to terrify the girls. The writer remarks that he cannot imagine "what satisfaction such a joke could afford even a morbid mind."[9]

Joke or not, the world was not yet done with Spring-Heeled Jack. If possible the reports became even more bizarre as the month continued. The worthy *Camberwell and Peckham Times* noted, on November 23, that the appearances of the ghost were getting more regular and stretching over a wider area, and that the police "maintained a dignified and taciturn mien; a mystified shake of the head, with compressed lip . . . and a significantly stolid silence which even the blandishments of reporters—to whom seeing through brick walls and round a corner are as nothing—can penetrate."[10] The same reporter observed how many people were taking care not to dress in any way similar to the ghost in case of being accused of being him.

The editor of the paper apparently received several threatening letters at this point, warning him not to attempt to expose the identity of the ghost. These included drawings of a heart pierced with a knife, a couple of skull and crossbones images, and a letter supposedly written in blood.

These were all ignored, and a selection from an apparently much larger cache of letters on the subject followed, among which we find a "Mr. F. S." who, catching sight of the ghost, delivered a blow with his stick "to no avail"[11] while another "well known resident" declared that he would be "on Goose Green from half past 8 pm until midnight, next Tuesday, to meet 'the ass of a fellow' face to face."[12]

JACK STEALS A WATCH

Further indication of the way in which the locals were beginning to react to the presence of the "ghost" include a fracas over a man carrying a pig who was accused of having stolen it. This event quickly drew a crowd of neighbors, loudly crying "The Ghost! The Ghost!" A few days before this, on November 18, a case was heard before the magistrate of a young woman named Maria Horgan, aged twenty, accused of stealing a watch and chain from a Mr. George Wells. The story has more the feeling of poltergeist activity than of a mysterious ghost. The piece is enticingly headed: "Capture of a Ghost in the Camberwell Road."

Camberwell and Peckham Times

NOVEMBER 23, 1872

CAPTURE OF A GHOST IN THE CAMBERWELL ROAD

Sargent Ham, of the detective force of the P Division, stated that for some weeks past a deal of excitement had been caused in the neighborhood of prosecutor's house, 135, Camberwell Road, by the report that a 'ghost' was committing all sorts of damage. Flowerpots were thrown about, trees damaged, and persons struck by all sorts of missiles, without the originator of the mystery being discovered. Detectives Puttock and Neville were instructed to investigate the matter, and on Monday [November 18] they went to the house of prosecutor. The mother of [the] prosecutor had shortly before been struck by a flowerpot on the arm and injured. A vine was found torn down and a water pipe cut. The prisoner appeared in a very excited state, and showed a bruise on her forehead, which she said had been inflicted by a man she found concealed in the washhouse. The detectives searched the place, but failed to find any trace of a man. During the time they were searching, flowerpots were thrown in a most mysterious manner, and the prisoner screamed out and begged to be allowed to leave the house, as she was afraid to stay. Her mistress told her not to be afraid, as she would be protected. She, however, made earnest appeals to be allowed to leave. Just at this time a watch and chain were missed from the breakfast room; and the detectives, having a suspicion about [the] prisoner's conduct, followed her upstairs. She ran into a bedroom, quickly followed by Detective Puttock, who discovered the watch and chain concealed in the bed. The prisoner was then taken into custody.

So far, so good; however, the second part of the article reveals an apparently everyday explanation. Martha Platz, another servant in the service of Mr. Wells, having told the court that her mistress had instructed her to hang up the watch in the breakfast parlor, noticed that soon afterward, while the detectives were still occupied in searching for the mysterious attacker, both watch and chain vanished. She then told how Maria Horgan

CAMBERWELL AND PECKHAM TIMES, NOVEMBER 23, 1872

came to her and said, 'I must do something to make Missus believe somebody has got into the house'. The prisoner then opened the kitchen window as though it should be enforced, and told [the] witness to scream out and call the young master. The witness went upstairs and called him. Prisoner told her not to say anything about what was done, and to throw some flowerpots so as to alarm the house. She declined to do so. On Monday the prisoner said, 'I must do something else to make Missus think a man is in the place', and then, taking up the head of the broom, struck herself heavy blows on the forehead. Shortly afterwards she rushed in from the washhouse, screaming, and said a man concealed in the washhouse had struck her.

On the face of it, this is very clearly a story of a recently employed housemaid (Horgan had only been in the employment of Mr. Wells for six weeks) creating the ghostly activities to enable her to carry out the theft of the watch and chain. The testimony of her fellow maid certainly points to this, and on the strength of this evidence, she was committed for trial.

The fact that Maria Horgan was able to get away with this indicates just how much the neighborhood felt the power of the supernatural sightings, and beyond this of the strength of the belief among Victorians of many walks of life in the existence of ghosts and spirits.

Several of the letters received by the editor of the *Camberwell and Peckham Times* struggle with a reluctance to accept the overly dramatic stories in circulation. One gentleman, a Major J. W. Erlam, suggests that a loaded gun might prove a strong deterrent, while a Mr. R. E. R. J. of Honor Oak Road, goes further with the idea that a gun loaded with saltpeter shot might be even more effective!

This particular strand of activity ended when, a few days later, a report came in that the "Ghost" had been arrested and taken to Lambeth Police Court. Understandably, there was a rush to view the captive and discover the true nature of these events. The man in custody proved to be named Joseph Munday, a person of no fixed abode, described by the ever-present *Camberwell and Peckham Times* for November 30, 1872, as

Camberwell and Peckham Times

NOVEMBER 30, 1872

A middle-stature fellow, brawny built, with no expression on his face, saving occasional twitching however, indicative of being 'not such a fool as he looks'. Occasionally a grotesque air of injured innocence pervaded his features, no longer shrouded by feathers or such like screen, but exposed in the healthy bright sunshine. . . . Nothing of the Bill Sykes was evident. On being brought into the court— which was very inconveniently crowded—he was ... charged with 'loitering for an unlawful purpose, and also terrifying certain witnesses by gestures and menaces, whereby they were put in bodily fear'.

Several witnesses were called to support the arrest. The first, Mathilda Ayers, described as "an interesting child of twelve, who was evidently suffering from the apparition of that previous evening, and was accordingly told by Mr. Chance [the magistrate] in a fatherly tone, to come up toward the Bench,"[13] told how she had been with her father and how they had killed a rabbit. Instructed to dispose the part of the animal not required (presumably the guts), she had gone out of the house and there, close by The Alliance, a tavern located in Summer Road, had been confronted by a figure that

CAMBERWELL AND PECKHAM TIMES, NOVEMBER 30, 1872

all of a sudden opened a great black thing, and outspread his arms, and was all white. He frightened her dreadfully, because he was black and then white, and he made a queer 'bo-o-oing with his mouth'; that frightened her too. She ran away home and told [her] father, and in half an hour's time she saw the man in John Street and a lot of people shouting 'They've got the ghost!' Two policemen had him. She had also seen him throwing peas at windows and shutters. That was when she began to run home.

At this point the accused was instructed to open his coat, disclosing the "much dreaded white" beneath it, though unfortunately we are not told exactly what it was. Following this, an Inspector Gedge, who must have been in charge of the capture of Joseph Munday, informed the magistrate that "he had already twelve witnesses to call"[14] and that the whole affair had "given rise for weeks and weeks past to the most undesirable state of things about the neighborhood, and the details given week to week in the local paper prove that it was of the most serious character, and calculated to cause great discomfort, to say the least."[15]

Police constable Hills next gave evidence that he had taken Munday into custody in Bath Place where he found him in a house to which he had fled to escape an apparent mob of ghost hunters. Hills described Munday as wearing "a dark coat with a long white sort of 'smock' underneath,"[16] and carrying "a huge stick, two foot long, wrapped up in another very long black over-coat, which he carried over his arm."[17] It seems possible there was some kind of struggle at the police station, as the stick became "broken." The prisoner when called upon asserted his innocence, and said that he had called at the house to see a man named Hall, and finding him out "he took a stroll; the boys set upon him, and he sought protection in the house where he was arrested. He had no witnesses."[18]

The magistrate saw no reason not to remand Munday for a fortnight while further information was gathered. The account of the trial continued:

CAMBERWELL AND PECKHAM TIMES, NOVEMBER 30, 1872

Yesterday at the Lambeth police Court, Joseph Munday, 43, of no abode, was brought up on remand, charged with loitering for unlawful purpose; and also terrifying people. Matilda Ayers having again given her evidence, which was identical to that published in our last, Arthur Ridgeway was next sworn, and stated that he lived at 2, Bath Place: 'As I was passing with a bottle of beer along Camden Street by the corner of Cato Street, prisoner walked out of the dark corner. He walked into the road and opened his black coat and showed me a white jacket under, made a noise with his mouth, but said nothing. I passed, but I was so frightened that I dropped my beer, when after running for five yards I went back and pick it up. The prisoner never moved or spoke, but had his arms open. I wasn't frightened, when I went back. The man had a wig on, a grey curly wig which hid his face. I was on the path and he in the road, and he stood there with his arms out. I saw him after he was caught, in the house'.

The possibly unintentional humor of the man first dropping his beer but then going back for it was not lost on the court, which had to be silenced. The next witness was one John Coles, of 12, Cowley Place, Peckham. He told how

---

CAMBERWELL AND PECKHAM TIMES, NOVEMBER 30, 1872

"at twenty minutes to eight on Thursday evening, the elder brother of last witness told him that the Ghost was close by. Witness with others went to Cator Street where they saw the prisoner walking up and down. He rushed to a house and called out to its inmates, 'Let me in! Let me in!'"

PRISONER: It is utterly false!

WITNESS: We got a constable and saw him taken into custody. He had a stick with him.

THE CLERK: What sort?

WITNESS: I can't quite say, sir. I only saw the end of it, as it was wrapped up in a coat on his arm. He used to live next door but one to me. I never heard of his going about like this.

THE MAGISTRATE: Have you ever before seen the prisoner dressed as he is now?

WITNESS: Yes sir, but with a white slop [a smock-like coat] underneath. I saw no wig, but he had a hat on.

James Ridgeway, of 2, Bath Place, Peckham was the next to speak.

"On the evening in question my brother John told me we could catch the man who is frightening children. We could not get him to come out of the dark place although we threw stones. After we had gone about a hundred yards we saw the prisoner crawling along by the wall toward Cator Street. We then followed him, and my brother called out, 'There goes the man'. He had a coat on his arm and a stick wrapped up in it. He made for a house and was let in, and the door shut. We had heard on the previous night that he had frightened children."

There is something unnerving about the description of the man "crawling along by the wall," though this aspect never occurs again in reports of Spring-Heeled Jack or his imitators. It also appears that Munday was known to the police, who told the magistrate, Mr. Gage, that they had heard of him "being about during the week."[19]

The evidenced now resumed and James Ridgeway noted that they had found some peas outside number 7, Bath Place. Ridgeway said that his brother, who lived there, had 'heard a jingling when the peas were thrown against the shutters'.

MATILDA AYERS RECALLED: I saw the prisoner throw the peas at the shutters. After he had frightened me, I saw him throw them at Ridgeway's house. He threw none at me. I was very much frightened at him.

Mr. Gage, in reply to His Worship, said that he had no one else who had seen Munday frightening people.

In reply to Mr. Chance the prisoner said he hadn't been in the parish an hour.

MR. GEDGE: He has been a working man in Peckham for twenty years. Nothing known against him. He had been away in the country looking for work, and only come to Peckham that evening.

Mrs. Cook, of Bath Place, was here called at [the] prisoner's request, but the name was not answered to.

PRISONER: I was walking about to see a young man on whom I called, and whose mother said he wouldn't be long. That's why I went into his house. I never was within twelve yards of the dark corner. I had the peas to eat, and for nothing else. Witnesses had promised to attend, but he saw no one in the court to speak for him.

A man here came forward with enviable coolness, and said that for the last nine days [the] prisoner had been in his company.

THE MAGISTRATE: How so? The prisoner has not been out on bail. He has been in jail.

So have I, sir, and am fortunately innocent of my charge. He quite denies the whole affair, and has written to his late employers in the country to speak for him. In fact, in my opinion—

The speaker was here ordered to stand back. After referring to sundry tomes, and speaking to the Chief Clerk for some minutes, Mr. Chance addressed the prisoner, and observed that the case presented certain difficulties; he (the Magistrate) had no doubts in his own mind that the prisoner had frightened the witnesses as testified. It was very odd that he had peas in his pocket for the purpose of throwing at people's windows; and if there had been any previous case of his like conduct, committal for trial as a common nuisance would most unquestionably have followed. The evidence was not sufficiently strong to justify that, but the prison that must find surety for his good behavior. 'Doubtless', continued Mr. Chance, 'to you and such as may be doing like you have been, there is a great joke and in thus frightening the public. What is sport to you maybe death to others, and at the least very serious mischief may arise. The public must be protected from such annoyances, and, whilst requiring you to find surety for £10 of your good behavior for six months, I shall certainly commit to the Sessions any similar future case whatever which may be brought before me'.

The fine was a considerable amount for the time, the equivalent of nearly £1,000 today, and as Joseph Munday was unemployed, we are not told how or if he paid up. Indeed, we hear nothing more of him beyond an outraged letter to the paper, in which the writer, signing himself "E. E. S.," records his astonishment at the account of the trial and proceeds to ridicule the entire case.

CAMBERWELL AND PECKHAM TIMES, NOVEMBER 30, 1872

Now, Sir, I ask you; ask your readers; ask all who are interested in the sensation, do you really believe the unfortunate man arrested last week, and bourn off to the police court in triumph . . . to be the bona fide perpetrator of the ghostly outrages? Surely, Inspector Gage and his fleet of foot myrmidons are this time on a "false scent," and have run down the cat instead of the hare. Perhaps, however, the worthy inspector . . . has determined to take whom[ever] may bear the slightest resemblance to the "ghost." Woe unto those unfortunate persons say I, who, being clad in the habiliments not usually worn among men should show themselves, even in the heart of Peckham "after dark." Let the adventurous countryman who may visit his friends in our neighborhood at Christmas, leave his "smocks" at home, or perchance, he may be invested with the order of the bracelet [handcuffs]. Mr. Gage tells us he has many witnesses to produce. Can those witnesses prove the identity of the arrested clodhopper, who could not run the length of the street without being captured, with the ugly customer whose nimble gait and spring heels have struck terror into the hearts of all who have met him? Can this man of forty-three summers be identified by the navvies as the hero of the reservoir wall? I fear not. Peckham, I fear, is not rid of her bugbear, And before long, no doubt, Mr. Ghost will crop up in a new costume, especially prepared for "a limited number of nights." But let us not repine; if the real culprit is still at liberty we can at least comfort ourselves with the certainty, "that all spurious imitations," such as old women returning with the clothes basket, men in smocks, the old gent with a handkerchief of extraordinary dimensions etc., will be run in, and we Peckamites supplied with the "real article only." I will say no more (as my supply of gas is running short, and I am threatened with total darkness) save, that your insertion of the foregoing may induce your readers to keep their eyes and ears open still.

Yours etc.

E. E. S.

There is no reason to question any of these statements. Looking back at the case, one can only see how much fear had been engendered in the minds of the people of Peckham and Camberwell. As E. E. S. rightly observes, it was better to stay indoors, and if one had to venture out to avoid wearing anything that might be perceived as pertaining to the "ghost." Perhaps he should have added that one should refrain from carrying peas! Whatever Joseph Munday was really up to—and one suspects nothing at all—the magistrate was clearly in the right to set him free.

Given the general aura of fear and suspicion, it seems surprising that the whole matter suddenly vanishes from the newspapers. Despite a brief summary of the recent happenings in the *Illustrated Police News* for December 28, 1872, there are no further sightings until May of the following year. When they do occur the "ghost" has moved some distance north, to the industrial city of Sheffield, Yorkshire.

JACK GOES TO SHEFFIELD

In May 1873 accounts began to appear in the newspapers serving the area in question. The journalist David Clarke summarized these in an article published in the magazine *Contemporary Legend* in 2006. He recalled hearing stories during his own childhood from his maternal grandparents, who remembered stories told by their parents of the dramatic appearances of Spring-Heeled Jack—a fascinatingly direct chain of reportage unique in Jack's history.

One of the most interesting aspects of these sightings is the way they combine what is really a ghost story with the idea of a man actually dressed as a ghost—or at least behaving in the manner of a specter.

CONTEMPORARY LEGEND
NEW SERIES
VOL. 9, 2006

The most striking of my grandmother's memories were those concerning eccentric local characters and notorious criminals. These stories were regularly recited alongside those describing the activities of ghosts and bogeymen that haunted country lanes and parks. Easily the most unusual character described by my grandmother was the odd one out—a being who seemingly had supernatural powers but at the same time was believed to be a real man—disguised as a ghost or demon.

Clarke's grandmother remained adamant in her belief that the being she remembered was a supernatural creature who had yet, at some time, been a man. Yet her description is a familiar one to us—and one that would have been just as familiar to the population of the area: "a tall figure in white—wearing some sort of mask and cape—who possessed 'Steel springs hidden inside his boots.'"[20]

Fig. 4.2. A modern version of Spring-Heeled Jack
with springs in his boots

This Jack haunted parts of the city that were remote and usually quiet at night. He attacked seemingly random passersby, moving with "uncanny speed" and leaping over walls with ease or even from rooftop to rooftop. He did not seem to be responsible for either serious physical assaults or even burglary but had left a number of women in a state of shock. Clarke's paternal grandmother added a further incident in which a policeman pursued Jack though an area of the city known as Pitsmoor, finally cornering him in the Bumgrove Cemetery. However, he escaped by leaping over the gates of the graveyard.

Dozens of stories began to circulate from the center of Sheffield as far out as the nearby town of Rotheram—then a center for industrial activity—along the River Don. The effect was to draw forth gangs of armed vigilantes, who roamed the streets looking for the strange attacker.

Despite this, no one was ever caught, and when Clarke asked his grandparents if they knew why the attacks took place at all, he was told it was almost certainly "just done for devilment, or for a bet, to see if he could scare people,"[21] an argument once again familiar from the appearances in London.

Fascinated by these accounts, Clarke began his own investigation years later, searching the archives of local newspapers for reports of Spring-Heeled Jack. What he found amounts to a detailed narrative of events that took place between Easter and Whitsuntide in 1873, mostly localized around an area known as the Park, from which the mysterious figure of the leaping figure acquired an alternative title: the Park Ghost. Formally part of a medieval hunting estate belonging to the Earls of Shrewsbury, as late as 1910 this area was still being described as a place of fearful reputation, linked in the minds of many to the use of the medieval Manor Lodge as a temporary jail for Mary, Queen of Scots. Ghostly activities centered in particular around the Cholera Monument, a memorial to the hundreds who perished in the cholera epidemic of 1832. Rumors of underground caverns beneath the streets, leading to Manor Lodge or nearby Sheffield Castle, added color to the stories, making this a spot ripe for ghostly activities and strange events.

On May 23 a lengthy account of the Park Ghost's activities was reported.

Sheffield Daily Telegraph

MAY 23, 1873

During the last few days quite a sensation has been caused in the Park, and more particularly in the vicinity of the Cholera Monument, by the circulation of reports that 'a ghost was to be seen!' The rumor first gained currency about a month ago, but as in all ghost stories was discarded by sensible people. A few of the more curious however, watched but without success, although women and children complained of seeing a tall man covered with a sheet who met them in lonely places; occasionally too, when the husband was out, women have been startled by the sudden appearance of the strange[r] into their dwellings. These complaints became numerous, and as the complainers had really been frightened . . . it was taken for granted that a ghost was appearing in the neighborhood. The subject was well cultivated by newsmongers, and ultimately it was rumored that a man, whose name has not been made public, wagered in Easter week to frighten a certain number of individuals between then and Whitsuntide.

Here, once again, we have the repeated story that the whole matter was a hoax perpetuated by someone (name withheld, of course) who was behind the manifestations. Furthermore, the report states, "another party" was on the alert, expecting to capture the "ghost" at any moment. What happened next is again a mirror of events in London. According to the report,

SHEFFIELD DAILY TELEGRAPH, MAY 23, 1873

[f]rom 8 to 11 o'clock last night, Norfolk Road and the adjoining thoroughfares were filled with people from different parts of the town [who] betook themselves to the quarry beneath the cholera monuments, and as tokens of their presence made fires of all matting and other rubbish deposited there. It is needless to say the ghost did not appear, but it was reported that he had been visiting very near.

The police made several attempts to disperse the crowd, and at this point things turned ugly, when

SHEFFIELD DAILY TELEGRAPH, MAY 23, 1873

for want of amusement more than anything else the mob began stoning the police, and for about a quarter of an hour mob law ruled. The police were compelled to retire, and while at the top of South Street, Police Constable Ironside was struck on the head with a stone with such violence as to cause him to fall. When picked up by his comrades, it was found he had sustained an ugly wound from which blood flowed freely, and it was deemed advisable to taking him off to the Town Hall. . . . When the police disappeared, the crowd dispersed apparently of their own accord.

The effects of this riotous behavior seem to have been passed over by the officers of the law, and apparently the well-named Constable Ironside was not permanently harmed. A rival newspaper ran the same story in greater detail later the same day, making it clear that the reporter regarded the whole affair as a piece of nonsense. He certainly made it an excuse to send up the story. There were, we are told, three or four hundred people who wished to amuse themselves with a bit of ghost hunting. The apparition did not respond as they might have wished.

Sheffield and Rotheram Daily Independent

MAY 23, 1873

So far from being of a sociable disposition, it refused in the plainest manner to have anything to say to anybody, and spent much of its time in scudding through the burial-ground aforesaid, and steeple-chasing in a breakneck way across the disused quarry. Many old ladies remained out of bed on set purpose till midnight, and left themselves open to the possibility of fatal attacks of influenza, with a view of gratifying a desire to see a bonit fide [sic] spectre; and yet this churl of a ghost declined to appear to them or to anybody else except persons of its own choosing.

The reporter ends with a brief appeal to the "ghost's" better nature.

SHEFFIELD AND ROTHERAM DAILY INDEPENDENT, MAY 23, 1873

If an appeal made to its higher feelings through the columns of a newspaper can have any effect, we beg of this 'ghost' to go to Hades or to the Red Sea—or anywhere, in short, out of Norfolk Road. The nightly battle between the police and the public on account of a 'something in white' cannot be gratifying to any well-organized supernatural being, and can only afford pleasure to a morbid-minded evil spirit not fit for decent society.

The lightness of the reporting continues in this manner for a day or so longer, until May 31 when the *Sheffield Daily Telegraph* ran an article bearing the title "GHOST HUNTING by the Impartial, Observer." This person claimed to be something of an expert on ghosts and, having heard of the appearances of the Park Ghost, set out in pursuit. Joining in what was apparently a large crowd, once again gathered near the Cholera Monument, the would-be ghost hunter was unsuccessful in his efforts. Once again no ghost showed itself, though "the impartial observer" did add some details, apparently gleaned from the crowd and not reported in the newspaper.

Sheffield Daily Telegraph

MAY 31, 1873

GHOST HUNTING BY THE IMPARTIAL OBSERVER

He was described as tall, gaunt, and of unearthly aspect, as 'skimming' over the ground with supernatural swiftness, and as making bounds into the air. . . . He had been seen stalking in stately fashion through St Paul's Churchyard—he had curdled the blood of the inhabitants of Upperthorpe, and frightened the residents of Daniel Hill into fits. He was here, there, and everywhere, and one could hardly meet a friend without being asked, 'Have you seen the ghost?' . . . One voracious eyewitness affirmed that he had seen the apparition clear a wall at a bound, said wall on subsequent measurement proving to be 14 feet 3 inches in height. Another told how, meeting two young girls, he had seized them, and after whirling them around, thrown them over a stone fence; a third affirmed that the night before, the ghost had been shot through the ankle by a volunteer, and notwithstanding this little mishap, had bounded off more merrily than ever.

Most of these details closely resemble the descriptions of Spring-Heeled Jack found in the London newspapers only a few months earlier, but during the actual events, no one seems to have made the connection—though one report in the *Sheffield Times* for May 31 described the ghost as possessed of "spring-heels and phosphorus face—spitting fire."[22]

This was almost the last reference to the appearances of the Park Ghost, leading many to assume it was indeed the work of a prankster who was frightened off by the appearance of the well-armed gangs patrolling the streets. By June 7 the *Sheffield Times* was announcing "the ghost has gone," though in fact a single further report, dating to November 8, 1873, suggests that the idea of the intruder had not entirely faded. It began with a letter from someone calling himself "Observer" who wrote to the editor of the *Rotherham and Masbrough Advertiser*, much in the way of the "Gentleman" writing to the Lord Mayor of London in 1838: "Can you enlighten the public as to there being any truth in the report that a man who goes by the name of "Spring-Heeled Jack" is frightening persons night after night in the vicinity of Rotherham?"[23]

The letter goes on to give a detailed account of ghostly activities in Kimberworth, a village some seven miles from Sheffield along the Don Valley.

Rotherham and Masbrough Advertiser

NOVEMBER 8, 1873

Whether there exists such an individual or not, it is certainly necessary that some step should be taken to dispel the alarm which has been excited. It is not to be supposed that the police have been unable to meet with anyone who corresponds to the descriptions given of this mysterious man, for scarcely two of them are alike, and their number is legion; in fact I never heard or read of anyone assuming the various characters given of him, and performing such wonderful feats. . . . First of all he is said to possess springs in his boots which enable him to jump over persons, walls, gates, hedges, with the greatest facility, he can also tap at second-story bedroom windows, climb up houses and disturb the inmates, by crying down the chimneys, all which things he is said to have done.

He then offers a description that reads as entirely borrowed from the earlier London accounts:

ROTHERHAM AND MASBROUGH ADVERTISER, NOVEMBER 8, 1873

[H]e wears a kind of white skull cap which is capable of being changed into a black cloud immediately he confronts any person. . . . He carries a lamp which can be converted into the imitation of a man's face, thus frightening people, and one woman actually thought that it was this wonderful lamp, which gave him power to jump over gas-lamps. Fourthly, he is reported to wear a coat of mail, which protects him from any ordinary blows that he might be subjected to.

And then we have the "Observer's" summary of the ghost's modus operandi, a description of Spring-Heeled Jack that reads as though straight from the pages of the *Times* and other newspaper accounts.

ROTHERHAM AND MASBROUGH ADVERTISER, NOVEMBER 8, 1873

He chiefly confines himself to attacking women, sometimes in a ghostly manner by suddenly making his appearance and then departing. At other times he assumes the more human form and condescends to touch them, and occasionally deprives them of some article of clothing as a memento, and even last night he was said to have had a desire for beer, and so took a jug filled with that beverage out of a child's hands—thereupon a man seized him, but he was found to be super-human, and could not be held. . . . Whether there be any truth in the story or not, great fear is excited. Parties are going about with revolvers, and perhaps someone who is compelled to go out in the dusk, and bears any resemblance to the descriptions given, may meet with an unwelcome salute.

No response seems to have been forthcoming to this, and we hear no more of the story in this area. David Clarke, however, when looking into these accounts, found that an unpublished manuscript dating from 1936 by a local historian named Henry Tatton (1861–1946) included a note titled "Spring-Heeled Jack or the Park Ghost." He, or it, appeared "at all times of the night and disappeared suddenly—before anyone could get hold of it. It mostly came out of the Cholera Monument Grounds. Springing and jumping about the quarry and over walls. The crowds that went to see it and try to capture it got too hot for the Ghost and it ceased its antics. It never came out who it was."[24] The implication being, once again, that the ghost was a human being in disguise.

Following Clarke's write-up of the events of 1873, Spring-Heeled Jack seems to have become something of a focus for local folklore. As a consequence, the hostelry The Old Queen's Head bears his likeness, carved on one of the walls, and a local "Ghost Tour" includes several designated streets supposedly following the route of the sightings.

THE WESTBURY STREET PROWLER

The story of Spring-Heeled Jack's connection with Sheffield did not end here.

A reporter, writing in March 2007, was investigating alleged UFO sightings and asked his subjects if they had any other paranormal experiences. He began to hear about strange events in the Carbrook Hall area of Sheffield, in particular Westbury Street. The area had been the focus for UFOs, ghosts, and Black Dog sightings throughout the early 1970s until the area was cleared by the local council to put up new houses. In 1997 however, people began to report a "prowler" in the area who knocked on windows, struck men on the back, and grabbed hold of women. One young woman told how she and her boyfriend had been walking home one night when they saw a shadowy figure slip into a side street. They decided to walk down the middle of the road for safety and, as they passed the side street, became aware of two brilliant red lights, which they then realized were gleaming eyes. Terrified, they fled, pursued by the figure, who threw something after them. It struck the young man on the back, and when he stopped to look, he found it was a kind of gardening fork. The figure had vanished, and they hurried home and called the police, who took away the fork as evidence but offered no explanation.

This prompted the girl's father to tell a story that had happened twenty years earlier in the 1950s. One night he heard laugher coming from the attic and rushing upstairs witnessed a strange scene. His house was one of a row in which the attics were not separated but ran all the way along the street above the upper rooms. There, running and leaping along the rafters, laughing maniacally, was a figure—tall, well over six feet—dressed in black and sporting a cape. He had glowing red eyes, and the man was convinced he was the devil. Several householders had given chase and the girl's father remembered one of them missing his footing and almost falling through the ceiling of one of the houses. But the laughing figure never missed a step. Apparently this lasted for nearly half an hour, before the prowler vanished.

At first the reporter was disinclined to believe this story, until a few weeks later he received a call from another man, concerning a possible UFO sighting in the same area. While they were talking the reporter asked the man if he had ever heard of a prowler around Westbury Street. The man replied at once that he had heard of a figure that "ran up the side of buildings." He then went on to say that when he had lived in the area, he heard a story from a very nice older woman who lived next door who told him how she had been looking out of the window across Attercliffe toward the famous Sheffield Steel Works when she saw a figure jumping across the rooftops. She thought at first that it was a burglar but then realized he was clearing distances of thirty feet at a time. She watched him for about five minutes until he finally ran down the wall of a pub into a scrap yard.

Intrigued, the reporter began to look for reports of this and any other sightings. He found nothing specific, though he did notice the high number of unexplained deaths in the area. He did not think these related to the Spring-Heeled Jack figure, but wondered why it had not been reported. He went back to talk to the original witnesses and heard from them that the police had been called out to catch the leaping figure and had chased him across the rooftops into the yard of the Drexel Tyre company. Apparently the constables surrounded the figure and had him trapped in a small room—but when they broke in he had vanished. Nothing more was heard of the Westbury Street prowler, and the police told the residents of the area not to talk about the events. The reporter remained skeptical, but the stories are once again so similar in tone to the majority of Spring-Heeled Jack sightings that it seems appropriate to include them here.

A year after the last of the Sheffield appearances of the 1800s, there is one further report of a ghostly sighting near Richmond, Yorkshire.

𝔑𝔬𝔯𝔱𝔥𝔢𝔯𝔫 𝔈𝔠𝔥𝔬

AUGUST 1, 1884

Some consternation has been caused among certain timorous people of Richmond (writes our reporter) by the rumor that a ghost of the Spring-Heeled Jack type has been seen. A night or two ago Mr. John Bradley was driving, with his servant, up the Reeth Road, when (so the story goes) the horse suddenly shied, and the figure clad in white was observed to emerge from near the Convent. With remarkable swiftness, and accompanied so far as could be made out by no sound, the ghostly figure glided up the road, and the horse was put to its utmost speed with the view of discovering the nature of the Spectre. But in vain. The white figure sped on, and by the mode of its progression caused considerable uneasiness to the observers. At the top of the road it turned to the left, and was last seen disappearing rapidly toward the West Field. Much controversy has taken place as to what the white object consisted of, but in the old town there are still those who firmly believe in ghosts, and confidently assert this to have been the uneasy spirit, mayhap, of one of the Warriors slain long ago in one of the many gallant struggles fought hereabouts.

This is the only instance I have found where a "Spring-Heeled Jack" type ghost is compared to the ghosts of warriors fallen in battle. The area is certainly one that has seen many conflicts, including battles at Northalerton, Scotch Corner, and Myton. After this we hear no more of Jack's ghostly appearances for a number of years—to be explored in more detail in chapter 7.

THE POP-UP VILLAIN

As mentioned earlier, aside from the possible human characters who may have adopted the name and shape of Spring-Heeled Jack, or even the folkloric figures who are a clear source of much of his story, there is another (previously unnoticed) example of a Jack-type figure, which could have had a powerful influence on his supernatural appearance and actions.

Until more recent times, many children in the West possessed a toy called a Jack-in-the-box—a box with a lid, usually held in place with a hook, which, when opened, allowed a figure to pop out suddenly on the end of a coiled spring. Some of these boxes had a musical aspect: when a handle was turned, a tune played, and at a certain juncture, "Jack" would spring out. Often the accompanying tune was "Pop Goes the Weasel," with the word "pop" occurring when Jack popped up.

Often, these Jacks were clowns, which in itself gives one pause for thought, as many people find clowns sinister, so that even a word, "coulrophobia," has been coined for the fear of clowns. In older versions of Jack-in-the-box, the clowns had an especially sinister look, appearing both devilish and terrifying.

Fig. 4.3. The "evil clown"
Jack-in-the-box

According to a pamphlet held by the Nuremburg Toy Museum, one of the earliest documented Jack-in-the-boxes was made by a German clock maker named Salomon de Caus in the early 1500s. He had studied ancient automata and used pressurized water as a means of powering his creations. In this account he was commissioned to make a new toy for the son of a local prince on the occasion of the boy's fifth birthday. Caus came up with the idea of a simple wooden box with metal edges and a handle that turned a crank. It played a simple tune, and the Jack that popped out was a comical devil with a leering smile. Other nobles were so taken with this new device that they began to order copies of the "devil-in-a-box" for their own children.

The idea caught on, and sometime during the Renaissance, the devils began to be replaced with jesters with bell caps and mile-wide grins. As the pop-up figure inside the box became more and more popular, and toy mechanisms improved, Jack-in-the-boxes began to be mass-produced. By the eighteenth century it was available to virtually every child and became a common plaything (see plates 7 and 8).

During this time the image of the Jack changed again, now represented by caricatures of unpopular politicians and finding a clientele more among adults than children.

By the 1930s and 1940s, Jack-in-the-box toys were made from stamped metal. These were gradually replaced by plastic, which made the toys lighter in weight and easier to mass-produce. Clownlike figures remained popular and have continued to be so into our own time—though modern "Jacks" can be anything from dragons to ninjas.

Even the song closely associated with the Jack-in-the-box has a curious history. There are a number of different versions native to Britain but also appearing in the United States. The best known begins:

> *Half a pound of tuppenny rice,*
> *Half a pound of treacle.*
> *That's the way the money goes,*
> *Pop! goes the weasel.*
>
> *Every night when I get home*
> *The monkey's on the table,*
> *Take a stick and knock it off,*
> *Pop! goes the weasel.*
>
> *Up and down the city road,*
> *In and out the Eagle.*
> *That's the way the money goes,*
> *Pop! goes the weasel.*

The American version added the following:

> *All around the cobbler's house,*
> *The monkey chased the people.*
> *And after them in double haste,*
> *Pop! goes the weasel.*

From the viewpoint of our present examination, we can note two interesting things. First, that the song began to be popular around the 1830s, when the Spring-Heeled Jack phenomenon was at its height, and second that it seems to have been particularly popular (appearing in dance halls and being played on street-corner barrel organs) in the areas of London that coincide with the appearances of the leaping figure. These areas were a focus for the textile industry, and one suggestion relating to the song is that the "weasel" refers to a measuring device attached to spinning wheels. This "popped" when a certain length of cloth had been spun. This association with the mind-numbing activity of the spinner may have become connected with the sudden appearance of the Jack, and it is, of course, no distance at all from the springing forth of a devilish character from within a box and the appearance of a hideous being with blazing eyes who sprang out at people from behind walls and hedges.

The other references within the song are mostly to do with the hardships endured by the Victorian poor, including their frequent repairing to public houses such as The Eagle, named in the song. (An actual public house still exists in London with this name, which proudly bears the lyrics of the song inscribed on its walls.)

Beyond the story of Salomon de Caus, the origins of the Jack-in-the-box lie beyond record and are lost in the mists of time, but there are references as early as 1563. In John Foxe's *The Actes and Monuments,* Bishop Nicholas Ridley discusses the uninformed attacks on the sacraments and remarks that "[there are] railing bills against the Lords supper, terming it jack of the box, the sacrament of the halter, round Robin, with like unseemly terms."[25]

To the Protestant world, the Mass was a mysterious, suspicious activity, and the fact that the priest stood at the altar with his back turned to the congregation suggested to many non-Catholics that he was hiding something or engaging in perverse actions.

From the sixteenth century onward, the term "Jack-in-the-box" was used for a swindler who cheated tradesmen by substituting empty boxes for the full ones that were expected; in other words, the tradesmen were left with "jack," or nothing—a term that sounds curiously modern and would be recognized today. In an anonymous work, *The Bird in the Cage,* included in a collection of satirical poems from the time of the Reformation and dated 1570, reads:

> *Jak in the bokis, for all thy mokis*
> *a vengeance mot the fall!*
> *Thy subteltie and palzardrie*
> *our fredome bringis in thrall.*

Which roughly translated means:

> *Jack in the box, for all thy mocking*
> *Revenge must on you fall!*
> *Your cunning and your falseness*
> *Our freedom threatens to thrall.*

Jack's tricks, his cunning and subterfuge, are well in line with those of his spring-heeled namesake. We should also notice in passing that Jack In The Box is the name of a type of firework that is still current today in Britain, first mentioned in John Babington's *Pyrotechnia* of 1635.

THE DEVIL IN THE BOOT

A further theory regarding the origin of the Jack-in-the-box introduces yet another aspect of the character and actions of Spring-Heeled Jack. An account from the twelfth century describes a pious country rector named Sir John Schorne of North Marston, Buckinghamshire, who was something of a wonder-worker. Among other things, he discovered a well with miraculous properties, but his undoubted claim to fame is the story of how he "conjured" the devil into a boot. He is often pictured holding this example of stylish footwear, from which the devil is peering forth. Pilgrim badges dating from the fourteenth century onward show the same image.

Fig. 4.4. Sir John Schorne

How this idea came to be associated with the Jack-in-the-box is uncertain, but it seems likely that the idea that the devil could somehow be contained in a vessel, from which he was still able to pop out, remained in people's minds, so that when the earliest Jack-in-the-boxes were made some five hundred years later, complete with devilish faces, the link was made. Later still, cockney rhyming slang made Jack-in-the-box a term meaning venereal disease, widely known as the pox.

What is of greatest interest here is, of course, the fact that the demonic figure leaping from the box is perceived as a devil. We have already seen that many of the reported sightings associated Spring-Heeled Jack with the devil and referred to him in this way. The devilish Jack-in-the-box neatly brings the imagery of both figures together in one place, presenting us with not only the leaping, terrifying figure of the Jack-in-the-box but also a satanic connection. This may, as we shall see, have influenced a very much more sinister, current manifestation from our own time (see chapter 7). One thing remains clear: once the stories of Spring-Heeled Jack's appearances began to be reported, there would have been many who remembered the child's toy and recognized in it a far less innocent figure.

Thus, an anonymous text dating from 1702, *The Infernal Wanderer, or The Devil Ranging upon Earth,* tells the story of Satan setting out on a journey through the world in search of sinners to carry off to hell.

> The Sable Monarch of the Subterranean Dominions, having with wonderful alacrity received the News of the Wars and Confusions which are now on foot among his Christian Enemies in the upper World, hath of late thought fit upon the Joyful Tidings thereof, to proclaim a Jubilee for a whole Year thro' the vast Extent of his Infernal Territories, his Penal Laws are suspended for the Time, his Fire's extinguished, the Furies lay aside their Scorpion Scourges, and a general cessation of all activities are graciously commanded through his Sultry Regions.[26]

When news of this reached the upper world: *"Up started everyone in his seat, like a Jack-in-a-box"* (my italics). The devil was already well on the way to being identified with the sinister pop-up figure of the child's toy.

There are also clear references to another character, who was to be found across England from beaches to village greens to city street corners. This was the sinister figure of Mr. Punch, puppet-hero of a thousand miniature plays in which he not only behaved outrageously but was seen to be wicked enough to beat the devil.

This is not the place to go into the remarkable history of the Punch and Judy shows, but a few words must be said to put the shows in context. Based on characters from the sixteenth-century Italian commedia dell'arte, Punch epitomizes the trickster figure, a Lord of Misrule, whose origins go back into the mists of time (see plate 10). He makes his first recorded appearance in 1662, when the diarist Samuel Pepys mentions an Italian puppeteer named Pietro Gimonde (or Signore Bologna) playing to audiences in Covent Garden in London.

Here Punch is represented as a hunch-backed, hook-nosed figure with a strange, squeaky voice produced by the use of a device known as a swizzle, which the performer holds in his mouth, making his voice high and rasping. He carries a stick, known as a slapstick—the origin of this word commonly used for outrageous physical comedy—with which he beats most of the characters during the show. There is nothing PC about Mr. Punch; he is a complete savage. He beats his wife, ill-treats his child, knocks down a policeman, and, significantly for us, beats up the devil.

Apparently the earliest Punch and Judy productions (the latter name applied to Punch's wife only after several years of her being called Joan) were marionette shows, but the cost of transporting and setting up these shows became untenable, and the marionettes were soon replaced with a set of glove puppets operated by a single performer in a canvas booth. In this form the plays were free to travel and became popular in locales as far apart as Paris and Washington, DC, where President Washington himself bought tickets for a Punch and Judy show.

To this day, Punch and Judy shows follow this form; the characters have remained, for the most part, unchanged. During the Victorian era efforts were made to sanitize the shows, especially as these shows, originally intended for adults, began to be aimed more at children. For a while the devil vanished from the cast, along with Mr. Punch's mistress Pretty Polly, but Beelzebub was soon back. Significantly, the red-skinned, black-horned puppet that represented the devil in these shows was, in several places, briefly replaced by Spring-Heeled Jack himself, who took over the role of chief bugaboo during the height of the sightings.

In this cluster of imagery, we can see just how far the influence of the figure of Spring-Heeled Jack spread and how readily adults and children alike would have recognized him. Though we cannot say with absolute certainty that the leaping figure of Jack originated with the demonic occupant of the Jack-in-the-box, there can be no doubt that many of his characteristics were influenced by this child's toy.

Having thus far explored the supernatural aspects of Jack's character, it is time to look at the more ancient strata from which he ultimately emerges.

CHAPTER 5

Roots in Myth and Folklore

. . . gaunt and weird, with a tangled beard,
And a mark is on his brow.
His heels are light and shod in steel,
His arms are thin and worn
He buttons his coat to the height of his throat,
But his sleeves are short and torn.
SIR JOHN HAMMUND, *SPRING-HEELED JACK,* 1900

There are essentially three streams of material from which Spring-Heeled Jack receives his unique nature: Victorian and Gothic ghost stories, the traditions of folklore and myth, and the exaggerated newspaper reporting of the time. We have already seen how the stories grew and developed over a comparatively brief period of time and how belief in the supernatural fueled a belief in this aspect of his character. Here, we look behind these aspects to the deepest layer of all—the living traditions of the people who, for the most part uneducated, relied on perceived events from the past to give form to more current stories.

Spring-Heeled Jack shares a number of such points of origin—influences that gave him a name, a face, and a character. Most date from much older times and show that Jack is, among other things, a fairy being like Puck, from whence he derives his tricksterish nature; a ghost, from which he derives his fearful aspect; and a devil, from which he draws some of his nature and occasional appearance with horns, tail, and glowing eyes.

Though the newspapers treated Jack as a human being in a costume, the majority of the public looked to these older archetypes. For them Jack represented the dim (or not-so-dim) memory of devils and demons or even more folkloric figures like the Green Man, or Green Jack. They looked to these ancient traditions of fairy and wildness, seeing behind the character of Spring-Heeled Jack a more ancient face.

IN THE NAME OF JACK

The name chosen for the fantastic leaping figure of the tabloids is not without significance. There have been many "Jacks" in fairy tale and folklore traditions throughout Europe from the pagan Jack-in-the-Green to the Jack Skellington of Tim Burton's story *The Nightmare before Christmas*. Most have several things in common—principally their tricksterish nature and unorthodox life and acts. Many can be seen to feed into the evolving character of Spring-Heeled Jack.

Right from the start there were things that struck a familiar chord in the minds of people who read or were told about the mysterious leaping figure. Whoever or whatever he was, a need to identify his nature and possible purpose filled out the bare outlines of his character to create a complete image. Some would have thought of the so-called London Monster, a killer whose terrible acts had brought terror to the streets of London between 1788 and 1790 (see chapter 6). But to many, especially those living outside the environs of the city, there were other, older Jacks whose stories added details to his character and gave him a more powerful and lasting presence.

The appearances of the name "Jack" in phrases and sayings widely used throughout England tell their own story. The name appears in more examples than any other—perhaps due to the fact that John, of which Jack is a diminutive, was the most popular name over a huge stretch of time. But there is more to it than this: Jack was a name with its own particular range of associations and stories. The following names show how each in its own way lends itself to interpretation as an echo of the Spring-Heeled Jack sightings, or as an influence on the way he was portrayed.

JACK THE GIANT KILLER

Anyone who has read a collection of European folktales, or attended pantomimes or films about a hero who climbs up a beanstalk, will be familiar with stories featuring a young man named Jack, whose cleverness and cunning enables him to slay a variety of threatening creatures— usually giants. Stories of Jack the Giant Killer abound over a huge expanse of Britain, originating in Celtic myth and legend. The best-known version of the story was published in 1760 by John Cotton and Joshua Eddowes, based on an earlier chapbook dated to around 1711.

In this tale we are taken back to the time of King Arthur, when giants roamed the land. Jack, a Cornish farmer's son and a young man of considerable wit and cunning, earns himself a place in legend as the slayer of giants. His first encounter is with a cattle-raiding giant called Cormoran, whom Jack lures to his death in a pit full of sharpened stakes. This earns him his putative title, along with the giant's gold, a splendid sword, and a belt bearing the words

Here's the right valiant Cornish man,
Who slew the giant Cormoran.

However another giant, known as Blunderbore, hears of the death of Cormoran and vows vengeance. He lures Jack to an enchanted castle and prepares to cook and eat him. But once again Jack succeeds in tricking not only Blunderbore but also his brother, Rebecks, and kills them both. He also sets free three ladies who were held captive in the castle.

Now enjoying the life and title of hero, Jack journeys to Wales where

Fig. 5.1. Jack
the Giant Killer

he kills a two-headed giant by tricking him into cutting himself open. At this point he encounters King Arthur's son and becomes his servant. Finding themselves near the castle of a three-headed giant, they plan to spend the night there and rob the giant of his treasure. This they succeed in doing, thanks to Jack's cunning. When the giant discovers his loss, he is surprisingly grateful that the two great heroes had spared his castle. In fact, he is so overwhelmed that he gives Jack a magic sword, a cloak of invisibility, a cap of wisdom, and shoes of swiftness!

Armed with these objects of power, Jack and the prince continue on their adventures, soon encountering a lady enchanted into serving Lucifer. Using his newly won magical accessories, Jack is able to break the spell. He then beheads Lucifer and carries the head back to King Arthur's court. The prince marries the lady, and Jack is invited to join the fellowship of the Round Table.

Jack's first adventure as a knight is to rid King Arthur's land of the giants who have been troubling it for some time. Armed with his magic sword, cloak, shoes, and cap, he sets forth alone and soon encounters a giant terrorizing a knight and his lady. After cutting off the giant's legs, he kills him and frees the giant's prisoners.

Now Jack becomes aware that the dead giant has a friend living in a cave nearby. Donning his cloak of invisibility, he creeps into the cave and cuts off the giant's nose. As the giant rolls about in anguish, Jack stabs him in the back and kills him. He frees more captives, and all return to the home of the knight and lady he had rescued earlier. As they prepare for a celebratory banquet, a two-headed giant named Thundedel attacks the castle, shouting the famous lines

> *Fee, fi, fo, fum!*
> *I smell the blood of an Englishman!*
> *Be he alive or be he dead,*
> *I'll grind his bones to make me bread!*

Jack traps the giant by leading him onto the drawbridge, which gives way, landing him in the muddy moat. From there, Jack throws a rope around both heads, drags the giant to the edge of the moat, and cuts off the head with his magic sword.

Tiring of the feast, Jacks slips away and heads off in search of further adventures. Along the road he meets an elderly man who tells him the story of a giant called Galigantus, who lives in an enchanted castle. Not only has this giant imprisoned dozens of knights and ladies, but also a duke's daughter, who has been transformed into the shape of a white doe by a sorcerer.

This is Jack's greatest challenge, but aided by his magical gifts and cunning, he succeeds in killing Galigantus, freeing the prisoners, and restoring the duke's daughter to her true shape. He then returns to King Arthur's court, dispatching several more giants along the way, marries the duke's daughter, and retires to a splendid estate to live out his days happily.

This story, as anyone familiar with the Arthurian legends will recognize at once, owes much to the Round Table stories for its details. Thomas Green, who has studied the relationship between the two strands, believes that the Jack story was an attempt to restart interest in the legends of Arthur, perhaps for a less sophisticated audience. The casual savagery and broad humor of the story is a far cry from the elegant romances of Chrétien de Troyes and Thomas Malory, but the character of Jack, the know-it-all lad with a vast stock of native wit and cunning, became an overnight success.

During the eighteenth century, Jack became a familiar figure both on stage and in literature. A farce called *Jack the Giant-Killer* was performed at the Haymarket in 1730, while John Newbery printed fictional letters about Jack in *A Little Pretty Pocket-Book* in 1744. A political satire, *The Last Speech of John Good, Vulgarly Called Jack the Giant-Queller*, was printed 1745. Eventually, his fame crossed the Atlantic, and in the southern Appalachians of the United States, Jack became the generic hero of a series of popular stories anonymously adapted from the writings of the Brothers Grimm.

Although this Jack bears no exact resemblance to Spring-Heeled Jack, he is included here to illustrate the associations that would have been made by any country dweller on hearing the name. Such instances of folklore transference were by no means unusual during the nineteenth century, and memory of the resourceful Jack, climbing beanstalks and slaying giants, could easily have influenced the way the leaping man was perceived—especially on the part of those who saw him as a kind of antihero of the poor.

How easily this could happen is demonstrated by the historian Henry Mayhew, who first drew attention to the plight of the poor in Victorian London. In his seminal book *London Labour and the London Poor* (1861), he wrote how a sixteen-year-old boy from the workhouse related a story to him of a boy called Clever Jack who outwitted the police at every turn. Mayhew related how the men in the general wards often told tales among themselves featuring clever criminals who always escaped the law. They were, he wrote, "romantic tales, some; others, blackguard kind of tales, about thieving and roguery; not so much about what they'd done themselves, as about some big thief that was very clever at stealing and could trick anyone." He added that "the best man in the story *is always called Jack*"[1] (my italics).

Other Jacks may be listed and described here as an indication of just how deeply rooted in early folk tradition the Victorian "fiend" really was.

Jack O' Lent was a huge puppet made of rags stuffed with straw and herring skins who personified the Lenten feast in Tudor and Jacobean times. Paraded through the streets on Ash Wednesday, the puppet was pelted by sticks and stones and finally consigned to a bonfire just before Easter. Curiously, the custom was revived in Cornwall around the same time as the Spring-Heeled Jack appearances. One cannot help wondering if the reports then in circulation throughout the country brought back memories of the huge puppet burning brightly in the fire.

Jack Frost is a personification of snow and ice and generally freezing weather. His origins probably begin in Anglo-Saxon and Norse traditions, where winter itself was perceived as a spirit of huge power. In Russia he is known as Grandfather Winter. However, there is something about the way he is depicted as a leaping, glowing, sometimes frightening character that is very reminiscent of Spring-Heeled Jack. Despite a more ancient and shadowy portrayal in myth, he evolved into a spritelike, mischievous, trickster figure who left exquisite frost patterns on windows to show he had been by and given noses and ears a tweak to remind people of his presence. Much of this may derive from a popular poem by Hannah F. Gould (1789–1865). It appeared, coincidentally, around the same time as the sightings of Jack in London. Here is the beginning:

Fig. 5.2. Jack Frost

JACK FROST

The Frost looked forth one still, clear night,
And whispered, "Now I shall be out of sight;
So, through the valley, and over the height,
In silence I'll take my way.
I will not go on like that blustering train,
The wind and the snow, the hail and the rain,
That make such a bustle and noise in vain,
But I'll be as busy as they!"

So he flew to the mountain, and powdered its crest;
He lit on the trees, and their boughs he drest
With diamonds and pearls; and over the breast
Of the quivering lake he spread
A coat of mail that it need not fear
The downward point of many a spear
That he hung on its margin, far and near,
Where a rock could rear its head.

*

He went to the windows of those who slept,
And over each pane, like a fairy, crept;
Wherever he breathed, wherever he stepped,
By the light of the morn were seen
Most beautiful things; there were flowers and trees;
There were bevies of birds and swarms of bees;
There were cities with temples and towers; and these
All pictured in silvery sheen!

Here we have a Jack who not only moves everywhere at speed but also wears a coat of mail—a detail mentioned more than once in the descriptions of Spring-Heeled Jack.

Jack-o'-Lantern, also known as Jacky Lantern or Jack-a-Lantern, is today most familiar from the Halloween holiday when a turnip or pumpkin carved with a wild and grinning face is called by this name. The origin is lost in the mists of time, but some investigators see the jack-o'-lantern as a fairy that lives in hedges and leaps out at passersby—a device familiar to us in our investigation of Spring-Heeled Jack. Perhaps it is no more than coincidence that the modern-day pumpkin carvings usually have grinning mouths and eyes that glow in the darkness when candles are placed inside them. In East Anglia the name is applied to will-o'-the-wisps, fairies who shine their lights out on dark roads, to lead travelers astray into bogs or pits.

Jack-o'-Legs was a notorious robber believed to have operated near the village of Weston in Hertfordshire in the eighteenth century. He was said to be tall enough to look in the upstairs windows of the houses he intended to rob. Very much a Robin Hood figure, he seems only to have robbed the rich and to have given his ill-gotten gains to the poor. Again, like Robin, when he was eventually captured and sentenced to hang, he requested that he should be buried wherever an arrow he fired from his bow landed. Two stones still lie in Weston churchyards, some fourteen feet apart.

Plate 1. Steampunk Hero. Spring-Heeled Jack crouches on the rooftops of London. (Illustration by Wil Kinghan)

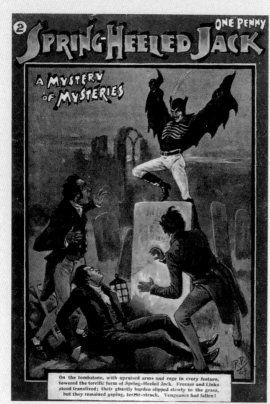

Plate 2. With upraised arms and rage in every feature, Spring-Heeled Jack towered on the cover of this penny dreadful.

Plate 3.
*Spring-Heeled Jack,
A Leap for Liberty*

Plate 4. As Spring-Heeled Jack appeared, an explosion shook the building shown on the cover of this penny dreadful.

Plate 5. Spring-Heeled Jack causes another victim to swoon.

Plate 6. The Green Man, one of thousands of statues dedicated to this ancient symbol

Plate 7.
An ornate
Jack-in-the-box

Plate 8. Jack turned into a toy for children.

Plate 9. A Victorian-era advertisement for a Jack-in-the-box

Plate 10 (above). An old-fashioned Punch and Judy show in Islington, UK

Plate 11. *Robin Shoots with Sir Guy* by Louis Rhead

Plate 12 (above). Spring-Heeled jack as a "spaceman"

Plate 13. Mothman statue in Point Pleasant Park, West Virginia (Bob Roach, sculptor)

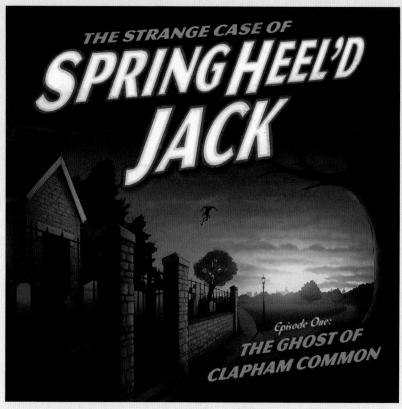

Plate 14. Poster of Episode One (Art by Jamie Egerton)

Plate 15. Advertisement for shoe springs from a 1960s Eagle comic book

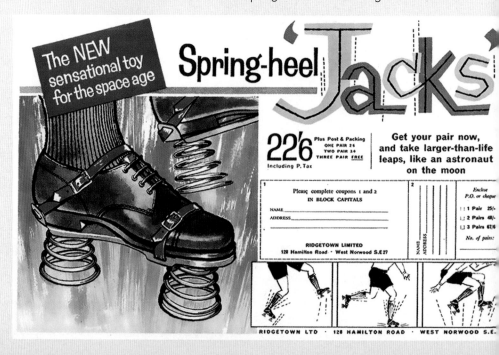

These stones are said to mark the head and foot of this Jack's last resting place. He was certainly taller than his Spring-Heeled namesake and was thus able to stride over walls and hedges.

Jack-in-Irons was a malevolent giant from the county of Yorkshire who was said to have haunted lonely roads. He carried a great, spiked club and wore a number of huge chains with the heads of his victims hanging from them.

More general terms applied to a random range of less significant individuals include:

Jack-the-Lad—a self-opinionated young man with a tendency toward trickery, which is still in use today in Britain.

Swearing Jack—mentioned in Shakespeare's *The Taming of the Shrew,* circa 1616: "A mad-cap ruffian and a swearing Jacke."

Characters named Jack, who are generally young and mischievous and are also featured in nursery rhymes, include:

Little Jack Horner—familiar from nursery rhymes.

Jack Sprat—name given to any dwarf from the sixteenth century onward.

Jack and Jill—names used for any young couple from as early as the 1450s.

Another nursery rhyme first published in 1798, only a few years before the first appearances of Spring-Heeled Jack, might also have been in the memory of many people when they responded to the initial stories:

> *Jack be nimble,*
> *Jack be quick,*
> *Jack jump over*
> *The candlestick.*

GREEN JACK

But the oldest image of a "Jack" that we have is Jack-in-the-Green, a figure who is part of an even more ancient and powerful archetype—the Green Man. This being—who in general terms is best described as a spirit of nature, perhaps *the* spirit of nature—can be found in many parts of the world. For some he is an ancient symbol of fertility representing humanity's connection with Earth. To others he shares something of Spring-Heeled Jack's own wildness, the untamed spirit that lives within most humans, as well as reflecting the wildness at the heart of nature.

The idea of the Green Man as a representative of the natural world probably dates back to the first agrarian peoples of the ancient world who felt the power of nature and gave it a face and form. We have only to look at the way in which the green thrusts through the earth, rampantly overcoming and glorying in its strength, to understand why a masculine image was chosen. Certainly among the tribal people who lived in the vast woodlands that once covered much of the European continent, the Green Man ruled supreme as a spirit of these woods, a representation, in semihuman guise, of the abiding life force of the trees.

Fig. 5.3. One of the many Green Man statues of Rosslyn Chapel

In our severely deforested world, it is hard to imagine just how dense the woodlands once were. Forests were places of awe and mystery into whose depths few would venture during the day, although the resources of the woodshore were useful to those who lived nearby. In northwest Europe, these dense forests often contained groves of sacrifice or spiritual mystery. From trees in the groves dedicated to the Norse cult of Odin, both human and animal offerings were hung, indicators of the powerful force of the ancient forest gods. Similarly, the oak groves of the Celtic world were the haunt of strange forest beings and tree spirits, their mysteries known only to the Druids, whose knowledge and understanding of the natural world were second to none.

Wildness is an essential part of the Green Man's character, just as it is of Spring-Heeled Jack. Leaf-mask carvings discovered in the Middle Eastern cradle of civilization lead us to the Sumerian epic of Gilgamesh (ca. 700 BC) where we encounter a figure that represents just such a power: Enkidu, a wild and primitive being whose great strength and passionate soul embody the energy of nature itself. Jealous of his power, the gods condemn Enkidu to die, prompting his friend, the hero Gilgamesh, to undertake a journey to the otherworld in search of a cure for death itself, a magical plant called "How the Old Man Once Again Becomes a Young Man." Although Gilgamesh finds the plant, he loses it again to a serpent, which at once sloughs its skin in a symbolic act of rebirth.

In the classical world the orderly deities of Mount Olympus were not the only ones to hold sway. There were older, wilder forces also; each tree, stream, hill, and grove had its own dryad, nymph, and tutelary spirit. The god Pan, whose name literally means "universal," was a major deity of nature. As the protector of the wild, he could appear anywhere in the natural world. Those who came across him at lonely, unfrequented places were consumed with panic at the sight of him, just as were the people who witnessed the bizarre appearance of Spring-Heeled Jack. Like Pan, Jack could not be tamed or controlled, and he became, for many, another representative of unfettered nature—though more of human than forest or field.

The gradual loss of the forests and the building of the great cathedrals coincide. The church tried to make people believe that the woods were full of evil from the start, but it was partly in acknowledgment of the importance of the ancient tree-scapes that so much of the architecture of medieval churches was designed to make them look like stone forests. It is not surprising to find the Green Man there, carved in stone in the form of foliate heads that decorate the ceilings and columns of so many of the great European cathedrals. His presence was too deeply embedded in the consciousness of the ordinary people to be forgotten.

The building of the cathedrals entailed the cutting down of prime trees to provide scaffolding for the huge stones to be raised. This enormous undertaking required its own harvest of men, skilled craftsmen who learned their trade through respect of their materials—stone, iron, and wood. It was they who carved the foliate heads and placed them high above the heads of the worshippers. And, like all men engaged in dangerous work, they needed their talismans, carving their protectors in places of honor in acknowledgment of their powers. Lest the woodland spirits be offended, their green images were set higher than the holy images upon the altar.

The presence of such figures in the European folk plays and the festivals of Mayday and midsummer bears witness to the continuing presence of the Green Man. Jack-in-the-Green was a wild and sometimes comical figure who accompanied the dancers and minstrels at many of these seasonal celebrations. In most instances the man portraying Jack carries a framework made from woven branches and leaves, sometimes bedecked with flowers. This often heavy costume covers both head and body so that it gives the appearance of a moving bush or tree (see plate 6).

Often the Green Man is led about through towns and villages by groups of supporters, who collect money to pay for the celebrations in this fashion. One account, which describes the celebration of Garland Day in the town of Castleton in Derbyshire, shows that a darker theme underlies the procession. Here the Garland King is lead in procession through the streets on horseback. On reaching the local church, the framework of greenery and flowers is hooked up to a winch, which then hauls it to the top of the tower, where it is left to swing in the wind until the elements gradually demolish it. At one time, the body or head of a sacrificial victim was hauled aloft, maybe to swing from the topmost branches of a tree. Such things link more recent folk traditions with a far older time, when propitiating the gods of nature was a far more serious business.

Such celebrations may seem a far cry from the landscape of Victorian Britain, but they signified a part of life that was important then, as it still is in some parts of the world today—the spirit of the forest emerging from the wildwood and coming into the streets and among the houses to be hailed and honored. When men cover themselves with leaves and align themselves with the green spirit of growth, this act engenders a feeling of uneasiness. Such overlapping margins where civilization and wildness meet is tinged with awe and an uneasy hilarity that tries to cover the fear that can be woken by embodying the sacred in anthropomorphic form.

Ideas and realizations of this kind passed into the folk life and customs of ordinary people, along with the distant memories of devotion to the power of nature. Scraps of lore and imagery became embodied in dance, story, song, and legend, underpinning the traditions of a world that still acknowledged the presence of the Green Man despite an increasing sense of separation from nature. It was still present in the nineteenth century and fed into the imagery of Spring-Heeled Jack through the ideas of his wildness, unbridled behavior, and even, to some extent, his appearance.

REBELS IN GREEN

A significant aspect of Spring-Heeled Jack's reputation was not only his wildness but also his lawlessness—and the inability of the police to capture him or even lay hands on him. This made him something other than a figure of fear—it made him a hero of the people.

Fig. 5.4. Nottingham statue of Robin Hood

One character in particular, though he bears no other significant relationship to Jack, unites the characteristics of the spirit of the wildwood with the outsider figure of the outlaw. The name of Robin Hood, the leader of a band of twelfth-century outlaws in Sherwood Forest, still resonates for us today (see plate 11). In fact he is a far more complex, myth-based character than he seems at first. His historical existence is at best doubtful, but his life, as told in medieval ballads, follows a universal pattern.

Of unknown or doubtful parentage, Robin appears fully fledged, living in the greenwood with his outlaw band, the Merry Men. Their tricksterlike adventures, which conceal a darker historical truth in which Norman overlords ruthlessly oppressed their Saxon serfs, mark them out as semidivine beings hiding behind the appearance of medieval freedom fighters. The eventual death of Robin Hood in which his blood is shed in a semi-ritual fashion, prophesied by a mysterious woman identifiable with the Washer-at-the-Ford in Celtic tradition, shows him to be another representative of the Green Man, sharing the same wildness and abandon as the ubiquitous Jack, and possessed of his otherworldly status.

Robin Hood's tricksterlike activities link him with another dweller

Fig. 5.5. Robin
Goodfellow, alias
Puck, alias Hob

of the Greenwood—Robin Goodfellow. He shares his name and nature with the famous outlaw and in addition is firmly embedded in fairy lore. This Robin is better known to us as Puck, the wild and uncontrollable spirit of Shakespeare's *A Midsummer Night's Dream*, but behind these disguises lurk far older figures, dating back before the Middle Ages. Famous for their jokes and jests, mostly at the expense of foolish humans, these are the primordial trickster gods who appear in mythology all over the world; their fierceness and unbridled behavior are every bit as frightening as the sudden appearance and demonic laughter of Spring-Heeled Jack.

Shakespeare compares the two sprites by referencing

> *that shrewd and knavish sprite*
> *Call'd Robin Goodfellow. Are not you he*
> *That frights the maidens of the villagery,*
> *Skim milk and sometimes labour in their quern,*
> *And bootless makes the breathless housewife churn*
> *And sometimes make the drink to bear no balm,*
> *Mislead night-wanderers, laughing at their harm?*
> *Those that Hobgoblin call you, and sweet Puck,*
> *You do their work, and they shall have good luck*
> *A MIDSUMMER NIGHT'S DREAM, ACT 2, SCENE 1*

Most of what we know about Robin Goodfellow, apart from a few scattered references like the one above, comes from a seventeenth-century pamphlet that rejoices in the title *Robin Goodfellow, alias Puck, alias Hob: his mad pranks, and merry jests, full of honest mirth, and is a fit medicine for melancholy*. It was printed in 1628 but almost certainly drew on a whole range of earlier fairy lore from earlier. The story contained in the pamphlet may be summarized as follows:

Robin's nascence is described in a manner very reminiscent of the birth of Merlin. Oberon, the Fairy King, visits a maiden at night, but in the day vanishes "wither she knew not, he went so suddenly." The outcome of these nightly visits is a child, who shows no unusual traits until, aged six, he begins to be so troublesome and to play such knavish tricks upon the neighbors—startling them, then running away with loud ringing laughter—that his mother is in despair. Finally, she promises him a whipping, and since this did not please him, he runs away. A day from his home, he settles to sleep in a field and there dreams of bright-eyed folk who dance around him all night to music he deems as fair as Orpheus might have made. In the morning, he wakes to find a scroll beside him on which is written, in words of gold:

> Robin, my only son and heir,
> How to live take thou no care:
> By nature thou hast cunning shifts,
> Which I'll increase with other gifts.
> Wish what thou wilt, thou shall it have;
> And for to fetch both fool and knave,
> Thou hast the power to change thy shape,
> To horse, to hog, to dog, to ape.
> Transformed thus, by any means,
> See none thou harm'st but knaves and queans:
> But love thou those that honest be,

And help them in necessity.
Do thus and all the world shall know
The pranks of Robin Goodfellow,
For by that name thou called shall be
To age's last posterity;
And if thou keep my just command,
One day thou shall see Fairy-Land.

Robin at once tested the promise of wish granting by asking for food; a dish of fine veal was set before him. He wished for plum pudding: it appeared. Then, being weary, he wished himself to be a horse. At once he became a fine spirited beast, and thereafter changed himself into a black dog, a green tree, and so on, until he was sure he could change himself into anything he wished. Then he wished to try out his newfound skills by playing more of the tricks for which he had been recently chastised, and forthwith he set forth into the world, where he began to play so many merry jests that soon his name was known throughout the land. He played tricks on clowns, on burgers, on old and young; he turned himself into a chimney sweep (for which reason he was still the patron of sweeps in the Victorian era and appeared in procession with them in the Mayday games). Finally, so great was the noise about the world complaining of Robin Goodfellow's trickery, that his father Oberon summoned him to Fairy-Land with these words:

Robin, my son, come quickly rise,
First stretch, then yawn, and rub your eyes:
For thou must go with me to-night,
And taste of Fairy-Land's delight.

Robin rose from his bed at once and went where he was called. Here he met with Oberon and many other fairies, all clad in green. Throughout the night they danced to fairy music, and as they danced Oberon said:

> *"Whene'er thou hear the piper blow,*
> *Round and round the fairies go!*
> *And nightly you must with us dance,*
> *In meadows where the moonbeams glance,*
> *And make the circle, hand in hand—*
> *That is the law of Fairy-Land!*
> *There thou shalt see what no man knows;*
> *While sleep the eyes of men doth close!"*

After this Robin is said to have remained in Fairy-Land for "many a long year."

This curious little story, which on the face of it bears little resemblance to anything concerning Spring-Heeled Jack beyond the behavior of its hero, nevertheless offers us a clear portrait of the kind of trickster-ish nature we encounter at every point in Jack's saga. Robin Goodfellow's knavish ticks, his loud laugher, his ability to appear in several different shapes seem oddly familiar. The "letter" he receives from his father Oberon, listing the shapes into which he could transform, includes that of an ape—a form more than once associated with Spring-Heeled Jack's disguises. His appearance elsewhere seems reminiscent of Jack. The playwright and pamphleteer Samuel Rowlands (ca. 1573–1630) in his work titled *More Knaves Yet* refers to a demon

> *Known by the name of Robin (as we hear)*
> *And that his eyes as bigge as sawcers were,*

Like Robin Hood, Jack is a hero of the common people, with powers far greater than his pranks would suggest, and together they are lineal descendants of the Green Jack. Their sympathy for poorer folk is an aspect of the way that Spring-Heeled Jack was seen by the people of London as a kind of antihero. Like the clever boy named Jack in the story related by Henry Mayhew, or the irrepressible fairy Robin, he was deemed uncatchable by the clumsy efforts of the police.

JACK VALENTINE

Yet another Jack who bears some of these aspects is a mysterious figure known as Jack Valentine, who first appeared in Norwich, Norfolk County, UK, between the years 1830 and 1850. This curious figure would knock on doors and leave gifts in a bizarre echo of St. Nicholas at Christmas. He may possibly be the earliest manifestation of the now-familiar aspect of St. Valentine's Day as an excuse for gift giving, but although almost nothing more is known of him or his origin, the choice of name and the reports of his behavior are interesting. Local traditions from Norfolk County tell how this Jack, also known as Old Father Valentine or Mr. Valentine, would knock on the door and then hide, leaving a present on the doorstep to be discovered by the child of the house. In a variant version he is replaced by the trickier figure of Snatch Valentine, who also leaves a parcel on the doorstep, but when the eager child opens the door and reaches for it, the person posing as the trickster, hiding out of sight, tugs on the end of a string attached to the parcel and jerks it away. This action is repeated several times, until finally the hidden person takes pity on the child and allows him or her to catch hold of the gift.

When this story was reported on the Internet recently, a number of people responded to the account with their own memories, showing that the story of this Jack extended not only to Britain but also to America. One lady wrote that when she was a child in California,

we had a visitor on Valentine's night that left candy and a toy in a brown bag on the porch. My mom who is 82 also remembers the visitor on Valentine's, but the family never spoke of where the tradition came from . . . I have continued the tradition with my children

> going on 23 years [making] 8 generations passing on the tradition.
> My great-great-great-grandfather, David West [who came] from
> Derbyshire [in] 1824 . . . introduced it to my family.[2]

Though this may seem a far cry from the activities of Spring-Heeled Jack,
there is something curiously reminiscent of his behavior—especially when
taking the form of Snatch Valentine, who seems to have enjoyed playing
tricks not unlike some of those performed by the leaping man.

Such old stories do not die. They may vanish for a time, but they are
likely to recur almost anytime. As recently as 2014 a local report from
Norwich proclaimed that Jack Valentine had been caught on CCTV
wandering the streets of the town accompanied by an urban fox.

> For several centuries, Jack was famous for delivering gifts to fami-
> lies on valentines eve, tradition which is synonymous to Norwich
> Norfolk. One local historian believes he may have returned after
> hearing of interest from the curators Bridewell museum about his
> long-term absence.[3]

JACK AND THE MUMMERS

Another place where we encounter Jack figures is in the traditional folk
plays and dances that have been performed throughout Britain (and
more recently in America) from the Middle Ages. Known as mummers
or mumming plays, these involve a set of archetypal characters who
perform what is sometimes known as a "death and resurrection play,"
part of which involves the death of a hero (usually the patron Saint of
Britain, St. George) and his subsequent resurrection by a comic doctor.
Morris dances were incorporated into the performance, generally following the play: a team of varying numbers of men carrying sticks or
kerchiefs danced a broad variety of complex steps to the accompaniment
of fiddle or accordion.

The origins of these dances are vague. Even the derivation of the

Fig. 5.6. The Mummers death and resurrection play

name Morris has never been agreed upon. One early authority identifies the word "morisco" as the origin, which means "a Moor; also a dance, so called, wherein there are usually five men, and a boy dressed in a girl's habit, whom they call the Maid Marion, or perhaps Morian, from the Italian Morione, a head-piece, because her head was wont to be gaily trimmed up. Common people call it a Morris Dance."[4]

This derivation, frequently repeated since the eighteenth century, has been brought into question recently. Douglas Kennedy, the late director of the English Folk-Song and Dance Society, in his book *England's Dances* suggests that the confusion arose from the tradition of the Morris teams blacking their faces, which gave rise to an association with the Moors and possibly even the renaming of an older dance.

Jacks abound in the mumming plays. Among the list of characters from the various plays, which differ slightly according to which area they are found, include Johnny Jack, Jack Straw, Happy Jack, Jack

Finney, Little Johnny Jack, and so forth. Though it would be stretching the idea too far to suggest any direct link with Spring-Heeled Jack, it should be noticed that many of these characters, who generally perform a knock-about or mischief-making role, are to be seen jumping and leaping into and out of the action. As with the other folkloric aspects of Jack's saga mentioned here, they would have been very much in the mind of the people who experienced the strange manifestations of the Spring-Heeled man.

LUCIFER AND OTHER DEVILS

Spring-Heeled Jack was frequently compared to and even identified with the devil, and we should take a brief look at certain aspects of the devil's history and how the figure of Jack borrowed from it. First, it is important to understand that Spring-Heeled Jack personifies only one aspect of the devil—Satan, Lucifer, Diabolos, Beelzebub, whatever one wishes to call him—as promulgated in Christian mythology. The acts of Spring-Heeled Jack suggest another aspect of this ancient and complex figure—the devil of folklore. This devil takes many forms but bears more of the trickster elements than any other. He is constantly trying to trick humans into behaving badly, or signing their souls over to him in return for gold or power. The story of Faust is perhaps the most famous of these tales, outlining in grizzly detail the fall of its titular hero.

But Jack characters also figure frequently as clever, witty heroes who trick the devil. We may remember that in the oldest known story of Jack the Giant Killer (pages 144–48), the giant represents an aspect of the devil in the form of Lucifer, whom Jack easily beheads, at the same time rescuing a lady who had been enslaved to him.

Some of these heroic Jacks share aspects of the devil they best. One such story, told in Maryland, tells how Jack, an unpleasant fellow who used to beat his wife, was about to be dragged off to hell by the devil but managed to persuade Lucifer to share a last drink with him. As Jack had no money, the devil turned himself into a coin with which Jack

AN AUTHENTIC AND EXCITING GHOST STORY Nᴿ IVY CHURCH LANE

Fig. 5.7. Two examples of Spring-Heeled Jack portrayed as a devil

could buy beer. But Jack cleverly put the coin into a purse with a cross on it, so the devil was trapped.

Eventually, Jack let him out and got another year of life as a result. But at the end the devil came to get him, and as they were following the long road to hell, Jack saw an apple tree beside the road. He begged the devil for a last bit of fruit, and Lucifer agreed and climbed into the tree to get an apple. At once Jack drew a cross on the tree trunk with his knife so the devil could not get down.

Jack got another year from that, but when his time was up, he went to heaven and was sent away. Wearily, he went back down to hell. When the devil saw him coming, he said he was not welcome there either. "Go back home, Jack," said the devil. But it was dark, and Jack complained that he could not see how to get home. So the devil threw him a coal, and Jack placed it in his lantern. He can still be seen sometimes, wandering the world forever with his lantern unable to get into heaven or hell.

This story combines qualities later attributed to Spring-Heeled Jack and that were present in the folklore of the devil. The strange novel by Charles Sedley, *Asmodeus; or, the Devil in London: A Sketch,* published in 1808, describes a devil who wanders the earth for a hundred years and particularly haunts London, taking on whatever form he wishes. It is easy to see how this kind of imagery might have influenced the imaginations of those who saw Jack as a terrifying and essentially supernatural figure.

Fear of the devil spread across Europe during and after the Middle Ages, during which numberless stories were told that would later feed into the tales of Spring-Heeled Jack, the only trickster who can out-trick the greatest trickster of all. During the nineteenth century, he was more than once described as a demon, a goblin, or the devil himself. Though originally his only obvious connection with the devil was his fire-breathing abilities, his talons, and his sulfurous scent, as time passed he was depicted with horns, hoofs, and bat-like wings—especially in the Victorian penny dreadfuls, lurid and wildly dramatized stories plucked from the same depths of the Victorian imagination that gave us Frankenstein's monster and Dracula. In this form Jack belongs

Fig. 5.8. Spring-Heeled Jack: An early version of Batman?

with saucer-eyed dogs, phantom bulls, demonic cats, and other name-less beings that combined human and animal qualities, and it is even possible to see the shape of the later Batman of graphic novel fame as a modern incarnation in his costume and behavior (see also chapter 7).

THE MYSTERIOUS BULL

Several of the earliest accounts of the Spring-Heeled Jack phenomena describe not a man at all but a white bull—or at least a man clad in the skin of such an animal. This may seem odd, as it is both ordinary and extraordinary. Yet if one considers for a moment the symbolic and folk-loric significance of a bull—especially a white bull as seen by several peo-ple in the Barnes area of London in September 1837, just before the main Spring-Heeled Jack sightings began—it actually makes perfect sense.

British tradition speaks often of the idea of a horned god, dating from ancient times and perhaps aligned with gods such as Pan, which was later widely associated with witchcraft trials. Medieval witches were said to worship such a wild deity, which was very much a part of the Green Man/Green Jack traditions. Leaders of witch covens at the time were said to don a horned costume in order to enact the primitive rites of an older time. This gave rise to the belief that the witches worshipped the devil, who appeared, complete with horns and cloven hoofs, at their sabbats. A bull's hide would be seen as especially appropriate: the animal not only represented an extreme element of fertility but was also associated with traditions stretching back many hundreds of years, such as the Tarbfeis, or bull feast, of Celtic tradition, in which a white bull was sacrificed and a seer or shaman would encase himself or herself in the bull's mantle and incubate a vision. Memories of this survived into the early twentieth century, and during the period of Spring-Heeled Jack's activities, a figure garbed in a white bull's hide would have instantly evoked memories of ancient rites and horned devils.

The poet Kathleen Raine in her autobiography *Farewell Happy Fields* (1973) describes her father telling the story of a farmer who kept an ox hide, complete with horns and tail, in his loft. On certain fine evenings "he would sometimes put on this theriomorphic disguise, lurk behind hedges, and frighten his neighbors in whose souls, as in his own. . . . The horned god still reigned."[5] The outcome of the story is darker, as a young man who had only recently arrived in the area happened to be returning home by a darkened road. He had been sent to have the blade of his master's plough sharpened. Upon seeing the ghostly apparition of the bull-man, and hearing it bellow, he attacked the creature and slew it with the sharpened blade—only afterward discovering it was the farmer's blood that darkened the earth.

Having explored the supernatural and folklore origins of Jack's legend, it is time to turn to the actual people who have been, at various times, identified with the leaping man. In the process we shall see how fear of the unknown nature of the mysterious attacker prompted researchers to seek out physical embodiments of Jack's inexplicable qualities.

CHAPTER 6

Who Was Jack?

Oh, jolly is the night when the stars are shining bright,
And the moon is hid from sight beneath the sea,
Then I'm out upon the track,
For my name is Spring-Heel Jack,
And I love the winter darkness for a spree.

POPULAR SONG, CIRCA 1838

Not all the forerunners or parallels to the phenomena of Spring-Heeled Jack are ghostly or folkloric. A handful of real people—none of them real contenders for the identification of Jack—can nevertheless be seen to have influenced the way he was perceived.

The long-standing romance with the figure of the highwayman likely prefigured the Victorian public's reaction to Spring-Heeled Jack, and there were several figures whose adventures may have contributed to his. Once the initial hysteria had died down, Jack became, for a time, something of an antihero. His ability to run rings around the police made him a figure of admiration to some. Unlike the Ripper, whose terrifying crimes were briefly associated with Spring-Heeled Jack, the older figure was seen as a relatively harmless crank, bent upon nothing more serious than frightening women and girls (and some men) with his garish appearance and uncanny laughter.

The almost mythic status achieved by highwaymen, known as Knights of the Road, who terrorized travelers on the roadways of Britain throughout much of the seventeenth and early eighteenth centuries, is a clear foretaste of the public attitude to Jack. Though the Spring-Heeled Jack sightings begin some time after the so-called golden age of highwaymen, there are aspects of his daring attacks and sometimes violent behavior that must have reminded people of the days when it was unsafe to travel without an armed escort, or at least a weapon of some sort, for fear of the cry of "stand and deliver."

Despite the fact that they were essentially thieves and sometimes murderers, the status of many highwaymen, especially to the poorer people of Britain, was that of heroes. The daring deeds and exciting adventures of such figures as Dick Turpin, Claude Duvall, and John Nevison became the subject of penny dreadfuls in the same way as Spring-Heeled Jack was to do years later. It should come as no surprise that two of the most renowned figures among this band of devil-may-care antiheroes bear the name Jack. These are Jack Sheppard and Sixteen-String Jack.

Sheppard (1702–1724) was really more of a common thief than a highwayman, but his deeds became so legendary that he is regularly listed alongside Dick Turpin and the rest. Much of his short life was normal. He apprenticed as a carpenter in 1723, but before he had completed his indenture, he decided that a career as a thief was more fun. After a series of burglaries, he was captured, sentenced, and incarcerated. However, over the following year he escaped, not once but four times, making him something of a legend and hugely popular among the poor and downtrodden. He even produced an autobiography, probably ghosted by the famous author Daniel Defoe, which became a bestseller following his execution in 1724.

Sheppard's fame continued for another hundred years when he became the origin of the character McHeath in John Gay's *Beggar's Opera* (1728), and in 1840, at the height of Spring-Heeled Jack's activities, he returned to public consciousness in a bestselling novel by Harrison Ainsworth. So popular was this tale of thievery and daring-do that plays, which included the name of Jack Sheppard in their titles, were banned on the London stage in the belief that they would incite others to follow in the bold thief's footsteps.

The second of our redoubtable Jacks is John "Sixteen-String Jack" Rann (1750–1774). Though born into a working-class family in Bath, Somerset, Rann seems to have acquired a liking for an extravagant way of life early on. Moving to London he became a coachman, but quickly began to live beyond his means, splashing out on expensive clothes and attending balls around the city. Running short of money, he took to pickpocketing and became so good at it that he decided to graduate to being a highwayman. Arrested six times he managed to escape imprisonment due to lack of evidence or witnesses. It was at this time he received his nickname Sixteen-String Jack, due to the many colored strings or ribbons he wore tied around the knees of his britches. He was known for his wit and devil-may-care behavior, but in the end he was caught and sentenced to hang at Tyburn. It is said that on the appointed day he wore a specially made pea-green suit, exchanged lively banter with the executioner, and danced a jig before the noose was put around his neck.

Like many another before and after, these "gentlemen of the road" were seen as dashing and even heroic by those who cared nothing for loss of jewelry and purses by the nobility, or indeed the not infrequent murder of their victims. Again, this had its own knock-on effect on the way in which Spring-Heeled Jack was perceived, while others were more direct contenders for the crown.

THE MAD MARQUIS

Over the years a number of researchers have explored the possibility of identifying Spring-Heeled Jack with an actual person. Not surprisingly, given his multifaceted personality and the undoubted influence of other cultural figures from folklore and myth, no one has succeeded in doing so. The most popular and long-lived of these identities is Henry de La Poer Beresford, third Marquis of Waterford (1811–1859), nicknamed the Mad Marquis due to his wild and unorthodox behavior.

The Waterford family—also known as the earls of Tyrone and Haverfordwest in Pembroke, Wales—are one of the great noble families of Britain and Ireland. The title was created in 1789 for George Beresford, 2nd Earl of Tyrone, who hailed from the English county of Kent but who chose to settle in Ireland in the seventeenth century; having sat as a member of the Irish House of Commons, he was rewarded with a baronetcy in 1665. He was later made Earl of Tyrone in the peerage of Ireland in 1746. Following this, he was created Baron Tyrone of Haverfordwest in the County of Pembroke, in the peerage of Great Britain, and three years later became Marquis of Waterford in the peerage of Ireland. The titles descended in a direct line until the death of his grandson, the third marquis, Henry de La Poer Beresford, in 1859. This third marquis is the figure that has been consistently identified with Spring-Heeled Jack, despite no real evidence beyond a characteristic flair for the dramatic and a wild sense of humor.

Henry was certainly a black sheep of the family, which otherwise provided a number of respected churchmen—one an archbishop of Armagh—and several army officers. Described as a dark, curly haired child with sturdy limbs and handsome features only slightly marred by protruding eyes, Henry inherited his title on his seventeenth birth-

Fig. 6.1. Henry de La Poer Beresford, 3rd Marquis of Waterford (1840)

day in 1828 while he was still at Eton. Despite his undoubted sporting abilities (he was supposedly the best oarsman in the College Eight of 1829), he left this prestigious school under something of a cloud. From here he moved on to Christ Church College in Oxford, but was sent down within a year for gambling and drunkenness. His reaction to this seems to have been to get into even more trouble—going back to his old school to steal the headmaster's whipping block, an unpleasant device over which more than one recalcitrant boy had been bent before receiving what was referred to as "a good thrashing."

Henry seems to have enjoyed fighting and got into several affrays for which he was more than once arrested and fined. His extensive fortune enabled him to pay these without concern, and in most cases he went back to causing more trouble. Along with two friends, Lord Methuen and Billy Duff, he seems to have actively sought out suitable opponents for a roundhouse. According to sports writer Ralph Neville, these three young men were "never so happy as when engaging butchers and draymen in fistic encounters."[1] His legendary gambling habit, which made him willing to bet upon virtually anything, became ever more extreme and to this he added the kind of "pranks" that were (as they still are) the stock-in-trade of undergraduates.

After this the stories get more and more wild, making it easy to understand how the association with Spring-Heeled Jack came about. Ralph Neville has left us a wonderful portrait of Henry in his book *Sporting Days and Sporting Ways* (1910), describing several wild events remembered in the history of the various clubs to which the marquis belonged. He is described, among other pranks, as putting aniseed on the hooves of a parson's horse and then pursuing the terrified man with bloodhounds, and of putting a donkey into the bed of a man staying at an inn!

He also rented a hunting lodge somewhere in the English countryside, where he "amused himself with shooting out the eyes of family portraits with a pistol."[2] On another occasion he solemnly proposed to one of the first railway companies in Ireland [that they should] start two engines in opposite directions on the same line in order that he might witness the smash, for which he proposed to pay.[3]

Henry was also capable of acts of outrageous foolhardiness, seeming not to care for his life at all. While sailing aboard his yacht *Charlotte* in the Bay of Biscay, the wind blew his cap overboard. At once the marquis ordered his first officer to put out a boat to retrieve the hat. Neville continues:

'My Lord', respectfully urged his skipper, 'no boat could live in such a sea'.

'The deuce it can't', was the rejoinder, 'then I'll see whether I can or not', and as he spoke he leapt from the taffrail into the seething waters. It was now no time for hesitation and the once caused a boat to be lowered, and went to attempt the rescue of his reckless master, who was eventually reached about a mile astern of the vessel in an exhausted condition, but clutching his cap![4]

Inevitably, the activities of this rakish young nobleman began to attract the attention of the newspapers. One of the earliest reports, from the *Stamford Mercury*, focuses once again upon the tollgate at Melton Mowbray, Leicestershire—clearly a favorite haunt of Henry and his friends.

𝔖tamford 𝔐ercury

MARCH 11, 1836

The Marquis of Waterford, whose pranks have frequently drawn him within the powerful attractive influence of police stations . . . has been showing off at Melton Mowbray during the last week.

After smashing several windows, and offering a bonus to some street passengers to fight with him, he turned his attention to a member of the medical profession, who is remarkable for his gentlemanly conduct and unoffending deportment, who happened to be riding up the street, and being near the turnpike gate, the noble Marquis seized the bridal and peremptorily demanded the toll. The gentlemen mildly replied to his rudeness by stating that he had already paid for going through the gate, and requested to be suffered quietly to proceed. Some blows hereupon where inflicted . . . and a certain epithet applied, too gross for utterance [here].

It is stated that a note of apology has been forwarded to the insulted party who, it is hoped, will refer the matter to the decision of the law, rather than by compromising so gross an outrage as to encourage . . . such conduct towards some who have neither spirit nor money to demand justice.

Whatever the outcome of this escapade, Henry was back in the public eye again shortly afterward, accused of having overturned the sedan chair in which an elderly lady was traveling and leaving its passenger stranded by the roadside. Shortly after he is reported to have stated an "unseemly incident" at a local inn in Hertfordshire, getting two servant girls drunk and then encouraging them to fight him for the amusement of his friends. Having easily defeated the tipsy young ladies, the marquis is then said to have placed them across his knee and to have soundly spanked them both "for presuming that even two women were a match for a man of . . . sport."[5]

By now Henry seemed completely out of control, and in his next escapade finally overstepped the mark sufficiently to end up in court, along with three friends—Sir Frederick Johnstone, the Honorable A. C. H. Villiers, and E. H. Reynard, Esq. The episode was deemed sufficiently serious to be reported in the *Times*.

All four men had attended the Croxton Park Races on April 5, 1837, continuing on to the nearby small town of Melton for supper. At around two o'clock, the town watchmen were roused to attend a noisy altercation. They found "several gentlemen attempting to overturn a caravan"[6] and as they drew near realized that there was a frightened man inside. The report continues:

The Times

APRIL 6, 1837

The watchmen succeeded in preventing the caravan being overturned, at which the Marquis of Waterford challenged one of them to fight. The watchmen declined.

Subsequently hearing noise in the direction of the toll-bar [a gate at which a fee was charged to gain access to the town], the men proceeded to that, and found the gatekeeper had been [locked up] in his house, and had been calling out 'Murder!'

On coming up with the gentlemen the second time, it was observed they had a pot of red paint with them, while one of them carried a paintbrush, which one of the constables wrestled from the hand of the person who held it; but subsequently they surrounded the man, threw him on his back, and painted with red paint his face and neck.

They then continued their games, painting the doors and windows of different persons; and when one of their companions (Mr. Reynard) was put in the lockup, they forced the constable to give up the keys, and succeeded in getting him out.

When the offenders were arraigned, none of them denied their actions and paid the large fine of £100 each immediately, before retiring again to the same inn where they had begun the actions of the evening in question.

This was perhaps Henry's most famous prank, earning him the doubtful honor of being the first person to literally "paint the town red"! Now, apparently tired of being hounded by the press and restrained by police and watchmen, the marquis and his friends decided to leave England for a while and seek adventure elsewhere.

For a while they considered undertaking an expedition to Africa, but perhaps wisely decided instead to sail Henry's yacht, the

Charlotte, to Scandinavia. Arriving in Bergen, Norway, on August 11, the young men lost no time in heading off to the nearest inn—a small public house in the district of Nostest. There, they quickly persuaded three serving girls to join them for supper. Henry was especially taken with a blonde and mischievous girl named Anne Uldenhoft, and as the evening proceeded, she and the marquis became increasingly intimate.

Around midnight Henry suggested they take a walk together, and Anne agreed. Outside, as the two twined arms and supported each other, laughing loudly as the marquis tried to drink from a bottle that still had the cork in. At this moment a watchman appeared, and events took on a darker tone.

A subsequent report filed by the local police chief, tells what happened next. The watchman, forty-four-year-old Brynild Larsen, came upon the couple, Anne Uldencraft apparently wearing her escort's hat, while he wore no hat at all. As the marquis was a stranger, the watchman took this as a clear sign of mischief and ordered them to be quiet. Not only did they ignore his request, but the marquis also picked up a stone. In response the watchman attempted to deliver "a light blow to the man's arm"[7] with his staff (called a morning star), in order to disarm the marquis. At the same moment the marquis bowed toward the watchman and "by chance" received the blow on his head.

The report continues.

THE TIMES, APRIL 6, 1837

The watchmen came up, abused them for making a noise, and, with his morning star, struck the Englishman on his back, at which the latter laughed louder than before. They then went over the Halvkands Height, passing the watchmen, but as the Englishman continued to laugh out loud, she [Anne Uldencraft] was not able to get away from him until the Watchman came up and struck him a blow, which threw him to the ground.

This is all far from clear, though it would seem that the overenthusiastic watchman decided that the local girl was under duress by the Englishman and decided to punish him accordingly. The fact that more than one blow was delivered, and with far more force than necessary, was revealed when Henry's friends lodged a complaint with the British consul who requested a doctor's report on the injuries sustained by the young marquis.

> D. A. Heiberg, town-physician, deposed on the 16th, [reported] that the blow had fallen on the right temple, and had inflicted a wound which had pierced to the bone. A considerable swelling and discoloring of the skin ensued subsequently, extending over the whole temple and eyelid. Nearer to the cranium were two superficial wounds of no importance. The blow must have been struck with extraordinary force, and had occasioned a severe concussion of the brain that the Marquise's life was still in danger. On the back there was no mark of a blow having been given; but on the loins there is a round blue spot of the size of a dollar, evidently occasioned by some external act of violence.[8]

Clearly this was far more than a light blow on the arm such as described by the watchman. It seems evident that Henry was severely beaten. Indeed, it took him almost a month to recover, during which time he had to suffer reports in the local newspapers such as the *Bergen Morgenavisen,* which proudly stated that,

> "The well-known Marquis of Waterford has attempted to play the pranks in our streets by which he has acquired a very equivocal reputation in the United Kingdom, but unhappily encountered a watchman who is one of the most vigorous of our guardians of the night, and a blow of whose staff felled the Marquis to the ground, when he was taken up half dead."[9]

More than happy to shake the dust of Norway off his shoes, the marquis and his friends boarded the *Charlotte* again and sailed for home, finally docking at Aberdeen on September 18. The *Caledonian Mercury* reported the affair briefly and declared that the young marquis seemed in good spirits. However, according to the memoirs of Henry's close friend Sir Frederic Johnstone, who had been a co-conspirator on many occasions before this, his mood was far from happy.

The Caledonian Mercury

SEPTEMBER 18, 1837

On the coach journey from Scotland, there were many efforts on the part of his friends to raise Henry's spirits. He evinced the most bitter hatred of the police authorities for their part in the matter and talked in the most depreciating terms of the servant girl whom, he said, was in part to blame. Try as we would to distract his mind to other things he kept to the subject as if the night Watchman's blows had somehow affected his reason. Only when the talk was of new wagers did he show any interest, and I believe his later return to good spirits was due to a daring venture the others proposed for his return to London.

What exactly this "daring venture" was remains a mystery as Sir Frederick, later a respected member of Parliament, said no more—but it is from this point that Peter Haining, the most determined advocate of the identification of Spring-Heeled Jack with the marquis, believes the evidence points to this conclusion.

To begin with he notes that Henry spent the next few months on the move from house to house around London, visiting and staying with friends. One of these was a place known as Vanbrugh Castle on Mazer Hill, Blackheath. From there, according to the *London Gazette* for October 11, "a party lead by the Waterford disported themselves with much merriment at Blackheath Fair. This event, known as the 'hog and pleasure fair,'"[10] took place every year in January and October in the area, and was the occasion of much merriment along with a brisk trade in the sale of hogs.

The site was not far from the place where the attack by Spring-Heeled Jack on the servant-girl Polly Adams took place, and Haining notes that she had referred to the "pop eyes"[11] of her attacker and his "loud, ringing laugh"[12]—both features of the marquis.

Next, Haining records that on Friday, November 24, of the same year, the *Times* reported the marquis indisposed with "a complaint of the eyes."[13] This, suggests Haining, could have been the result of his using a chemical that enabled him to appear to breathe fire, and Henry's convalescence coincides with a period of inactivity on the part of Spring-Heeled Jack.

Finally, he records that Mr. Ashworth's servant boy noted the initial *W* embroidered on his attacker's cloak and cites the evidence suggesting the attacker returned later to retrieve the cloak. Haining of course assumes this *W* stands for Waterford, but assuming the evidently distracted youth was correct, it seems unlikely that the perpetrator, if it was Henry, would have made the mistake of wearing anything so recognizable on any of his daring attacks.

Could the attack on Polly Adams have been Henry taking revenge for what he saw as the slight he had received from the servant girl in Norway? Was this the "daring venture" mentioned by Sir Frederick Johnstone? It is certainly not impossible to see Henry's previous wild behavior as a forerunner of the events, and the dates are a match. The idea has continued to surface through the years and was incorporated into the penny dreadful accounts of Spring-Heeled Jack published in the years following the reported sightings.

A series of letters printed in the journal *Notes and Queries* throughout 1907 all claimed that this was the best solution to the mystery. This monthly publication invited any and all comers to write in with their questions and comments, which were then dealt with by experts. In the correspondence in question, at least one writer, a Mr. Harry Hems of Fair Park, Exeter, claimed that his grandmother, who died at an advanced age in 1850 and thus had lived through the period of Jack's appearances, had personally told him of the identification. If there is

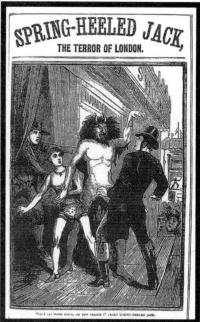

Fig. 6.2. Spring-Heeled Jack featured in the penny dreadfuls.

any truth in this, the old lady was almost certainly recalling the newspaper reports of the time.

But it seems a long stretch to connect the essentially harmless pranks of the young Irish nobleman with the terrifying attacks of Spring-Heeled Jack, and there is so far no solid evidence to confirm the identification. The identification of Henry de La Poer Beresford with Spring-Heeled Jack seems to have been almost entirely invented by the press, based on the rowdy escapades of the young marquis, coupled with his penetrating laugh, which some chose to compare with the maniacal laughter of Spring-Heeled Jack. The whole matter seems to have emerged from a deep-seated perception of social inequality and the idea of the rich preying on the poor. The newspaper reports seemed to take delight in suggesting, over and over again, that the attacks were carried out by "young gentlemen" out for a good time at the expense of the less well-off. The fact that Spring-Heeled Jack preyed upon every level of society seems to have been conveniently forgotten.

Certainly, if Henry was indeed connected with the sightings of Spring-Heeled Jack, his wild ways finally came to an end in 1839 when he was twenty-eight. In that year an event took place that changed his life when he took part in a famous event organized by the 13th Earl of Eglinton (1812–1861) at Kilwinning in Scotland. The event, known as the Eglinton Tournament, was an attempt to re-create a medieval jousting match in intricate detail. The earl, a lifelong fan of the Arthurian legends, spent almost £40,000 on the event—a vast sum at the time—and it was an unqualified success, bringing thousands of spectators to watch Victorian gentlemen dressed in plate armor tilting against each other in a life-size re-creation of the medieval lists.

Henry took part in this, though it is not certain whether as a combatant or simply a spectator, but it was here that he met the beautiful Louisa Stuart (1818–1891), daughter of Lord Stuart of Rothesay. Henry seems to have fallen head over heels in love with her on the spot and almost immediately asked for her hand in marriage. Not surprisingly perhaps, given Henry's reputation as a hell-raiser, it took three years to convince the Rothesays to agree to the match, but during this time the young marquis seems to have made every effort to mend his ways.

After the wedding, to all intents he became a model husband and seems to have remained so. The couple settled on the marquis's extensive estates in Ireland, and it was there that we hear, again from the London *Times,* a very different report about the marquis, headed simply "The Marquess of Waterford."

The Times

NOVEMBER 24, 1842

THE MARQUESS OF WATERFORD

It is a pleasing duty to record a truly noble and humane act upon the part of this nobleman. A few days ago, as his lordship was travelling in the neighborhood of Kilsheenan, in Tipperary, he was struck with the appearance of a farmer's horse, which his carriage overtook on the road. After a few preliminaries the animal changed owners, and became the property of the noble Marquis.

The farmer, however, belated no doubt by his ready sale, was resolved to show off the merits of the horse, but in doing so the animal became so restive and irritated that he broke to pieces the vehicle to which he was harnessed, and fractured the arm of the farmer, beside inflicting other injuries upon him.

Upon witnessing the accident, the Marquis of Waterford immediately left his carriage and, causing three gentlemen who with him at the time to do the same, he had the sufferer placed within it, then drove with him to the house of the neighbouring gentlemen, where he had every attention paid him. Not content with this, his lordship, in the most generous manner, gave him £5 and returned him his horse. He further directed no expense to be spared, to have him removed to Clonmel, and to have the best surgeon there employed for him. He is now under the care of Dr. Burgess and rapidly recovering. We will not add a word of comment.

The last sentence makes it clear that the reporter was well aware of Henry's earlier behavior, which his failure to comment upon doubtless reminded his readers of the same.

This is a far cry from the wild youth splashing red paint on passersby and picking fights with tradesmen. If he was Spring-Heeled Jack—and I would say that the very best we can do with the theory is that he might have been one of several men who chose to adopt the style and persona of the fearsome Jack—there is no evidence to suggest that he ever attempted anything similar again.

THE LONDON MONSTER

Another character whose behavior bears a striking resemblance to that of Spring-Heeled Jack is the so-called London Monster, who haunted the streets of the metropolis between 1788 and 1790 and was responsible for attacks on more than fifty women. In fact, this was a far more sinister and serious offender who, according to the testimony of his victims, stalked them, shouted obscenities at them, and slashed at them with a sharp-bladed weapon. His modus operandi was far more dangerous than Spring-Heeled Jack. The London Monster—so dubbed by the press—seriously wounded several of his victims. He always attacked women of the upper class, aiming particularly at the buttocks or legs. He is also said to have worn knives attached to his knees, with which he also inflicted wounds. Still more horrible was his trick of presenting an innocent woman with a nosegay, and on inviting her to smell it, stabbed her in the face with a blade hidden among the flowers. Interestingly, given the parallels with Spring-Heeled Jack, he was said to smile widely, grinning and laughing as he struck out at his victims.

The Monster's appearance varied widely according to the accounts of his various victims in much the same way as the sightings of Spring-Heeled Jack. One described him as "a large dark man," another as a "villainous looking fellow with a narrow face." Yet another described him as a small, thin, big-nosed man, while another had him as six feet tall with pale skin and sallow features. This variety of appearance seemed to add to the fear running rife in the streets. Anyone, it seemed, could be the Monster.

Once it became clear that the mysterious attacker only targeted beautiful women, this had the effect of causing some to claim they had been attacked, even faking wounds in order to get sympathy, when this was actually not true. At the same time, many men were afraid to speak to any passing woman, especially after dark, for fear of being identified as the sinister attacker. Some indeed founded a "No Monster Club" and wore a pin to identify themselves and ensure they were not accused of the attacks.

As the year dragged on, the Monster escaped apprehension, always seeming to vanish before the screams of his victims brought help on the scene. Fashionable women took to wearing copper guards over their petticoats, while the poor hung frying pans from their belts. Just as with

Spring-Heeled Jack almost fifty years later, there was a great outcry from the public, and efforts were doubled to capture the Monster.

Finally, a well-known art collector and philanthropist, John Julius Angerstein, offered a reward of £100 for the capture of the Monster—a considerable sum at the time. Thus encouraged, gangs of armed vigilantes began to patrol the city. Inevitably people were falsely accused, and men who were seen as behaving in a suspicious manner were attacked in the street. Pickpockets and other petty criminals used the ensuing panic to their advantage, snatching a wallet or purse and shouting "Monster!" before escaping in the resulting confusion.

In the end it was a casual event that ended the Monster's reign of terror. On the June 13, 1790, one of the Monster's earliest victims, Anne Porter, thought she sighted the attacker while walking with an admirer in St. James Park. Her companion, a young man named John Coleman, immediately began to pursue the man who, strangely, made no attempt to run off despite the fact that he was clearly aware of being followed. He made his way to a house where Coleman confronted him and challenged him to a duel. The man, who gave his name as Rhynwick Williams, an unemployed twenty-three-year-old, protested his innocence even when Coleman forced him to confront Anne Porter. When the lady promptly fainted at the sight of him, Williams's fate was sealed.

Williams, portrayed as a gentle-looking man in the contemporary engraving on page 186, continued to claim his innocence even after the police were called and he was arraigned before a magistrate. Given the general atmosphere of terror gripping the city, the outcome was inevitable—especially once Williams admitted to having approached Anne Porter on an earlier occasion. Given that the recorded words he was said to have uttered were: "Oho, is that you?" The suggestion that he had known Anne earlier seems reasonable. However, further investigation by the police discovered that Williams had an unshakable alibi for one of the attacks. Shortly after this, one of the supposed victims admitted she had not been attacked at all but had invented the incident.

Fig. 6.3. Rhynwick Williams

These two factors enabled Williams's advocate, the redoubtable Irish poet and satirist Theophilus Swift, to get the offense changed from one of assault to one of "defacing the clothing of his victims." Curiously, though we may find it hard to believe today, the law of the time made this a more serious offense than attempted murder! It thus made Williams's case worse and could have earned him the Victorian punishment of transportation—being transported to the colonies, usually Australia, to serve out a sentence. In the end the offense again became one of assault, and he was sentenced for two years each for three of the attacks, receiving a total of six years in prison.

Though Williams never admitted his guilt, the attacks ceased following his imprisonment, and as life in the city returned to normal, it was widely assumed that he was guilty as charged. Experts who have examined the case and the evidence presented have found it to be very flimsy, and some have suggested that the whole affair was the result of lurid reporting, which instigated panic following one or two isolated incidents.

It is extremely unlikely that Williams, who vanished from history after his imprisonment, could have been Spring-Heeled Jack. The timings alone are wrong, as Williams, twenty-three at the time of his arrest, would have been over seventy by the time the sightings of Spring-Heeled Jack began. However, there is no doubt that memories of the London Monster would have returned to haunt the citizens of London, and Spring-Heeled Jack's attacks, though actually less serious than those of the Monster, were sufficiently similar to cause people to draw their own conclusions. Given the supposed supernatural nature of the new attacker, many may have believed it to be the ghost of Rhynwick Williams returned to cause further havoc in the city.

We may remember that other suspects, in particular Millbank and Paynes and James Priest, were arraigned and questioned regarding their part in the mystery (see chapter 1), but none of them were convicted of anything more than a breach of the peace.

These are the main figures that have been, at various times, identified as the people behind the growing myth of Spring-Heeled Jack. All can, with reasonable doubt, be dismissed. It is more than likely that the activities of people like Waterford and Williams contributed to the story, while those of Joseph Munday (see chapter 4) suggest how easy it was to be mistaken for Jack, or perhaps to imitate him. In the end it is perhaps pointless to try to pin the identity of Jack upon a single person. He was, it seems, not one but many, each seeking, for whatever reason, to be associated with the mysterious leaping menace.

CHAPTER 7

Jack's Back
Twentieth- and Twenty-First-Century Appearances

*The tortures of the damned shall be implanted in your
heart by me—the wretched, despised outcast whom you
have christened Spring-Heeled Jack!*

ANONYMOUS, *THE TERROR OF LONDON*

Though most of the stories that have gathered around the figure of
Spring-Heeled Jack tend to be focused either in Britain or (more recently)
parts of the United States, there is one significant Jack-like figure that
warrants our attention and who comes instead from the heart of Europe.
This is Pérák, a shadowy hero who appeared in Prague during the
German occupation of World War II. Callum McDonald and Jan Kaplan
in their 1995 book, *Prague in the Shadow of the Swastika: A History of the
German Occupation 1939–1945,* describe this figure as leaping out from
shadowy alleys, frightening passersby, and then vanishing as mysteriously
as he had appeared.

Oral tradition suggests that some of Pérák's leaps were of an
extraordinary magnitude, including the act of jumping over train car-
riages, obviously parallel to the jumps achieved by Spring-Heeled Jack.
However, there seems to be no actual evidence for the existence of this
character. Not even police records, examined by George Zenaty, an
expert on police activity of the period, showed anything.

This does not, of course, mean that no such records existed, or that Pérák himself did not exist, but it is hard to get any kind of picture of him beyond these few sparse details. Certainly, if he were real, he was flouting the German curfew by being out on the streets. If he existed at all, it is possible that he was a figure of the resistance movement, or perhaps simply an imagined hero invented to give the citizens of occupied Prague hope. Certainly he was to become a hero of the Czech people after the war, when the animator and puppeteer Jiri Trnka (1912–1969) created a cartoon called *Springer and the SS* (1946), in which a character dressed in black with a mask and springs in his shoes challenged the Gestapo to capture him as he sprang through the narrow streets of Prague. These stories suggest the way in which Pérák was seen at the time. It is possible that the story of Spring-Heeled Jack had spread this far and inspired the creation of Springer, or it may simply be a coincidence.

THE JUMPING MEN OF SAXONY

A similar story is told of a character known as the Hippemannchen (Little-Hopper-Man) or Spiralhopser (Spiral-Hopper), who was active in the East German provinces of Saxony and Thuringia as recently as the early 1950s. The writer Dietrich Kuhn first described them in his book *Sagen und Legenden aus Sachsenn* (1994). According to the book, there were in fact several of these leaping figures, dressed in white in a manner familiar to us from some of the descriptions of Spring-Heeled Jack, who terrorized the area. In response to an inquiry from *Fortean Times* correspondent Ulrich Magin, Kuhn replied:

The Hippemannchen and Spiralhopser in Saxony were reported 1950–1951 and considerably disquieted people. There are no written reports from that time. I remember this mass hysteria from being a youth at that time. In Erfurt, for example, a chef of a famous hotel was almost beaten one night because he returned home in his

working dress to save time. It cost him quite some effort to convince
the excited masses that he was not one of the Hippemannchen.[1]

He goes on to say that he knows of no one "who could really claim a
personal sighting of one of the mannequins . . . [they were] a nearly
contemporary manifestation of mass hysteria."[2] Whatever the truth
of the matter, there is little difference between this description and
the contemporary reports of Spring-Heeled Jack. Even the poor chef
chased through the streets because he went home wearing his white
work clothes is reminiscent of similar confusions during the hunt
for Jack.

VISITOR FROM ANOTHER WORLD

It is not really surprising that Spring-Heeled Jack should eventually
become associated with UFOs and alien visitors. His appearance, in
a tight-fitting suit and voluminous headgear, his blazing eyes, and the
blue fire issuing from his mouth share a good deal with images of
visitors from other worlds who have been part of the world of mystery seekers from the late nineteenth century to our own time (see
plate 12).

The first person to make the connection was the actor and radio
personality Valentine Dyall, also known as Britain's Vincent Price and
the Man in Black. Between 1943 and 1955, he was the narrator of BBC
Radio 4's gothic horror show *Appointment with Fear,* which dramatized
spooky and supernatural tales for an eager public. At the height of its
popularity, the show recorded a listenership of several thousand. In
1954 Dyall wrote an article for *Everybody's Magazine,* "Spring-Heeled
Jack—the Leaping Terror," which catapulted Jack once more into everyday consciousness. Dyall's article was sensationalized to an extreme
level, describing Jack in lurid and garish terms and making free use of
the nineteenth-century reports. Rehearsing the attack on Aldershot
Barracks, he described Jack as

Fig. 7.1. Valentine Dyall, the British Vincent Price

a tall, thin figure in a tight-fitting suit and huge, gleaming helmet of fantastic design . . . rising from the ground with the ease of a bird. As it swooped over Regan's head a stream of blue flame spurted from its mouth.[3]

Regan is the name given by Dyall to the soldier on duty on the occasion of the first sighting. Peter Haining later took this up and added it to his own equally overblown account. No such name had been attached to the story before this, and no amount of searching through the army records of the time has brought forth such a person. Nor do we find any reference to the "gleaming helmet of fantastic design" anywhere else. But it is Dyall's summing up that suggested an extraterrestrial connection, which was swiftly taken up by ufologists:

Today we are still without a likely answer to the question: who—
or what—was the fabulous, ubiquitous creature that terrorized a
huge section of the British public for nearly sixty years? One thing
is certain—he was no ordinary mortal. It is significant that a high
proportion of those who saw him were convinced that he was not of
this world, but either a spirit or a visitor from some distant planet.[4]

Everybody's Magazine received a postbag of theories from its readers,
among them that Jack was actually a mad circus acrobat, an eagle, or
a kangaroo! They also included a letter from someone signing himself
"Inman Race of Sheffield," who had a theory of his own in response to
Dyall's question. It was obvious to him that Spring-Heeled Jack was an
alien who had crashed his ship and remained stranded on Earth. This
alone explained his ability to leap to such heights and over such distances.

The downward thrust needed to allow any spring to hurl a grown
man many feet could never be obtained. But a Being, reared on a
planet where gravity was far greater than on earth would be able
to leap colossal distances on THIS planet. . . . I suggest that the
alleged monster was a visitant from Space who had been marooned.
His birth on a greater gravity planet would enable him to live longer
on Earth, and perform all the feats attributed to the oddity.[5]

Seven years later, in 1961, the ufologist John Vyner wrote an article,
"The Mystery of Spring-Heeled Jack," for the influential London-based
journal *The Flying Saucer Review*. Responding to an inquiry into the
existence of alien visitors before the 1940s, Vyner suggested that Jack
was the most obvious contender. Taking his cue from the more dramatic
contemporary newspaper reports, and very clearly building on Valentine
Dyall's earlier speculations, Vyner summarized Jack's appearance:

The intruder was tall, thin, and powerful. He had a prominent nose,
and bony fingers of immense power which resembled claws. He was

incredibly agile. He wore a long, flowing cloak, of the sort affected by operagoers, soldiers and strolling actors. On his head was a tall, metallic seeming helmet. Beneath the cloak were close-fitting garments of some glittering material like oilskin or metal mesh. There was a lamp strapped to his chest. Oddest of all: the creature's ears were cropped or pointed like those of an animal.[6]

We can see immediately that most of these details are borrowed from various descriptions, in particular the attack on the Alsop girls, with a few details (such as the cropped ears) added for good measure. He also describes the blue flames issuing from the "Spaceman's" mouth as "stupefying gas," coupled with "a magnetic effect transmitted along a beam of polarized light from Jack's mysterious lantern." He then theorizes:

Intense magnetic fields produce effects comparable to those experienced by Jack's victims—and by those who have ventured near to grounded saucers. Though the inverse square law governing radiation is commonly thought to prevent development of paralyzing ray devices small enough to be easily portable, a concentrated beam might trigger off a magnetic disturbance in the vicinity of its target.[7]

Considering the appearances of Spring-Heeled Jack around specific areas of London, Vyner suggests that the spaceman was "desperately trying to locate a 'safe house' or a friendly 'agent' who could help him locate his misplaced flying saucer."[8]

Not done with this strand of speculation, Vyner adds:

The enigma of Spring-Heeled Jack's astounding leaps is, like the siren song, not entirely beyond conjecture. It is possible that a being from a high gravity planet might be able to duplicate some of his feats on our own; likewise, there is the possibility of his employing an individual rocket device, such as U.S. Army engineers have developed. Such a device could carry a man over wide rivers and standing trees, but what happens on landing?

All the accounts of Jack's feats seem to indicate that he had perfect control of his mighty bounds. In fact, his silent landings indicate buoyancy. The buoyancy of the balloon jumper with the gasbag attached a shoulder harness. But, despite observations of Jack carrying 'something on his back', I am inclined to think the solution must lie in the possession of a device for neutralizing gravity. Normally, the user would reduce his weight to a point at which he could walk normally while retaining the capacity for tremendous leaps. Increasing the power would enable him to soar, or even float. That he would then use control . . . unless he had wings. Light, collapsible wings, serving as controls surfaces, requiring little muscular effort to use.[9]

Inman Race's idea of a visitor from a planet with lighter gravity has not gone away; it has become, instead, part of the story, while Vyner's speculation of the way in which Jack was able to make his prodigious leaps harks back to the idea of theatrical illusions posited years earlier. Whether Jack is regarded as a supernatural character or a fake with means of projecting himself though the air, the desire to explain his abilities remains.

In a 1971 issue of *The Flying Saucer Review,* Roger Sandell comments that if the reports published in the nineteenth century had appeared in twentieth-century newspapers, "it is possible that the creature would have been described as a 'man from outer space.' The helmet and oilskin garment may well have been described as a 'spacesuit.' Even the luminescence and the incredible jumping ability can be paralleled in many modern reports."[10]

Further suggestions come from the excellent Internet site "The Complete Spring-Heeled Jack Page." Here our attention is drawn to the Great Moon Hoax of 1835, which took place two years before the first recorded sightings of Spring-Heeled Jack in London. The hoax burst onto the scene via a series of six articles published in a New York newspaper called the *Sun,* beginning on August 25, 1835. The claim of the author, anonymous in the newspaper but since almost certainly identified as Richard Adams Locke, a Cambridge-educated reporter then working for the *Sun,* told of the discovery of a richly detailed civilization on the moon. The discovery was attributed to none other than Sir John Herschel (1792–1871), one of the most famous astronomers of his time who had apparently been able to study the flora and fauna of the moon through a great telescope of a unique design.

The articles that followed were attributed to one Dr. Andrew Grant, a personal assistant to Herschel. Grant, however, was fictitious, as was the whole story. At the time it was sensational, even backed by Yale University, who hailed the story as the greatest discovery of that orb.

The articles offered a detailed account of the fantastic sights viewed by Herschel, accompanied by some astonishing illustrations. The lunar landscape included vast forests, inland seas, and quartz pyramids. Herds of bison ranged across the plains, and blue unicorns were seen on hilltops, while spherical, amphibious creatures rolled across its beaches. But perhaps most important of all was Herschel's discovery that intelligent life existed on the moon. These were a tribe of primitive, hut-dwelling, fire-wielding bipedal beavers and a race of winged humans. Herschel dubbed these latter creatures *Vespertilio-homo,* "man-bats," and illustrations appeared showing these strange beings.

The entire affair was revealed to be a hoax by 1837, when the supposed authors were challenged to produce the evidence for Herschel's discoveries. Their response was to claim that the rays of the sun, focused though the telescope, had caused the observatory to be consumed by fire, and soon after the whole story fell apart, despite the fact that many people refused to believe the articles were not real.

Although there are no specific references connecting the man-bats with Spring-Heeled Jack, memories of the dramatic accounts of winged men on the moon almost certainly remained in general consciousness strongly enough to influence the depiction of Jack as a winged, horned, fire-breathing being. Indeed, when a picture was later printed depicting the appearances at Aldershot, the image of Jack is clearly based on *Vespertilio-homo.*

Once these details, such as Jack's "helmet" and the other details of his unearthly attire, were received into the UFO community, the idea of Jack as an alien was established for all time. Ufologists such as Jacques Vallee and John Keel seem not to have questioned Vyner's description and ensured that it has been repeated ever since. Thus, when Jerome Clark, one of the great collectors of ufology, compiled his monumental *Emergence of a Phenomenon: UFOs from the Beginning through 1959: The UFO Encyclopedia* in 1992, his summary of the available information on Spring-Heeled Jack as an alien visitor was almost exactly the same as those printed earlier by Dyall and Vyner and developed by Keel and Vallee.

Stories of strange creatures and alien beings have continued to haunt the legacy of Spring-Heeled Jack to the present. Again and again, reports are offered as proof that "Jack is back." Some of these are worth looking at for the simple reason that they seem to be a product of the same instincts that turned a series of newspaper reports into a countrywide phenomenon. In 1904 there were several accounts of a "ghost," rapidly identified with Spring-Heeled Jack, frightening residents in Liverpool and drawing a sizable crowd of onlookers. The behavior of this being seems more like that of a poltergeist, but a report in the *News of the World* for September 25, 1904 suggested otherwise. The article is headed "Spring Heel Jack [sic]—Ghost with a weakness for ladies."

News of the World
SEPTEMBER 25, 1904

SPRING HEEL JACK—GHOST WITH A WEAKNESS FOR LADIES

Everton (Liverpool) is scared by the singular antics of the ghost, to whom the name of Spring Heel Jack has been given, because of the facility with which he has escaped, by huge springs, all attempts of his would-be captors to arrest him. William Henry Street is the scene of his exploits, and crowds of people assemble nightly to see them, but only a few have done so yet, and 'Jack' is evidently shy. He is said to pay particular attention to ladies. So far the police have not arrested him, their sprinting powers being inferior.

It is very possible that this is a fake report, based on the fact that one of the original sightings of the leaping man took place in the same street in 1888. The similarities between the appearances and the "interest in ladies" seem to echo the older reports, but no further evidence has so far come to light.

THE MAN IN WHITE

It was in 1926 that the next series of Jack sightings took place—this time in the industrial town of Bradford in West Yorkshire. The first report was printed in the *Bradford Daily Telegraph* for September 10, 1926.

The Bradford Daily Telegraph

SEPTEMBER 10, 1926

This afternoon the Bradford police announced that the people living in the Manchester Road area of the city have during last few nights been terrorized by a man garbed from head to foot in white.

The 'ghost' made his first appearance in Grafton Street around midnight last Sunday, and every night since then the white figure has been seen on numerous occasions in Grafton Street, Earl Street and Fitzgerald Street.

Those who have seen the white figure state that it is that of a man at least six feet two inches in height.

Several young men have during the nights of Wednesday and Thursday stayed out of bed in order to attempt the man's capture.

This morning at 2 o'clock the ghost appeared in Grafton Street, and a young man, William Jordan, of Butterfield Terrace, ran for the police. Six officers hurriedly appeared on the scene, and gave chase, but their efforts to catch the man proved in vain. He is extremely fleet of foot.

Already several women had been frightened by the ghost, and one woman, who saw the man at 4:45 yesterday morning, fainted, and had to receive assistance.

Over the next few days, the story developed dramatically. A thunderous headline announced a much fuller story and was every bit as fascinating as this clarion call and is strongly reminiscent of the ordinal sightings from the 1880s.

The Bradford Daily Telegraph

SEPTEMBER 11, 1926

BRADFORD 'GHOST' HUNT THRILLS. WELL-ARMED SEARCHERS. POLICE AND FLYING SQUAD JOIN IN. HOT RECEPTION TONIGHT

Pokers, choppers, copper sticks, lead piping and fender-ends figured prominently last night in one of the most extraordinary ghost chases ever known in Bradford.

The 'infected area', as it is now named, lies in the Fitzgerald Street, Grafton Street, and Earl Street quarter of Manchester Road. The apparition taking the form of a tall white figure, gifted with wonderful agility, and the fleetness of foot comparable, according to one witness, to that of an 'Olympic champion'.

As exclusively reported in the *Telegraph* yesterday evening, the white figure was first seen in Grafton Street about 2 o'clock on Sunday morning. And every night since then it has made terrifying appearances in that street or in Fitzgerald Street and Earl Street.

There are a great number who swear to have seen the figure. They state that it is completely dressed in a white garment, with the head covering slitted near the eyes, and the majority are unanimous in declaring that it is at least 6'2" in height, and makes practically no noise when running.

Following Sunday's visitation, seen by a young man . . . the ghost again appeared at two thirty on Tuesday morning, startling another young man . . .

Toward 5 o'clock the same morning the white figure was seen by a young woman going to her work, and when it approached her she ran screaming down the street, and eventually fainted.

Fortunately her cries woke residents in the streets, and on bedroom windows being raised quite a number saw what seemed to be a 'ghost' standing near the prostrate woman. A number of the aroused men rushed to her assistance, the white figure slipping speedily away into the darkness.

Since then the figure, unterred apparently, by the eager crowd who seek his blood, has made further appearances, the haunting being chiefly carried out from . . . house roofs.

Early yesterday morning the city police were given the alarm by a scared young man who rushed into the charge office at the Town Hall, and a posse of six policemen dashed at full speed to Fitzgerald Street, only to find that the ghost had decided to retire.

There is a distinct ring of truth to this report so far. Whatever, or whoever, the figure in white was, he was clearly seen and the response, both from those who were frightened by his appearance and those who fled from him, seems completely in tune with an actual event. The story continues with a breathless description of "heavily armed" gangs patrolling the streets, delving into shadowy back alleys and yards, accompanied by "savage looking bull terriers" who sniffed out nothing like a ghost. Then, as the evening wore on, a woman returning home from the theater saw a tall white figure that appeared to "sway backward and forward with arms outstretched and then vanished into nothing."

Despite this rather obviously "ghostly" behavior, the woman in question, backed up by two men who were in the same street, claimed to see a very solid man in a cap walk hurriedly from the garden of a dark house and hurry off down nearby Horton Lane. A girl walking nearby claimed to have almost collided with a man answering this description in an adjacent street.

As the night progressed, the scene became noisier and rowdier, with cries of "It's here!" being frequently raised—always with no result— and quarrels breaking out between the tired posse of ghost hunters. To make matters even more difficult, groups of youths built a barricade of tin cans and empty jam jars across the darker alleys, which many of the searchers subsequently fell afoul of, much to the delight of the youths.

The police seem to have spent much of the night running from place to place, summoned by various outcries. The report ends by promising that the "apparition" would receive an even warmer welcome should it appear the following night, with help promised not only by the Criminal Investigation Department, by the elite police force known as the Flying Squad, but also the force's champion runners, who are promised to appear dressed in shorts!

Next day the *Yorkshire Observer* picked up the report, concluding that the "ghostly figure" was real enough to be reported upon by a large number of people. But it was the *Bradford Daily Telegraph* that once again scooped the next dramatic part of the story on September 17. Here we read that the "ghost" had extended its area of activity to the Bierley Estate, an area close to the previous appearances and where a local tram driver named Harold Fishwick had a direct experience of the figure in white. His wife told the *Telegraph* reporter the story, which began after her husband had taken their dog for a walk.

The Bradford Daily Telegraph

SEPTEMBER 17, 1926

He returned home about at 9:15. A few minutes later, a gentle knocking was heard on the glass panel of the back door leading to the kitchen. Mr. Fishwick went to the door to see who was there, and on opening the door was amazed and startled to see a figure garbed in white standing a yard or two back from the door.

'My husband told me that he had a clear view of the figure', said Mrs. Fishwick. 'It was the figure of a tall man, and it was all in white. There was a hood over the head and face, and only slits for the eyes. A second after my husband opened the door, and before he could say a word, the figure turned and ran rapidly around the side of the house to the front. My husband ran after it, and on reaching the front of the house, was just in time to see the ghost disappear in the darkness'.

Mrs. Fishwick then related how shocked everyone was, and how neither she nor her children could sleep that night. It was all very strange. Even their dog, which usually barked at strangers, had not done so. This detail makes one wonder if the "ghost" was known to the Fishwicks—or at least to their dog. This is supported somewhat by the next report, which described the reappearance of the ghost some thirty minutes later, around a quarter of ten, at the house adjacent to the Fishwicks.

The resident of this house, a Mrs. Robinson, related how she had been taking a bath when she heard a knocking at the door. She called out to her lodgers, a young couple called Mills, and her friend and neighbor Mrs. Walker, who was also in the house, and soon heard sounds of excitement. She got out of the bath, dressed, and hurried downstairs, where she heard what had happened.

THE BRADFORD DAILY TELEGRAPH, SEPTEMBER 17, 1926

Jim Mills then told me what had happened. He said that Mrs. Walker had been sitting in an armchair, which is set near the door separating the dining room from the back kitchen. She heard somebody knocking and on looking round was horrified to see dimly through the clear glass panels of the door a white figure that seem[ed] to be waving its arms slowly above its head. The figure had on what looked like a white sheet, and the head and face were covered. Mrs. Walker told Mr. Mills, who was standing in front of the fire, that there was some strange person at the door. She did not say more as Mrs. Mills is a highly nervous and delicate woman, and she did not wish to alarm her. Jim Mills hurried to the door, and caught a clear glimpse of the awesome figure, but as soon as he opened the door the figure turned and ran swiftly across the backyard and vanished.

The redoubtable Mr. Mills followed the figure round to the house of a neighbor, a Mr. Winch, and together they called the police. Detectives came and went, having found nothing, and Mr. Winch decided to keep watch. At about one thirty in the morning, just as he was thinking of giving up his vigil, Winch caught sight of "a white-robed figure" at the bottom of his garden.

THE BRADFORD DAILY TELEGRAPH, SEPTEMBER 17, 1926

Just for a moment, Mr. Winch was staggered by the suddenness of the apparition, but he quickly recovered, and rushed in the direction of the cowled 'ghost'. The latter, however, must have heard his approach and broke into a swift and noiseless run.

The man in white made off in the direction of some houses in the vicinity which are in course of construction, and once again succeeded in making good his escape.

Here the story simply peters out. The *Yorkshire Observer* printed a summary next day of the facts so far described and came to the conclusion that it was "someone carrying a white garment in his pocket and donning it on occasions to terrify women and children, afterward returning [it] to his pocket and joining in the chase." No further reports of this ghostly figure have so far turned up. It seems safe to assume that it was a man who decided to have some fun with his neighbors, and after succeeding in frightening everyone and raising the alarm to such a pitch that armed gangs of residents and police thronged the streets, he decided he had done enough and retired. The fact that the dog belonging to the Fishwicks did not bark suggests that it may have been a local man.

It is very much up to the reader whether we choose to see this as evidence of a series of similar jokes played on Londoners during the period of Spring-Heeled Jack's first recorded visitations. Even if one strips away the more obvious imitators, we are still left with a core of inexplicable sightings with enough commonality to suggest a very real presence.

JACK LEAPS BACK

The persistence of Spring-Heeled Jack stories may have abated after this, or become more widely disseminated, but they certainly did not go away. Over the years there have been scattered sightings of a cloaked figure that leaps into and out of the lives of individuals. In each case, at some point or other, the name Spring-Heeled Jack is introduced, sometimes as no more than a point of comparison, but often as an actual identification.

His appearances in the United States are distinctive, though they may have no actual connection to Jack at all. Only the dating of these gives pause for thought, as they appear to synchronize with the last known sightings in England in the nineteenth century. Thus, the earliest recorded appearance of a Jack-like figure appears to have taken place in Louisville, Kentucky, in 1880, at a time when there are no recorded sightings in the United Kingdom. Several women came forward reporting attacks by a sinister, humanoid creature wearing a cloak and possessed of long fingers and pointed ears and nose, who leapt prodigious heights and spat blue flames from his mouth.

These reports read like echoes of the Victorian newspaper articles in Britain and may once again be either copycat crimes or a product of the imagination perhaps suggested by the stories that crossed the Atlantic with travelers and emigrants.

Fig. 7.2. A leaping Spring-Heeled Jack (Art by Jamie Egerton)

Between 1938 and 1945, a mysterious character made a number of appearances in the Cape Cod area of Massachusetts. According to one report, originating in Provincetown, a leaping figure forced pedestrians off the pavement on a busy street. This excited the attention of a guard dog, which is said to have cornered the dark-clad figure. But when the dog's owner took a shot at the figure, he later reported, "The darned thing just laughed and jumped my eight-foot fence in one leap."

Similar sightings are reported haphazardly in the same area until 1945, when they stop abruptly, perhaps as a result of America's entry into World War II.

A somewhat more protracted set of visitations were reported from Baltimore in 1951. Over a three-week period beginning in July of that year, it was told of a black-clad, caped figure that terrorized the residents of O'Donnell Heights. Accordingly, "hundreds" of people took to the streets in pursuit of the interloper. A report in the *Baltimore News-Post* suggested that the "phantom prowler" had been seen in the area for several weeks before—though there seem to be no earlier reports. Here, a man named William New described an up-close-and-personal encounter with the phantom.

𝕭altimore 𝔑ews-𝔓ost

JULY 23, 1951

He went to O'Donell Heights early Monday to see a friend working on the night shift and waited until 2 a.m. in a tavern in Dundalk Avenue and O'Donnell Street.

Leaving the tavern, he heard a scream, ran toward it, and saw a man in a yellow T-shirt and brown trousers leap from a roof in Elliott Street near Urban. He gave chase, and two and a half blocks later, was gaining on the phantom when he was stopped.

Mr. New cruised through the area with the police, but found nothing. James White of the 6200 block of Plantview Way, saw the Phantom leap down from the roof there, but the man was gone before he could raise the alarm.

Two days later the *Baltimore Sun* presented a much longer account of the affair, listing a number of sightings, along with the efforts of various residents to capture the phantom prowler. It is clear from these reports that the matter was a cause of some concern and was taken seriously. The account begins with a colorful description of the local residents preparing for the worst.

𝔅altimore 𝔖un

JULY 25, 1951

At the rear of the house in the 1200 Block of Gusryan Street, a man kept watch on a garbage can with a .12 gauge shotgun. In an upstairs bedroom on Carbore way, Hazel Jenkins, still suffering from the time the black robed prowler grabbed her last week, tried to sleep.

The report goes on:

BALTIMORE SUN, JULY 25, 1951

In other houses, residents stretched out on the floor, too frightened to go upstairs. Police squad cars prowled the streets. Somewhere in the darkness the dog barked, a baby cried. Every now and then a face appeared at a door window to enquire fearfully of bands of patrolling youths: "Has anybody seen him yet?"

At the home of Mrs. Agnes Martin, 1211 Gusryan Street, 30 or 40 people, varying in ages from 5 to 50 years old, had gathered on the back stoop to wait for daylight.

"For the last two or three weeks since that man began appearing around here," said Mrs. Martin. "People are afraid to go to bed."

"I haven't closed my eyes since Thursday night," declared Mrs. Melvin Hensler, a neighbor of Mrs. Martin's. Since her home was broken into last Friday, Mrs. Hensler has been staying with her sister-in-law . . .

William Buskirk, 20, of 6542 Fait Avenue, described his encounter with the phantom, which took place around 1 a.m. last Thursday.

"I was walking along the 1100 block, Travers way with several of my buddies when I saw him on a roof," related Mr. Buskirk. "He was a tall, thin man dressed all in black. It kind of looked like he had a cape around him. He jumped off the roof and we chased him down into the graveyard."

"He lives in that graveyard," remarked Jack Cromwell, of 1203 Joplin Street. "Yeah," put in Lynne Griffiths, of 1217 Wellsbach way. "One night I heard someone playing the organ in that chapel [out] there. It was about 1 o'clock."

"He sure is an athlete," said one of the other boys. "You should have seen him go over that fence—just like a cat." (The fence bordering the graveyard in question is about 6 feet tall and trimmed barbed wire along the top.)

Most of the people who have seen the Phantom describe the ease with which he leaps on and off roofs—a feat made all the more remarkable by the fact that the roots of most houses in Donald Heights are a minimum of 20 feet from the ground.

The story continues in this vein for several more column inches, adding details of the number of people who had seen or encountered the phantom. One, a child named Esther Martin, claimed she saw the stranger "under an automobile. He was beckoning to her, 'Come here little girl,' he said."[11] This sounds a lot more like a predator of another kind than Spring-Heeled Jack, but the stories continued. Though no report of the earlier attack on Hazel Jenkins, who still could not sleep because of it (see above), Mike Dash reports seeing a photo of a teenage girl with two superficial slashes across her stomach.

A more detailed report appeared in the *Baltimore News-Post* the following day, which made it clear that the residents were seriously concerned by the presence of the prowler.

𝕭𝖆𝖑𝖙𝖎𝖒𝖔𝖗𝖊 𝕹𝖊𝖜𝖘-𝕻𝖔𝖘𝖙

JULY 26, 1951

Two hundred angry, aroused residents of O'Donnell Heights chased the areas of the phantom prowler around midnight Tuesday. But the wraith of the rooftops again eluded them.

He was spotted on the roof at 6200 Plantview Way by the Heights' self-formed "vigilante committee," searching for him since he started terrorizing the area, several weeks ago.

When a .22 caliber automatic pistol was discovered in a field, events escalated, with husbands mounting guard at night and housewives keeping baseball bats and clubs close to hand.

BALTIMORE NEWS-POST, JULY 26, 1951

About midnight he was spotted again, a dark cloaked figure against the black sky of the night. An immediate hue and cry drove him fleeing into the graveyard to escape from his pursuers.

Patrolman Robert Clark and Elmer Powell, of Eastern district police, rushed to the scene in answer to phone calls from terrified residents.

They said they found about 200 persons milling around in the community, hunting for the prowler.

Cruising around the north side of O'Donnell heights, alongside the old German cemetery, they found Marvin Fink, 21, U.S. Navy Patuxent River base, walking along the street, wearing dark clothing and carrying a hammer.

Fink told police he had been visiting in the neighborhood and had heard there was a reward for the capture of the phantom, so he was hunting for him.

He received a suspended $5 fine Wednesday morning on a disorderly conduct charge.

The same thing happened the following Wednesday, where again sightings of the phantom were reported. The police searched but found none; however, several people informed them that he was in the German cemetery. When the police searched the area, they found five older youths and a fifteen-year-old hiding among the tombstones.

The boys were each fined five dollars, and the juvenile was released into the custody of his parents, pending a hearing. The police rather dryly stated that they doubted whether any of the six were the actual phantom, but a Sergeant Sandler expressed the opinion that "publicity about the prowler is drawing prowlers and youngsters from all over town." He added: "They should stay away. They only aggravate the situation and it is very dangerous for them. Those people out there are angry and really aroused. Somebody is very likely to get hurt."[12]

The following day the *Baltimore Sun* reported that three more teenagers had been arrested on disorderly conduct charges, and this was followed by a number of further sightings, along with a clutch of prank calls, most deemed to be from teenagers. A few days later the story petered out, with no more visitations noted and the whole thing written off as the product of overactive imagination.

What is curious about this is the similarity between the Baltimore sightings and those around London in the 1880s. Though only one person, Hazel Jenkins, appears to have been physically attacked, the randomness of the appearances and the association with a local graveyard are reminiscent not only of the London attacks but also those that took place in Sheffield. Could there be a connection? It seems less likely now than at the time. Possibly this is yet another example of the night prowler whose appearance becomes elaborated to include fanciful aspects. It is worth noting that by this time the character of the Caped Crusader, aka Batman, who first appeared in 1939, was familiar to many, especially the younger generation, so that the idea of a dark figure leaping from rooftop to rooftop might well have rung bells for fans of the comic-book hero.

Some ten years later, in the earlier 1960s, the *Baltimore Sun* reprised the whole story, adding several details not found in the original reports—such as that the phantom was last seen jumping into or over a large sarcophagus, going "back to his grave" as one onlooker apparently remarked. The story had remained in the memories of the local residents far beyond that of any ordinary news story, demonstrating once again how such tales may continue to be told and retold to a new audience, ever eager for fearful events that had taken place around where they lived.

In John Vyner's influential article, which set out the claims for Jack being an alien, he wrote about a sighting in Houston, Texas, on June 18, 1953, at 2:30 a.m., when three people who had gone outside to escape the heat claimed to have seen a black-clad figure crossing their back-yard and leaping easily into the branches of a tall tree. According to one Hilda Walker of 228 E. Third Street, it appeared that the mode of this being's movement was a pair of black wings, which makes him slightly different from the original sightings of Spring-Heeled Jack. "I thought at first it was the magnified reflection of a big moth caught in a nearby street light," she said, but on closer examination she and her compan-ions saw what appeared to be "the figure of a man . . . dressed in gray or black tight-fitting clothes. . . . He was about six and a half feet tall, looked like a white man, and was wearing a black cape, skin-tight pants and quarter-length boots."[13]

The report in the *Houston Chronicle* for the time added that the figure in the tree remained there for fifteen minutes, then slowly melted away. Soon after, something resembling a rocket rose into the sky from the other side of the street. It left behind what was described as a fiery tail as it headed off along the northeastern horizon.

THE MOTHMAN

A far more intriguing story, which in its own way bears a resemblance to the Spring-Heeled Jack saga, is that of the Mothman, a bizarre crea-ture that made its first appearance in the Point Pleasant area of West Virginia, on November 5, 1966. The story was told that five men were digging a grave at a cemetery near Clendenin when they saw what appeared to be a man-sized bird fly overhead.

Ten days later two young couples from Point Pleasant went into a local police station and described seeing a large white creature whose eyes "glowed red" when the car headlights picked them up. They described it as a "large flying man with ten-foot wings," (see plate 13) which followed their car for several miles.

No one took this very seriously, but over the next few days, several other sightings were reported. A couple of volunteer firemen said they had seen "a large bird with red eyes" near their station, while a local contractor described catching sight of a large white creature in a field near his house whose eyes reflected redly when he turned his flashlight on it. He blamed the disappearance of his German shepherd dog on the creature, but no further evidence came to light.

Following these first appearances of the creature, soon dubbed the Mothman, several people came forward with accounts of their own encounters with the creature, which seemed to grow larger with each retelling. When the Silver Bridge collapsed in West Virginia on December 15, 1967, resulting in the deaths of forty-six people, stories began to circulate that this was somehow connected to the Mothman.

When Gray Barker published a book called *The Silver Bridge* in 1970, he made an even more explicit association between the disaster and the Mothman, adding a number of strange supernatural events believed to have taken place in the area around the same time. His ideas were expanded by the ufologist John Keel, who had already written about Spring-Heeled Jack in a book called *The Mothman Prophecies,* which became an overnight bestseller and was later filmed under the same title with Richard Gere as a man haunted by the Mothman. Keel claimed that residents of the Point Pleasant area had premonitions of the collapse of Silver Bridge and that UFOs had been spotted in the area. He has since been accused of faking much of his information.

It was even claimed that the Mothman was sighted again just a few days before the events of 9/11, and as with the stories of Spring-Heeled Jack, these tales have been described as urban legend. The most well-known writer about such legends in the United States, the folklorist Jan Harold Brunvand, describes these stories as ones that are told and retold, each time growing larger, often attributed to a friend-of-a-friend rather than as a direct experience. Such tales, he writes, "have a persistent hold on the imagination because they have an element of suspense or humor, they are plausible and they have a moral."

In his controversial book *The Vanishing Hitchhiker* (1983),

Brunvand noted that as many as a hundred reports were recorded during the first few months of the Mothman sightings, with others apparently too fearful to come forward. He also draws attention to a number of points of similarity between the descriptions of the creature and Native American traditions that were localized to the area. As with Spring-Heeled Jack, Brunvand sees these older tales as having a direct influence on the stories.

A less fanciful explanation comes from a wildlife biologist from West Virginia University named Dr. Robert L. Smith. He told reporters that descriptions of the Mothman exactly fit the sandhill crane, a bird that stands almost as high as a man and possesses a seven-foot wingspan. The bird also has reddish circles around its eyes, which could account for the red eyes reported by those who claimed to have encountered the Mothman.

Others have been less convinced by such prosaic explanations, however; some modern ufologists, such as Jerome Clarke and cryptozoologist Loren Coleman, claim to have interviewed many of those who sighted the Mothman in the 1960s and that these people remain convinced that what they saw was a tall winged creature of some seven feet in height with red glowing eyes. Evidence of the seriousness with which these claims are taken is the Annual Mothman Festival that has taken place since 2002 and a Mothman Museum and Research Center, which opened in 2005.

Alien, monster, or bird, the Mothman stories continue to attract attention and are very much a part of the resurgence of interest in the Spring-Heeled Jack phenomena. Perhaps we shall one day see a Spring-Heeled Jack research center in London?

THE MONKEY MAN

One of the most curious among the recent stories is that of the Monkey Man, which takes us all the way to the continent of India and the sprawling city of Delhi. There, in 2011, the police received over 350 eyewitness reports of attacks by a strange creature—half man, half monkey. It would spring out of dark corners, swing from rooftop to rooftop, and attack people in a seemingly random manner. At least thirty-five people reported injuries of a kind that could have been made by an animal, though the police were of the opinion that none of these were serious and could have been self-inflicted. However, a kind of mass panic gripped the city for three months, and several people became victims of attacks by mobs roaming the streets in a manner reminiscent of the days when Spring-Heeled Jack's attacks were at their height. Two people died from falls apparently resulting from being pursued by the specter, and the police took it seriously enough to offer a £1,000 reward. Despite this, not a single photo or detailed description of the supposed Monkey Man ever appeared, and when the attacks ceased as abruptly as they began, the whole incident was written off as "mass hysteria."

THE SLENDER MAN

A much darker, more sinister story is that of the Slender Man, a creation that began life, ostensibly, as a fictional character, but which subsequently took on a life of its own, with terrible consequences.

The first appearance of the Slender Man took place on an Internet site that hosted the "Something Awful" forum, a discussion group dedicated to stories of the paranormal. It was, to all intents and purposes, created by a man named Eric Knudsen, writing under the alias Victor Surge in 2009. The intention was to create a character that could be shared among the community of forum users and to extend from there into the world. Members of the original forum created fictional stories, art, and even videos, which soon extended beyond this limited field. The Slender Man became a familiar figure in video games such as *Minecraft* and even spawned its own games such as *Slender: The Eight Pages* and *Slender: The Arrival*.

The description common to these stories was of a thin, unnaturally tall man with a featureless face, wearing a black suit. His central

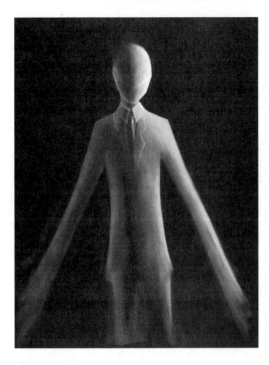

Fig. 7.3. The
Slender Man

purpose seems to be the abduction of children, while spreading fear to all who come upon him. We should, of course, recall how many of the averred sightings of Spring-Heeled Jack described him as tall and thin, dark clad, and (often) faceless.

The original thread began as a Photoshop contest in which users were challenged to manipulate ordinary photographs to give the appearance of paranormal activity. One of the first photos to appear were two black-and-white images of children showing a tall, thin, blank-faced figure observing them. In addition, Surge added fragmentary texts that seemed to relate to the abduction of several children and gave the character the name the Slender Man. The first read: "'We didn't want to go, we didn't want to kill them, but its persistent silence and outstretched arms horrified and comforted us at the same time . . . —1983, photographer unknown, presumed dead."

The text beneath the second photo read: "One of two recovered photographs from the Stirling City Library blaze. Notable for being taken the day

[on] which fourteen children vanished and for what is referred to as 'The Slender Man.' Deformities cited as film defects by officials. Fire at library occurred one week later. Actual photograph confiscated as evidence—1986, photographer: Mary Thomas, missing since June 13th, 1986."

This transformed the photographs into a work of fiction and invited other users to add to the story. Before long an entire subculture of Slender Man stories and art sprang up, continuing to the present, despite the tragedy that was to come.

Knudsen cites among his influences the work of the horror writer H. P. Lovecraft, the occultist Zack Parsons, and the film series *Phantasm* directed, written, coproduced, and edited by Don Coscarelli. The series, of which there have so far been five feature films, introduced audiences to the Tall Man, aka Angus Scrimm, a malevolent undertaker who turns the dead into zombies.

Others have suggested the Gentlemen, which are pale, bald, black-suited demons from the TV show *Buffy the Vampire Slayer,* or the Question, a blank-faced superhero from the DC Comics franchise, whose secret identity is Victor Sage, a name very close to that of the Slender Man's creator Victor Surge.

Professor Shira Chess, of the University of Georgia, in her book *Folklore, Horror Stories, and the Slender Man: The Development of an Internet Mythology* has looked more deeply into the possible origins of the character and found that there are frequent connections to folk-lore and fairy mythology, in particular the stealing of children. Chess also makes an interesting comparison between the way in which folk-lore is disseminated, mostly by word of mouth, and the "open source" approach of the Internet. Whatever the ultimate origin of the Slender Man, the spread of the story and the way in which it grew and developed is entirely separate from any single individual. In the same way, Spring-Heeled Jack, who began as a frightening but indistinct character in newspaper reports, grew into the distinctive leaping figure with the red eyes and breath of blue fire, which in turn became a part of the alien visitor theories of the ufologists.

The sheer vagueness of the Slender Man, his very facelessness—akin to Jack's masked face and undisclosed identity—seems to have made him all the more powerful. Inevitably, perhaps, he acquired followers, not only in the fabricated universe in which he was given birth but in the outer world as well. The creator of the disturbing YouTube web series *Marble Hornets* (2009–2014) gave them the name "proxies"—ordinary humans who fell under the influence of the Slender Man. It was perhaps only a matter of time before an impressionable person or persons attempted to become a proxy in the real world.

This happened on May 31, 2014, when two twelve-year-old girls from Waukesha, Wisconsin, allegedly held down and stabbed a twelve-year-old classmate nineteen times. Their declared reasons, when questioned, were that they sought to become proxies of the Slender Man, and that this required them to commit murder. Their victim, fortunately, survived this horrific attack, but both girls, who despite their ages were tried as adults, are facing sentences of up to sixty-five years. Final sentencing has been held up while the courts decide whether they are competent to be tried. One girl claimed to talk with Voldemort, the dark lord of J. K. Rowling's Harry Potter books, and declared that the Slender Man, who was clearly a real person to her, could read minds.

The story brought other accounts to light. An unidentified woman from Hamilton, Ohio, described how her thirteen-year-old daughter had attacked her with a kitchen knife and that she had written stories involving the Slender Man. In addition, on September 4, 2014, a fourteen-year-old girl in Port Richey, Florida, set her family home on fire while her mother and nine-year-old brother were inside. When the police investigated the incident, they found that the teenager had been reading stories of the Slender Man online.

The activities of the Slender Man are, of course, fictional—but the disturbing activities of those who have declared themselves to be his followers suggests a deeper reason for the continued references in the press and contemporary fiction to Spring-Heeled Jack. We cannot say with any certainly whether Jack existed, or whether he was a real person in disguise, or whether his story spawned a collection of imitators, but he was, as we have seen, believed to be real. Some saw him as a ghost, others as a deranged man, but during the nearly forty years when he was most active, he was considered to be completely real.

The parallels between Jack and the Slender Man are not specific enough to identify them as the same being, but parallels exist within folklore and even more ancient myth that imply a deeper connection with the nameless, faceless demons that seem to have lurked in human consciousness ever since we emerged into the world.

NEW SIGHTINGS

Stories that associate Spring-Heeled Jack with sightings of running and leaping men never seem to be far away. The magazine *Haunted Scotland* included in its first issue for July 1996 the story of an ex-army officer named Francis Marshall, then a salesman, who, during a regular trip to Ayrshire ten years earlier, had encountered the figure of a man "physically leaping high hedgerows in great bounds,"[14] when passing through Herefordshire. Becoming aware of Marshall's presence, the figure leapt into the road and as he passed slapped Marshall "so hard across the face that he fell to the ground."[15] He then let out "an almighty cackle of a laugh"[16] and vanished across the fields.

A couple of things give one pause for thought here, as also noticed by Mike Dash, who includes the description in his collection of documents. Was Marshall in a car at the time, and if so, how did "Jack" manage to slap his face? It sounds as though he was riding a bike, but this seems unlikely if this was really part of a regular trip to the north. Dash also notes the similarity between this story and one found in a famous book by Elliott O'Donnell called *Haunted Britain*. This was published in 1948 and was one of the more recent books at the time to give an extended account of Spring-Heeled Jack. The description given by O'Donnell relayed to him by his old nurse is virtually identical and also took place in Herefordshire. Finally, we should note that Mr. Marshall did not wish to leave an address or telephone number, citing embarrassment at his story since he did not believe in ghosts or paranormal events.

As recently as 2012 a British family on their way home by taxi at around 10:30 p.m. sighted a terrifying, "featureless" figure who ran across the road in front of them before vanishing over a fifteen-foot-high bank on the road approaching Nescot Cottage on the bypass outside the town of Ewell in Surrey. So terrified were the couple that they sat up most of the night with their four-year-old son, who was too frightened to sleep alone, while the taxi driver declared that he had no wish to drive on that part of the road anytime soon. Interviewed later the family declared how at first they had paid no attention when the dark figure appeared by the roadside, but when he ran across the road, jumping the median strip, crossing two lanes, and finally scaling the fifteen-foot bank with ease, they were all deeply shocked.

Needless to say the newspaper did not take long to make the identification with Jack. Nearly two hundred years after the first sightings in London, in the peaceful countryside of Surrey, the leaping menace appeared again. Whether one takes this as a piece of invention, hyperbolic reporting, or a misunderstood sighting of an animal, what counts here is the way in which the memory of Spring-Heeled Jack still surfaces in our own time, just as in that of the Victorians, or even earlier, when Jack was a name to conjure with in any story of strange creatures from beyond the ordinary world.

DREADFUL JACK

No account of Spring-Heeled Jack would be complete without looking at his manifestation in contemporary culture. Like many before, including Sherlock Holmes, Jack the Ripper, Sweeney Todd, and others, Jack has made a comeback in the world of comic-book heroes and graphic novels. Fiction, film, stage, and TV have all given Jack his due, adding to the mystery by expanding it far beyond the limits of folklore and urban myth.

During the period in which Jack's adventures were the talk of London, and in the decade just after this, he became the hero of numerous penny dreadfuls, as noted previously. Here Spring-Heeled Jack was reinvented as the hero of a cycle of melodramatic stories. These popular pamphlets serialized sensational tales, sometimes based on actual events, but more often the product of feverish imaginations, dealing almost always with a struggle between good and evil, with evil more often than not represented by upper-class lords and ladies, while the good were the poor and downtrodden. In this, the penny dreadfuls and their theatrical partners represented a deep division between the classes and the gradual manifestation of rebellion that was to burst forth in strikes and rebellious gatherings across the country—most often put down with fierce and swift aggression on the part of the authorities.

If we look just below the surface of the stories, we see that Spring-Heeled Jack is all about rebellion, about being able to play fast and loose with the law and its representatives. The unpopularity of the police force of the time and their perceived inability to catch even the most dastardly of criminals made Jack something of a hero, especially among the poorest classes of society. The press might decry his actions as "monstrous," "terrifying," and so forth, but the average man in the street seems to have had a sneaking respect for him.

The fact that despite his attacks, Jack was never directly responsible for the death or even serious injury to his victims (if we ignore the exaggerated claims of fainting ladies who were unlikely to recover) makes it curious that he became the object of such ferocious searches. Perhaps his identification with the lawless element of society made him more of a threat to the upper classes. Certainly, his apparently carefree approach and ability to do more or less whatever he liked without capture added to his popularity among the lower-class workers of London.

Highwaymen, criminals of an earlier time, despite the fact that they frequently killed or maimed their victims, became romanticized as the "heroes" of the penny dreadfuls. In the same way the stories that were in circulation about Spring-Heeled Jack became unceasingly less negative.

The writers of these sensational documents took the shadowy form of Spring-Heeled Jack and turned him into something of a people's hero—though not everyone agreed. As a writer in the *Quarterly Review* of 1890, also referring to the story *The Terror of London*, thunders,

𝔔uarterly 𝔑eview

JULY, 1890

The story is what might be expected—a tale of highwaymen, murderers, burglars, wicked noblemen, and lovely and persecuted damsels whose physical charms and voluptuous embraces are dilated upon with exceeding unction. It is almost needless to say that the highwaymen of romance are not the sorry and sordid rogues we know them to been in real life, but always 'dashing', 'high-spirited', and 'bold'. It is equally a matter of course that the enemies of these gallant fellows— the constables . . . are ugly, stupid, ill conditioned, and cowardly; that it is a 'paternal government' under which 'things have reached such a pitch that a man may be fined, or perhaps imprisoned, for carrying a pistol to protect himself'; and that, in one word, all the offices are 'tyrants' and oppressors, whom it is the duty of 'spirited lads' to resist to the uttermost.

It was notable, in most of these instances, that where Jack actually robbed people (something he was never accused of in the original reports), it was always the rich who were targeted. He even seems to have been associated only with upper-class villains rather than the more usual lower-class criminals. Neither is he associated with the usual haunts of the underworld of London; rather, Jack plies his trade around the edges of the city, or even in the countryside. In addition, all of his attacks took place in a manner that draws attention to him, rather than the quiet and secretive methods of burglars, pickpockets, or murderers.

As Dr. Karl Bell notes in his study of Spring-Heeled Jack in

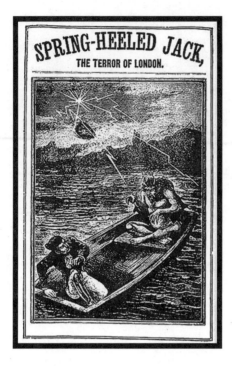

Fig. 7.4. Spring-Heeled Jack on the cover of a penny dreadful

Victorian culture, it is possible to see in the leaping man a symbol of anti-authoritarianism. His supernatural aspect made him the opponent of established religion precepts, and the mixture of wild naturalism and mechanized boots made him antiscientific, while his criminality clearly made him an opponent of the law.

It was the penny dreadfuls who took the basic shape of the agile, fire-breathing, red-eyed ghost and turned him into the fully fledged character of the daredevil that we may still see manifesting in contemporary graphic novels, where he appears as both hero and villain.

Needless to say the popularity of these publications, which made a number of people very rich, was not popular among the moralists who dictated every level of "respectable" society. One writer, James Greenwood, cited by Peter Haining, and who had dedicated himself "toward exposing and extirpating social abuses and those hole-and-corner evils which reflect society,"[17] reviewed a number of penny dreadfuls, describing them as "nasty feeling, nasty looking"[18] and thoroughly disreputable.

In an essay titled "A Short Way to Newgate," dated 1854, Greenwood examined one of the earliest penny dreadfuls dealing with the Spring-Heeled Jack saga. His description of the story gives one an idea of the typical kind of content to be found within.

Summary of contents: Jack indecently assaults a maiden lady, dragged from her bedchamber by her bed gown, which is pulled over her head, and finally thrusts her into another bedroom to pass the night with an elderly bachelor gentleman. Somebody springs a rattle, neighbors roused, bachelor's door forced, bachelor in night garment exposed, and maiden lady dragged nude from beneath bachelor's bed. Next chapter, the loves of a policeman and maid-of-work, and a 'spicy' scene of the pair in the shadows of a tomb in a churchyard at midnight.[19]

Ending with what Greenwood describes as a "disgusting" joke, the story is left "to be continued in our next [issue]." Today, this would seem very mild stuff, but in the Victorian era would have been sordid in the extreme.

In 1863 the Newsagents Publishing Company, which maintained a stable of hack writers equipped to pump out serials on every conceivable subject at the drop of a coin and which produced a huge number of serialized penny dreadfuls over a period of ten years, published *Spring-Heeled Jack—The Terror of London,* a forty-part penny dreadful reprinted in 1867. Only one almost complete set of all parts exists (missing episode fourteen) currently held by the British Library in London.

But it was in 1878 that there appeared what was to become the standard version of Jack's story for the time. *Spring-Heeled Jack—The Terror of London* was one of the most successful penny dreadfuls ever produced, selling hundreds of copies on street corners. The lurid illustrations portrayed Jack as a demonic character, scarcely human at all, bearded, horned, with a lion's mane of hair and bat-like wings growing from his arms, and—interestingly—no sign of boots with springs.

Originally serialized in a weekly paper aimed at the youth of the time and called *The Boys' Standard,* it ran for forty-eight episodes and was probably written by a writer named George Augustus Henry Sala (1828–1895), who later, when he began to write for high-class magazines like *The Illustrated London News,* fervently denied writing any of the penny dreadful texts. Another possible author was Alfred Burridge (writing as Charlton Lea) who was responsible for a number of sensational tales later reprinted in the *Boys' Standard* but became known later for his thrilling war books.

Whoever actually wrote the story, he changed it for all time. Rather than the random, motiveless attacker of young women, Spring-Heeled Jack now became a rescuer of helpless females as well as an opponent of those in authority who were abusing their power. In short, he was a kind of latter-day Robin Hood—something that seems appropriate when one considers that one stand at least of the remote origins of the character may indeed have been the famous outlaw of Sherwood Forest.

Chronologically Jack's next appearance in early pulp literature was a dime novel attributed to the martial arts expert and mercenary soldier Colonel Thomas Monstery (1821–1901) who turned to writing toward the end of his life and penned "Spring-Heel Jack; or, The Masked Mystery of the Tower." This marks the only known story of Spring-Heeled Jack to appear in America at this time.

The edition that most firmly stamped the image of Jack onto the imaginations of a newly literate audience was the reprint of the 1886 serial in forty-eight parts published by Charles Fox, one of the doyens of pulp literature, from his officers in Shoe Lane, off Fleet Street. These were later collected as a book, and it is this edition that forms the version included at the back of the present book.

The story set out to prove its authenticity by claiming to be based on a diary sent to the publisher by the family of the real Spring-Heeled Jack, here named Jack Dacre. It even drew upon the theory that he was somehow connected to the Marquis of Waterford, showing how far back this idea went. We should not forget that the serial was originally published while the reports of Spring-Heeled Jack were still appearing almost daily in national newspapers. To many people this would have appeared as true as any of the ongoing reports and may perhaps be compared to Dan Brown's *The Da Vinci Code* (2001), which, though Brown constantly declared it to be only a novel, was taken up by hundreds of followers who believed it to be true and sought for the reality behind the narrative by visiting every site mentioned in the book.

In *The Terror of London,* the blameless life of young Jack Dacre is blighted when he and his family, traveling home from India, are believed lost at sea. Though in fact Jack survives, his unscrupulous cousin Michael takes the opportunity to take over the business, and when Jack finally makes it home, he is turned away as an imposter. This destruction of his fortune turns Jack into the daring daredevil hero dubbed Spring-Heeled Jack whose friends help him to create the costume and spring-loaded boots. From here on, Jack Dacre becomes a hero, using his skills and bravery to help others who, like himself, have been tricked out of their rightful inheritance. Thus the leaping devil of London is given a purpose and a backstory that accounts for his behavior, incidentally turning him from a villain into a hero.

Much of the subsequent stories of Spring-Heeled Jack can be traced back to this penny dreadful text, and it is more than possible that its popularity influenced the way in which Jack was perceived by the legion of people who refused to accept the evil ghost or demon reported in the national dailies but as a hero who robbed the rich to serve the poor.

JACK TREADS THE BOARDS

A parallel to the penny dreadfuls were the penny gaffs, which were pop-up theaters, not unlike the "raves" of recent times. They were erected in derelict buildings around the poorer areas of the city and became hugely popular among the illiterate working class, who were too poor to pay London theater prices but were happy to pay over their pennies to be entertained with dramatic, sensationalized stories of murder and mayhem. Of course, Spring-Heeled Jack was a central figure in a number of these, and they played a significant role in the re-creation of the character and its dissemination far beyond the world of newspapers but ideally suited for Jack's illiterate audience.

Jack's first appearances on the streets of London happened to coincide with a huge upsurge of interest in melodrama. Plays such as *Jack the Giant-Killer*, which, as we saw, was performed at the Haymarket in 1730, and political satires, such as *The Last Speech of John Good, Vulgarly Called Jack the Giant-Queller*, which appeared in 1745, were forerunners of what was to come. In the nineteenth century Jack reappeared several times on the boards. He was the central figure of a play called *Spring-Heeled Jack—The Terror of London*, by John Thomas Haines in 1840, which reappeared as a penny dreadful novella and was subsequently developed into an early film.

Haines (ca. 1799–1843) was the author of a number of blood-and-thunder melodramas and seems to have been particularly adept at invoking current affairs. The appearance of *The Terror of London* would have come as no surprise—any more than its success, with over a hundred performances recorded. In part this seems to have been due to some of the first of what would later be termed "special effects," enabling Jack to literally spring several feet into the air and descend on his fainting female victims. Apparently, on more than one occasion, the "flying rope" used to enable Jack to hurtle above the stage became jammed, leaving the unfortunate actor to dangle in the air—much to the amusement of the audiences. Remembering the various suggestions offered by readers of the newspaper reports that Jack's antics were the product of stage trickery, we might see the danger of relying on such effects. Jack himself seemed able to perform his leaps and bounds without accident.

Haines retold the story of Spring-Heeled Jack more or less from the stories that had flowed from the pens of newspaper reporters, providing an ending that fulfilled the needs of his audiences for closure. Jack is revealed in the end to be an ordinary man jilted by his sweetheart and vowing vengeance on all women. He is caught, with a nice twist of irony, by one of his victims, who tricks him into revealing his true identity by flattering him.

The play's success caused it to be copied in the penny gaffs and then, in turn, by peep shows, small portable theaters not unlike the later Punch and Judy shows, which traveled from town to town, staging scenes from the popular dramas enacted by cardboard cut-out figures. To this day one may still purchase versions of these toy theaters from a company founded by Benjamin Pollock in 1888. Pollock's Toy Store, currently located in London's Covent Garden market, has produced replicas of the original peep shows since the nineteenth century.

The year 1863 saw a four-act drama, *Spring-Heel'd Jack, or the Felon's Wrongs* by Frederick Hazleton, which drew large audiences, but it was the Irish dramatist, novelist, and painter W. G. Wills (1828–1891) who seized upon the original play by Thomas Haines and completely rewrote it, changing the story and adding a considerable amount of detail. It was staged at the Lyceum Theatre in London in 1878 and was a marked success.

Here Jack is portrayed as a mad inventor, real name Philip Wraydon, and the setting is the period of the Napoleonic Wars. Banished from England after an unsuccessful assault on his brother's wife, Wraydon throws in his lot with the French and becomes a spy. Soon after, he builds a pair of spring-heeled boots to enable him to outdistance his pursuers and embarks on a career of murder and mayhem. In an attempt to further his schemes, he frames his nephew, Captain Jack Clayton, with several murders, but after a series of dramatic adventures, the stalwart hero triumphs, consigning Wraydon, aka Spring-Heeled Jack, to a grizzly death in one of his own inventions. This story was later to form the basis for the first and so far only feature film about Jack, *The Curse of the Wraydons*.

This was a far cry from the original stories of Spring-Heeled Jack, and in a pantomime of *Jack and the Beanstalk*, produced in Birmingham in 1886, things have drifted even further. Jack is here represented as one of a number of ghosts that hangs out on rooftops singing catchy songs—all designed to remove any trace of fearfulness from the character.

HOLLYWOOD JACK

The success of the theatrical outings of Spring-Heeled Jack meant an almost inevitable transfer to the cinema. In 1946, not long after the end of World War II, a British company, Ambassador Films, released *The Curse of the Wraydons,* starring the then king of melodrama, the appropriately named Todd Slaughter (1885–1956). Slaughter, who was by all accounts a fine character actor, got his first part in a stage play aged sixteen and went on to become what one newspaper described as "the most loveable multi-murderer on the British stage."

During his long career he starred in some five hundred plays and sketches, mostly melodramas in which he murdered pretty women or handsome men to the accompaniment of lively hisses and boos from the delighted audience. Among his many roles were Long John Silver from an adaptation of Robert Louis Stevenson's *Treasure Island,* Burk and Hare the body snatchers, the original "Bluebeard," serial-killer Henri Landru, a brief stint as Jack the Ripper, and, perhaps his most famous role of all, the lead character in *Sweeney Todd: The Demon Barber of Fleet Street.* Nicknamed "Mr. Murder," he liked to boast that he committed fifteen murders a day during the run of *Sweeney Todd.*

In 1956, reportedly after he gave one of his finest stage performances as William Corder, the villain of *Maria Martin, or Murder in the Red Barn,* one of the most famous melodramas of the time, he died, aged seventy-one, shortly after taking a final curtain call.

He made a total of sixteen films, including cinematic versions of his most famous stage roles, Sweeney Todd and Corder, but one of his undoubted successes was *The Curse of the Wraydons,* directed by Victor M. Grover with a script by Michael Barringer, based on W. G. Wills's stage play. The film was an undoubted success in Britain and played to full houses across the country, but the taste for melodrama was beginning to wane, and after a time the film faded from view. Having viewed one of the few remaining prints, it has to be said that it makes for hard viewing today. Perhaps the most surprising thing is that there has been, to date, no other feature film retelling Spring-Heeled Jack's story. Certainly, *The Curse of the Wraydons* with its elaborate plot line, much like the stage plays that preceded it, is a long way from the mysterious figure leaping over hedges and out of dark corners at an easily petrified Victorian public.

JACK IN PICTURES

In the 1930s the first comics, initially, loud, cheap, and highly colored, began to appear in the United States. They were in many ways the inheritors of the older penny dreadfuls and dime novels, but they came out of the period between the two world wars and were very much a grassroots reaction to the conflict. They became the foundation for a multimillion-dollar business and today run into hundreds of widely differing styles. Controversy reigned over their early days, raising all kinds of concern for the moral behavior of the young, at whom they were initially aimed. But this was soon swept aside in a rising tide of superheroes, evil villains, and complex plot lines that are still with us today. Though Spring-Heeled Jack does not have a huge place within the genre, he has made several notable appearances. These stories take him far from the original point of his appearance into fresh waters where his character undergoes a variety of strange twists and turns.

Among the first appearances by Jack in the world of comics and graphic novels is his role as a villain in the long-running DC Comics series *Knight and Squire*. Here Jack is the enemy of Percy Sheldrake, an important British superhero, known as the Knight. At age twenty Percy became the head of his family when both his parents died in World War II. At this time a character named Shining Knight, originally a member of King Arthur's Round Table and subsequently frozen in suspended animation until 1941, took Percy under his wing and trained him to become first of all his squire and later to take over as his replacement. Percy is eventually killed by Spring-Heeled Jack, who forces him to swallow a bomb. After his death his son Cedric takes up the identity of the Knight.

Several commentators have pondered the question as to whether Jack could have influenced the creation of one of the most enduring comic-book characters, Batman, to whom he bears a passing resemblance. There is no evidence whether Bob Kane and Bill Finger, the originators of the character, knew of Spring-Heeled Jack, though it could well be that Kane, as an artist, could have seen the many artistic renderings of the character from the world of penny dreadfuls and dime novels. If we think back to the *Terror of London* series, which we may remember, presented Jack as a well-to-do man of noble parentage whose disguise is as a masked, bat-winged figure who moves through the night saving people, we might well see parallels.

Jack is later mentioned in the first issue of *Justice League of America Classified* #1 (2005), created by Grant Morrison, one of the finest writers to join the more recent comic-book universe. He reappeared in Morrison's *Batman, Incorporated,* a continuing series featuring the Caped Crusader, which changed direction following the first of many relaunches of the franchise.

In Britain two miniseries featuring Jack appeared from Rebel Studios between 1991 and 1993. The first series is titled *Spring-Heel Jack: A Mystery of Mysteries,* written by David Barbour and illustrated by Wayne Tanaka. In this Jack is a Tulpa, or thought-form (based on the teaching of Tibetan masters), generated by a young woman named July who wants revenge on a terrorist group who had planted a bomb in her child's stroller. In this story Jack is noncorporeal; he can pass through walls, teleport, read minds, and, of course, leap great distances and breath blue flames. For most of the first series, Jack spends his time caching up with the terrorist group and killing them one by one in various unpleasant ways. The murders are investigated by Inspector Church who recognizes Jack's supernatural nature. Finally, Jack catches up with the leader of the terrorist cell and throws him off the roof of a tall building with a bomb attached to him. The leader's assistant is arrested by Inspector Church, but Jack manages to kidnap her, and the story ends with her screams drowned out by Jack's laughter.

Here Jack is represented almost as an angel of vengeance, but his sadistic cruelty is a far cry from the actions of the original figure, and one feels that the writer, David Barbour, had done little research beyond what could be easily found in any book on the paranormal.

The second series, titled *Spring-Heel Jack: Revenge of the Ripper,* sees the hero as a more benign figure, this time helping Inspector Church catch the Ripper, who has returned to his old haunts to carry out a further series of murders. Together with July, Jack aids the police in capturing the Ripper, and it is then revealed that Jack had been long since given the task of capturing the murderer by a gypsy who knew that the Ripper would return.

Neither of these series is very well written, but they do show how Jack was perceived in the pop culture of the 1990s.

By 2003 Jack's fame had spread far enough for him to appear as an adversary of the time-traveling Doctor Who, where he is represented as an alien, in a story from the *Doctor Who Magazine.* In 2006 another British company, Full Circle, produced *Springheeled Jack: A Strange Visitor,* written by David Hitchcock. It won an award for that year.

In this story, set in a version of the Victorian world, there are actually two Jacks—one is the alien visitor first suggested by John Vyner in 1961, and another who bears the name Jack Rackham (actually a well-known eighteenth-century pirate) who is trying to find his beloved Evalina, who has been carried off by the alien. He is helped by Dr. Henry Jekyll (of Jekyll and Hyde fame), wearing wings created for him by no lesser a person than Orville Wilbur (loosely based on the famous aviators, Orville and Wilbur Wright).

Jack Rackham pursues the alien across London, eventually tracking him to his lair and discovering several pods, each containing a pregnant woman—one of whom is Evalina. A battle ensues, and as human Jack and alien Jack battle it out, Jack Rackham realizes that the mask worn by the alien is in fact a breathing apparatus. When he rips the mask off, the alien dies. At this moment the scene is interrupted by the police, and as he escapes Jack dons the alien mask. The police see this and, thinking he is the real Spring-Heeled Jack, pursue him vigorously. Sheltering away from his pursuers, Jack realizes the mask is somehow alive and is fixing itself to his face. He rips it off but not before it has given him a vision of Earth under attack by more aliens.

On the whole, Jack's treatment in the world of comics is uneven. Most writers who have attempted to include him seem not to understand his true nature and rely, understandably perhaps, on the inheritance of the penny dreadful series, which gave him a more fully rounded personality.

FICTIONAL JACK

A curious idea put forward by Michael Anglo in his book *Penny Dreadfuls and Other Victorian Horrors* suggests that the origin (or partly so) of Jack's pranks could have been the famous Victorian adventure yarn *Mr. Midshipman Easy,* written by popular novelist Captain Marriott and published in 1836, two years before the first recorded sightings of Spring-Heeled Jack. This includes a scene in which the hero of the tale is returning home one evening after attending a masquerade in which he had been dressed as Mephistopheles (aka the devil), including a red suit, horns, and tail. In a fit of high spirits, he jumps into the window of a house he is passing and frightens the occupants half to death. Could this, if nothing more, have inspired the "prankster" who later appeared as Spring-Heeled Jack? Given the amount of evidence regarding the undoubted copycat Jacks, it is certainly not impossible, though on the whole the reference seems too fleeting to be a viable source.

There have, indeed, been a number of fictional treatments of Jack in the last few years. Most notable of these are Philip Pullman's *Spring-Heeled Jack, a Story of Bravery and Evil* published in 1989 and Mark Hodder's novel *The Strange Affair of Spring Heeled Jack,* one of a series featuring two Victorian detectives based on the historical figures of the famous explorer and adventurer Sir Richard Burton and the flamboyant poet Algernon Charles Swinburne.

Pullman's brief tale concerns three young orphans who escape and go on the run through the treacherous streets of London. They are shadowed by the threatening figure of Mack the Knife, borrowed from John Gay's famous *Beggars Opera* of 1798. Against this dark villain, Pullman sets Spring-Heeled Jack, presented here as a kind of Victorian superhero. The book was originally written as a play to be performed by the pupils of a school where Pullman worked. He describes Jack as "a character from Victorian penny dreadfuls, a sort of early Batman, who dressed up as the Devil to scare evil-doers."[20]

Hodder's imaginative and inventive tale, set in an alternative, steampunk Victorian world, features a time traveler from the distant future who goes back to 1840 to prevent an ancestor from attempting to murder Queen Victoria. When his attempt proves ineffectual, he travels back to 1837 and recruits no lesser a person than Henry de La Poer Beresford, the Mad Marquis himself, to seek out the murderer. The long-term result of this action is to cause a fracture in time that creates an alternate world where technological developments have far outstripped those of the real Victorian period. Sir Francis Burton becomes a King's Agent whose task, aided by the effete figure of Swinburne, is to investigate the activities of Spring-Heeled Jack.

The novel is the finest account of Jack's adventures to appear yet. Fast paced, detailed, and full of memorable characters, it brings the story to life and provides a believable explanation for Jack (he is created with future technologies) that goes far beyond any historical understanding of the phenomenon.

SYMBOLIC JACK

The symbolic meaning of Jack is something we have scarcely touched upon here. We may choose to see him as a representation of the deep-seated superstition of our ancestors, or the Victorian delight in the supernatural, and he is perhaps both of these and more. When the artist Wil Kinghan, Caitlín Matthews, and I devised *The Steampunk*

Tarot: Gods of the Machine (2013), Jack was placed in the position of the devil (card XV). We said of him that he is "the scavenger who sees off things that have run their time. No one knows whose roof he will land upon, whose house he will visit (see plate 1). Whatever is in a state of decay, he will kill, clear or dismember it. He spells closure to what no longer works, making way for something else to arrive. There is no arguing or bargaining with him. However glorious your carriage or apparel, however wondrous your career, no matter how happy your life, Jack clears it all away to make things new."[21] In the imaginations of those who believed in Jack or who encountered him, he stood for freedom, lawlessness, terror, and even, later on, a form of nostalgia that turned him into a strange kind of hero.

AUDIO JACK

This exploration of the more recent appearances of Spring-Heeled Jack in contemporary fiction and culture would not be complete without reference to an award winning series of audio plays: *The Springheel Saga*. Produced between 2010 and 2015, devised and written by Robert Valentine and Jack Bowman (under his pen name Gareth Parker), and released as audio files through The Wireless Theatre Company's website, they retell Jack's story with verve and panache. The idea began with Bowman in 2000 as an idea for a TV series in which a Victorian detective would spend his time hunting for Spring-Heeled Jack through the fog-bound streets of London. In 2007 Robert Valentine came on board, and the two set about creating a series of audio dramas that would have plenty of "chases and explosions but without the need of a Hollywood budget." They both elected to follow the historical story of Jack rather than creating flights of fancy such as the penny dreadful or comic-book storytellers had done. They also wanted the story to be "a love-letter to the city" of London, evoking a smoky, dimly lit world more in keeping with Charles Dickens than Sherlock Holmes.

The series, extending to nine episodes, manages to weave a huge amount of the original events of the 1800s, along with a fictionalized story of Spring-Heeled Jack, with some intriguing supernatural elements adding spice to the recipe. So densely is it woven that it seems appropriate to summarize the series in detail as an example of what remains the most fully worked-out story of Jack to date (see plate 14).

SEASON ONE

The first season of *The Strange Case of Springheel'd Jack* featured Police Constable Jonah Smith and sidekick Toby Hooks, who are drawn into the hunt for the leaping man when they are summoned to Clapham Churchyard to investigate an attack on Polly Adams, who insists she has seen the devil. A cloven-hoofed footprint, found by the wall of the church, suggests she may be right. Meanwhile, two vicious killers, Chough and D'Urberville, are seeking the whereabouts of Charlotte Fitzrandolph, who is on her way back to England from Europe, bringing with her a family heirloom, the Burning Truth—a pendant with strange supernatural properties.

Jonah Smith's investigations bring him to the attention of the powerful Lord Wayland, who is determined to capture Springheel'd Jack. He secures Smith and Hooks the task of looking into the case.

Meanwhile, Chough and D'Urberville are still in pursuit of Charlotte Fitzrandolph and mistakenly apprehend another young woman, Mary Stevens, thinking she is Charlotte. Responding to Mary's screams, Smith hastens to her rescue, while Mary flees, briefly encountering Springheel'd Jack himself. Together, Smith and Hooks drive off the two villains and interview Mary Stevens. They see a connection between the numerous sightings and the nearby Morgan Arms pub.

Elsewhere, Lord Wayland entertains none other than the Duke of Wellington, along with his distant cousin the Marquis of Waterford, at a lavish masquerade ball, before excusing himself to hold a secret meeting with Chough and D'Urberville, whom he has hired to find Charlotte and her mysterious pendant. Charlotte is herself drawn toward the area of the Springheel'd Jack sightings by the power of the Burning Truth. The mysterious jewel draws Jack also, and he attacks Charlotte's carriage in an attempt to possess the pendant. Charlotte drives him off, but her carriage crashes.

Smith, visiting the Morgan Arms, learns that the Duke of Wellington is to lead the hunt for Jack and is hiring locals as beaters. Hooks arrives and informs Smith of the attack on Charlotte's carriage. They learn that she is heading for Scratch Row, where Smith had grown up and where his parents had died in a mysterious fire.

Making their way to the site, they arrive just in time to save Charlotte from the attentions of Chough and D'Urberville in a deserted church. Overcoming the villains, Smith, Hooks, and Charlotte find their way to a secret underground chamber beneath the church, where a Black Mass in in progress, led by none other than Lord Wayland. As they watch from hiding, the Burning Truth omits a signal that alerts the worshippers to the heroes' presence.

As they flee to the bell tower of the church with Wayland and his followers in pursuit, Springheel'd Jack himself appears, summoned by the pendant. The satanists cower from him, allowing Hooks and Charlotte to escape across the roofs, while Smith chases after Jack, remembering how, on the night his parents died, he had seen a demonic-looking figure leaping through the flames. However, Hooks slips and falls to his death, forcing Smith to give up the chase. Jack, also injured in the chase, recovers in a side street, unintentionally frightening a young woman named Lucy Scales, who passes by his hiding place in Green Dragon Alley.

Smith and Charlotte escape, and realizing that the Burning Truth is somehow connected to Springheel'd Jack, approach the chief constable with what they have learned—only to hear that one Thomas Millbank has been arrested in connection with an attack on a girl named Jane Alsop and is to stand trial as Springheel'd Jack.

Knowing the real Jack is still out there, Smith and Charlotte return to the Morgan Arms, only to find themselves under attack by Chough and D'Urberville. Smith stalls them while Charlotte escapes, but Smith is overcome and taken to Lord Wayland, who tells him that Jack is really Lucifer and that it is he and his followers who have summoned him. Wayland reveals that he needs the Burning Truth to complete the invocation and suspends Smith over a vat of boiling oil to force him to reveal the whereabouts of the pendant. Watching this, Charlotte uses the jewel to summon Springheel'd Jack, and after a tense confrontation with Wayland, Jack reclaims the pendant, and Charlotte and Smith swing through a window in the building to the safety of the Thames. Driven mad, Wayland ignites the vat of oil and perishes in the fire.

Smith and Charlotte hurry to the court to clear Millbank's name, arriving in time to learn he has been released already because he cannot breathe the blue flames described by Jane Alsop.

With the case officially closed, Charlotte returns to Europe in search of answers. Smith is promoted on condition that he does not reveal the truth about Lord Wayland. His obsession to capture Springheel'd Jack has only just begun.

SEASON TWO

Seven years later, season two continued the ingenious weaving of actual Spring-Heeled Jack stories with fictional additions. Here, in a west-end pub, a writer of penny dreadful romances named James Malcolm Rymer frames the story with his own reminiscences.

Beginning in 1845 we hear how a thirteen-year-old pickpocket named Maria Davis is pursued and killed by a spring-heeled figure breathing blue fire. Inspector Garrick and Sergeant Skeres are already on the scene when Detective Inspector Jonah Smith arrives—tipped off by the alleged sighting of Springheel'd Jack. Finding paraffin on the corpse, Smith is satisfied that the killer is an impostor and leaves, bumping into the young Rymer, then still a freelance reporter.

In the period between seasons one and two, Smith has taken to drink. Frustrated by another dead end, he returns home to encounter an unexpected visitor—Charlotte Fitzrandolph. She has continued to search for evidence of Springheel'd Jack and has noted that sightings correspond with the appearances of a traveling theater company known as the Harlequin Players. Smith congratulates Charlotte on her discovery, but she admits she had help from "a remarkable man" she met in Paris.

Smith and Charlotte agree to meet at a nearby penny gaff, the Fighting Cocks Inn, where the Harlequin Players are due to perform that night. On his way to the meeting, Smith catches sight of Jack on the rooftops and gives chase, but his adversary escapes with speed. Hearing footsteps behind him, Smith ambushes his stalker, who turns out to be Rymer. Despite initial misgivings, Smith is convinced to allow the reporter, who is writing a book about Springheel'd Jack, to go with him to the pub.

They arrive at the penny gaff, but Charlotte is nowhere to be seen. The Harlequin Players' master of ceremonies, a man named Oscar Snitterfield, introduces a Punch and Judy show in which the character of Springheel'd Jack is substituted for the devil, and afterward they get chatting to the Punch and Judy man himself, "Professor" Elijah Hopcraft.

They observe a magic act given by a doddery magician named Cuthbert and his assistant, the pugnacious Lizzie Coombe. When Lizzie's charms indirectly trigger a pub brawl, Smith leaves and goes in search of Charlotte. When they meet she warns him that she has made a terrible error by trusting the man she met in Paris. As she is about to reveal his name, a figure in the shadows shoots her in the back. Charlotte survives just long enough to give Smith a cryptic clue to the mystery, before she dies in his arms. Found alone with the corpse, the pub's denizens mistake Smith for the killer, and he is forced to flee.

With Smith on the run, Inspector Garrick and Sergeant Skeres are given the job of tracking him down. Garrick believes Smith will be at the Bartholomew Fair.

Smith, meanwhile, has found an unexpected ally in the form of the magician's assistant Lizzie, who is also looking for Springheel'd Jack. It transpires that her parents had also died in the fire that claimed Smith's parents. Lizzie now reveals that she is actually Dreadful Penny, leader of an infamous pickpocket gang. Maria Davis had also been a member of the gang, and Lizzie seeks vengeance. In return for hiding Smith, she asks for his help capturing Jack. The two agree to work together, but Smith wants to attend the funeral of Charlotte Fitzrandolph.

Watching the funeral from a distance, Smith is surprised to find Hopcraft also present. Hopcraft admits he is the man that Charlotte met in Paris but goes on to reveal that he, like Smith and Lizzie, had also lost his parents in the Scratch Row fire. All three had seen what they now know to be Springheel'd Jack rise from the flames.

Hopcraft now tells them that there are two artifacts associated with the inferno: the Burning Truth pendant and a mysterious casket known as the Box of Emet. Hopcraft explains that while Springheel'd Jack has regained possession of the Burning Truth, he is still searching for this box, currently in the possession of the magician Cuthbert, who uses it as a prop for one of his magic tricks.

Hopcraft and Smith attend the next performance of the magic act at Bartholomew Fair in order to observe the so-called Box of Emet. Smith demands to know if Hopcraft killed Charlotte, and if so, why? Hopcraft doesn't deny the accusation but brushes Smith's accusation aside, urging the wanted policeman to join him as a "kindred spirit."

Smith refuses and, at the same time, spots Garrick and Skeres in the crowd, looking for him. He sees that Hopcraft has aimed his gun-cane at his side. Caught between the two, Smith does the only thing he can think of—he volunteers to help Cuthbert in his next trick! But when Smith has to place his hand on the Box of Emet, he experiences a rush of memories and psychic insights. At this moment the entire fair is thrown into panic as a fire-breathing, spring-booted copycat Jack appears, blowing flames at the crowds and making a beeline for the box.

At this moment the real Springheel'd Jack appears, and the two Jacks face off. Hopcraft flees, Smith escapes, and both Jacks leap away into the night, hunted by police and an angry mob.

Smith loses himself in the backstreets and suddenly feels the presence of the Burning Truth. The trace leads him to a deserted attic, which he realizes is Jack's rooftop lair. Jack returns and advances on Smith threateningly, but as an angry mob crashes along the street below, Smith finds himself comforting Jack.

Smith goes out onto the rooftop and draws the mob away until finally, on London Bridge, he is cornered by Garrick and Skeres. Garrick advances alone, and Smith protests his innocence. Garrick wants to believe him but knows that given the circumstances he is still likely to hang for Charlotte's murder. Swearing to solve the mystery once and for all, Smith throws himself off the bridge into the freezing Thames.

Next morning, at Paddington Station, Rymer is bidding farewell to Lizzie Coombe as she and the rest of the troupe depart en route for a performance at Windsor before Queen Victoria herself. As Rymer leaves the station, Smith pulls him into an alley and tells him they have to prevent Cuthbert from using the Box of Emet in the presence of the queen or havoc may ensue.

Hopcraft is also on the train, and just before it leaves the platform, Garrick leaps aboard, calling to Skeres to have a detachment of soldiers waiting for them when they arrive.

Smith and Rymer find Lizzie, and the three of them search the luggage van for the box. Instead, they find pieces of a copycat Jack costume among the Harlequin Players props and realize that the killer must be one of the troupe.

At this moment Cuthbert appears and shows them the trick with the box. Smith is now convinced that only certain gifted people can make the box sing; at that moment they are attacked by the copycat Jack, who seizes the box. Lizzie grabs her pistol and chases after the killer, determined to avenge Maria Davis's death. Cornering the copycat, Lizzie removes the mask to reveal Ethel, the troupe's fortune-teller. The box emits a signal that kills the old lady. Dying, she explains that the box had driven her mad.

Garrick now appears, but just as he is about to arrest Smith, Hopcraft arrives with gun-cane in hand and grabs the box. He fires a parting shot, which hits Cuthbert. Smith shows Garrick the abandoned gun-cane to convince Garrick of Hopcraft's guilt. The two policemen give chase.

Hopcraft hijacks the train and prepares to blow it up, but before he can uncouple the locomotive and escape, Smith reaches him. While they struggle for the controls of the train, Garrick, Lizzie, Rymer, and Oscar Snitterfield attempt to diffuse the bomb.

Smith recovers the box, but Hopcraft escapes by leaping from the train into Slough Weir. The others reach the locomotive, but the brakes have been damaged, and the train can't be stopped. Cuthbert helps them uncouple the locomotive and the carriage containing the bomb. Cuthbert dies in the explosion.

The rest of the train stops, and Smith spots the real Springheel'd Jack, who has been following them the whole time. Smith tries to return the box to the leaping man, but the soldiers arrive and take it to nearby Aldershot Barracks. Jack vanishes again, and Smith and the other survivors decamp to the nearby Ostrich Inn. As the story comes to a close, Rymer tells us that Smith and Lizzie eventually married. Though he never found out the truth about Springheel'd Jack for himself, what really matters to him is the legend.

SEASON THREE

Season three opened in 1877. Springheel'd Jack attacks Aldershot Barracks and, despite the resistance by the British military, steals the Box of Emet. Prime Minister Benjamin Disraeli believes the Germans or Russians may be behind the raid. But Anstruther, his foreign office adviser, remembers the old stories of Springheel'd Jack and a warning delivered by an agent, code-named Cheshire Cat, who has suggested the same thing. He suggests they seek out retired policeman Jonah Smith, who may be of help.

Anstruther finds Smith at his lodgings, now an aging, alcoholic widower, terminally ill with tuberculosis and no longer interested in hunting Springheel'd Jack.

Meanwhile, the news of the Aldershot attack reaches Prussian spy mistress the Countess de Sadesky, who is also looking for Springheel'd Jack. She and her right-hand man, the lethal Jaeger, arrive in London and send their henchmen to find Smith.

Jaeger and his agent Vecht kidnap Smith, spiriting him back to the German embassy. Despite torture, Smith tells them nothing, and the countess orders him killed. At that moment one of the German aides kills Vecht, revealing himself to be Anstruther's agent, the Cheshire Cat, none other than Elijah Hopcraft.

Smith and Hopcraft escape with the German agents close behind, but thanks to Hopcraft's ingenuity, they lose them. Safe from their pursuers, Smith plans to kill Hopcraft and then himself, but Hopcraft reveals that Sadesky wants to discover the secret of Springheel'd Jack's advanced weaponry and that they must find him before she does. Grudgingly, Smith agrees to join forces, and they report to Anstruther. He shares an intercepted German telegraph that points to the abandoned Scratch Row underground railway station as Sadesky's next port of call.

Smith and Hopcraft return to Scratch Row, the scene of the deadly fire that claimed Smith's parents as well as those of Lizzie Coombe. The denizens of the local pub tell them that Old Jack haunts the tunnels, and Smith and Hopcraft set out in search of their old adversary. Sadesky and Jaeger arrive and follow them.

Smith and Hopcraft find their way to the sewers and, via the lost river Effra, into an abandoned mine. Here, the Germans capture them. With no means of escape, Smith causes the roof to cave in. As the dust settles, Smith and Hopcraft find themselves on one side of the collapsed tunnel roof, with Sadesky and Jaeger on the other. Smith and Hopcraft fall through into a new tunnel lined with fused ceramic, created when something large and hot ploughed through the earth at high speed on the night of the Scratch Row fire. They follow the tunnel into a huge cavern in which they discover a strange vessel—Springheel'd Jack's spacecraft.

Entering the spaceship, Smith and Hopcraft discover Jack in an isolation chamber. He is sick, perhaps dying, but the Burning Truth, now set into the Box of Emet, is sending a signal out into the universe.

Sadesky and Jaeger now appear and attempt to take control of the ship. Sadesky reveals that she and Jaeger are leaders of a secret society of Bavarian Illuminati who plan to sell the secret of Jack's technology to the highest bidder.

Despite Smith and Hopcraft's warnings, Sadesky tampers with the controls of Jack's isolation chamber, and the ship's automatic defenses come on line and destroy her. Jack himself wakes and kills Jaeger, then communicates with Smith telepathically, explaining that he needs a second pilot to fly his ship home.

Hopcraft pulls a knife and threatens to kill Smith unless Jack takes him instead. Jack refuses and touches Hopcraft on the forehead, causing him to drop his knife and allow Smith to take his place in the cockpit. Understanding that Jack has done something to change Hopcraft, Smith gives his old enemy the Burning Truth and promises to return one day. Hopcraft flees as the ship takes off.

Hopcraft now begins a decades-long wait for Smith to return and realizes that Jack's touch has changed him forever. Tortured by guilt, he lives on until, in late 1904, the Burning Truth suddenly glows into life.

Drawn north to Liverpool, Hopcraft finds himself in Sefton Park during a fresh Springheel'd Jack scare and witnesses the return of the spaceship. Smith emerges, having aged only a few days, and together he and Hopcraft bid a final farewell to Springheel'd Jack. The two old enemies—now friends—walk off into the night, wondering if Jack will ever return.

The writers of this fascinating series have woven so much of the original accounts into their own dramatic story line. Here are all aspects of

Spring-Heeled Jack—monster, attacker, demon, even alien. Their use of the settings of the original stories, references to the Punch and Judy plays, even a sly ref to the Marquis of Waterford, add veracity to a story that one wishes were true.

THE END OR THE BEGINNING?

On the face of it, Spring-Heeled Jack should not exist—and even more should not have been written and talked about ever since his first appearance. Looked at head-on, he did very little, served almost no purpose, and is, on the strength of the evidence, virtually impossible to detect. He appears and disappears without a word spoken or an actually testifiable crime—unless we count jumping out at people and frightening them as such. Yet his story lingers on, even to this day, and we can see how tenacious and powerful it can become.

From 1870 onward, the decline in the stories was distinctive. People looked back upon the manifestations of Spring-Heeled Jack in the 1830s with something like nostalgia. What had once been seen as a fearsome and terrible specter now became a figure of fun, a minor terror of the kind that gave a delicious shiver rather than a genuine frisson.

It is impossible to see exactly how the next development in the continuing story of Spring-Heeled Jack will appear. Surely it can only be a matter of time before a feature-length movie based around this powerful archetype will be in production. But of one thing we can be certain, that the legend and mystery that is Spring-Heeled Jack will be around for many years to come.

APPENDIX 1

Spring-Heeled Jack—
The Terror of London

By Anonymous

Although normally ascribed to Anonymous, this text has been variously attributed to George Augustus Sala or Edwin J. Brett. It is one of the first serialized penny dreadfuls to deal with the subject of Spring-Heeled Jack. Though no literary masterpiece, it is competently written and begins with a lively summary of what is actually known about Jack. This is followed by the following statement: "we have been favored by the descendants of Spring-Heeled Jack with the perusal of his 'Journal' or 'Confessions,' call it which you will. The only condition imposed upon us in return for this very great favor is that we shall conceal the real name of the hero of this truly extraordinary story." This entirely fictional idea is then used as the jumping-off point for the sensational and at times lurid story (summarized on pages 221–23), which ultimately gave birth to other stories, plays, films, and eventually comic-book accounts and radio dramas. For this reason it is included here in its entirety, as a document of historical interest for all who seek to explore the mystery of Spring-Heeled Jack.

◙

Out of the enormous army of highwaymen, footpads, and housebreakers, who have made themselves famous or infamous in the annals of English crime, probably not one ever succeeded in gaining such a large amount of notoriety in so short a space of time as the subject of our present sketch, Spring-Heeled Jack.

This quickly acquired reputation was the result, probably, of the veil of mystery that shrouded the identity of the man who was known on all hands as the Terror of London. It was at one time generally believed that Spring-Heeled Jack was no less a personage than the then Marquis of Waterford. This, however, was distinctly proved not to be the case, although the manner of proving it does not redound to the noble marquis's credit.

That the Marquis of Waterford and Jack could not be identical is proved conclusively by the fact that the terrible apparition showed itself to many persons on the 4th, 5th, and 6th, of April, 1837. At this time we find from an indictment, which was tried at the Derby assizes on Aug. 31st, 1837, that the Marquis of Waterford, Sir F. Johnstone, Bart., the Hon. A. C. H. Villiers, and E. H. Reynard, Esq., were charged with having committed an assault on April 5th, 1837.

On that day it was proved that the defendants were at the Croxton Park Races, about five miles from Melton Mowbray.

The whole of the four had been dining out at Melton on the evening of that day, and about two in the morning of the following day the watchmen on duty, hearing a noise, proceeded to the market place, and near Lord Rosebery's place saw several gentlemen attempting to overturn a caravan, a man being inside at the time.

The watchmen eventually succeeded in preventing this. The marquis immediately challenged one of them to fight. That worthy, however, having heard something about the nobleman's proficiency in the "noble art," at once declined. On this the four swells took their departure.

Subsequently the same watchmen heard a noise in the direction of the toll bar. They proceeded there at once, when they found that the gatekeeper had been screwed up in his house, and had been for some time calling out: "Murder! Come and release me."

The watchmen released the toll-keeper and started in pursuit of the roisterers. When the "Charlies," as the guardians of the peace were called in those days, came up with the marquis's party for the second time, the watchman who had declined the challenge to fight observed that one of the swells carried a pot of red paint while the other carried a paint brush.

The man, who had by this time grown a little more valorous, managed to wrest the paintbrush from the hand of the person who held it. But his triumph was of short duration, the four swells surrounded him, threw him on his back, stripped him, and ten minutes later the unfortunate man was painted a bright red from head to foot. They then continued their "lark," painting the doors and windows of different houses red.

Some time later or rather earlier, Mr. Reynard was captured and put in the lock up. The marquis and his two remaining companions succeeded in making an entrance to the constable's room. Once there they had little difficulty in forcing him to give up his keys. Once having obtained possession of these they had little difficulty in releasing the prisoner. This done they bore their living trophy back to their lodgings in state, and the little town resumed its normal condition of quiet repose.

The jury found the defendants (who were all identified as having taken part in the affray) guilty of a common assault, and they were sentenced to pay a fine of £100 each, and to be imprisoned until such fine was paid. It is hardly necessary to add that the money was at once forthcoming.

So our readers will see that this disgraceful affair proves conclusively that the Marquis of Waterford and Spring-Heeled Jack had a separate existence, unless the marquis was gifted with the power of being in two places at once.

In the *Annual Register*, Feb. 20th, 1837, we find the following:

Annual Register

FEBRUARY 20, 1837

OUTRAGE ON A YOUNG LADY.— Frequent representations have of late been made to the Lord Mayor, of the alarm excited by a miscreant, who haunted the lanes and lonely places in the neighbourhood of the metropolis for the purpose of terrifying women and children.

For some time these statements were supposed to be greatly exaggerated.

However, the matter was put beyond a doubt by the following circumstance: A Mr. Alsop, who resided in Bearbind-lane, a lonely spot between the villages of Bow and Old Ford, attended at Lambeth-street Office, with his three daughters, to state the particulars of an outrageous assault upon one of his daughters, by a fellow who goes by the name of the suburban ghost, or 'Spring-Heeled Jack'.

Miss Jane Alsop, one of the young ladies, gave the following evidence:

About a quarter to nine o'clock on the preceding night she heard a violent ringing at the gate in front of the house; and on going to the door to see what was the matter, she saw a man standing outside, of whom she inquired what was the matter. The person instantly replied that he was a policeman, and said, 'For Heaven's sake bring me a light, for we have caught Spring-Heeled Jack here in the lane.'

She returned into the house and brought a candle and handed it to the person, who appeared enveloped in a large cloak.

The instant she had done so, however, he threw off his outer garment, and applying the lighted candle to his breast, presented a most hideous and frightful appearance, and vomited forth a quantity of blue and white flame from his mouth, and his eyes resembled red balls of fire.

From the hasty glance which her fright enabled her to get at his person, she observed that he wore a large helmet, and his dress, which appeared to fit him very tight, seemed to her to resemble white oilskin.

Without uttering a sentence he darted at her, and catching her partly by her dress and the back part of her neck, placed her head under one of his arms, and commenced bearing her down with his claws, which she was certain were of some metallic substance.

She screamed out as loud as she could for assistance, and by considerable exertion got away from him, and ran toward the house to get in.

Her assailant, however, followed her, and caught her on the steps leading to the hall door, when he again used considerable violence, tore her neck and arms with his claws, as well as a quantity of hair from her head; but she was at length rescued from his grasp by one of her sisters.

Miss Alsop added that she had suffered considerably all night from the shock she had sustained, and was then in extreme pain, both from the injury done to her arm, and the wounds and scratches inflicted by the miscreant on her shoulders and neck, with his claws or hands.

This story was fully confirmed by Mr. Alsop, and his other daughter said:

ANNUAL REGISTER, FEBRUARY 20, 1837

That the fellow kept knocking and ringing at the gate after she had dragged her sister away from him, but scampered off when she shouted from an upper window for a policeman.

He left his cloak behind him, which someone else picked up, and ran off with.

And again on Feb. 26th, of the same year, we find the following:

𝔄nnual 𝔚egister

FEBRUARY 26, 1837

THE GHOST, alias 'SPRING-HEELED JACK' AGAIN.—At Lambeth Street office, Mr. Scales, a respectable butcher, residing in Narrow-street, Limehouse, accompanied by his sister, a young woman eighteen years of age, made the following statement relative to the further gambols of Spring-Heeled Jack:

Miss Scales stated that on the evening of Wednesday last, at about half-past eight o'clock, as she and her sister were returning from the house of their brother, and while passing along Green Dragon-alley, they observed some, person standing in an angle in the passage.

She was in advance of her sister at the time, and just as she came up to the person, who was enveloped in a large cloak, he spurted a quantity of blue flame right in her face, which deprived her of her sight, and so alarmed her, that she instantly dropped to the ground, and was seized with violent fits, which continued for several hours.

Mr. Scales said that on the evening in question, in a few minutes after his sisters had left the house, he heard the loud screams of one of them, and on running up Green Dragon-alley he found his sister Lucy, who had just given her statement, on the ground in a fit, and his other sister endeavoring to hold and support her.

She was removed home, and he then learned from his other sister what had happened.

She described the person to be of tall, thin, and gentlemanly appearance, enveloped in a large cloak, and carried in front of his person a small lamp, or bull's eye, similar to those in possession of the police.

The individual did not utter a word, nor did he attempt to lay hands on them, but walked away in an instant.

Every effort was subsequently made by the police to discover the author of these and similar outrages, and several persons were taken up and underwent lengthened examinations, but were finally set at liberty, nothing being elicited to fix the offence upon them.

Articles and paragraphs of this nature were of almost daily occurrence at this period, and the public excitement rose to such a pitch that "Vigilance Committees" were formed in various parts of London to try and put a stop to the Terror's pranks and depredations, even if they could not succeed in securing his apprehension. There could be no possible doubt that there was very little exaggeration in the extraordinary statements as to Spring-Heeled Jack's antics.

A bet of two hundred pounds, which became the talk of the clubs and coffeehouses, did more to add to Jack's reputation for supernatural powers than all the talk of mail-coach guards, market people, and servant girls.

A party of gentlemen were travelling by the then newly-opened London and North-Western Railway.

As they neared the northern end of the Primrose Hill tunnel they observed the figure of Jack sitting on a post, looking exactly as his Satanic Majesty is usually represented in picture books or on the stage.

"By Jove! There's Spring-Heeled Jack!" cried Colonel Fortescue, one of the travelers.

"Yes," cried Major Howard, one of his companions, "and I'll bet you two hundred pounds even that he's at the other end of the tunnel when we arrive there."

"Done!" cried the colonel.

And sure enough as the train emerged once more into the open air there was Spring-Heeled Jack at the side of the line, his long moustaches twirled up the sides of his prominent nose, and stream of sulphurous flame seeming to pour out from between his lips.

Another instant and he had disappeared.

The whole party in the train was almost paralyzed for a time, although most of them had "et their squadron in the field," and hardly knew what fear meant.

Colonel Fortescue handed the major the two hundred pounds, and the affair became a nine-days' wonder.

The solution was, no doubt, simple enough.

Spring-Heeled Jack had sprung on to the moving train at the rear, and during its passage through the tunnel had made his way to the front, and then, with a bound, had made his appearance in front of the advancing train.

Be this as it may, the unimpeachable evidence of men of position, like the gallant officers, backed up, as it was, by the payment and receipt of the two hundred pounds, brought Jack with a bound, like one from his own spring heels, to the utmost pinnacle of notorious fame.

We have no particulars of the exact mechanism that enabled Spring-Heeled Jack to make such extraordinary bounds. To jump clear over a stage coach, with its usual complement of passengers on top, was as easy to him as stepping across a gutter would be to any ordinary man. The secret of these boots had died with the inventor, and perhaps it is as well.

We have no doubt that if those boots were purchasable articles many of our readers would be tempted to leave off taking in the *Boys' Standard,* so as to be able to save up more pennies toward the purchase of a pair. Fancy, if you can, what would be the consequence of a small army of Spring-Heels in every district.

To return, however, to our hero. His dress was most striking. It consisted of a tight-fitting garment, which covered him from his neck to his feet. This garment was of a blood-red colour. One foot was encased in a high-heeled, pointed shoe, while the other was hidden in a peculiar affair, something like a cow's hoof, in imitation, no doubt, of the "cloven hoof" of Satan. It was generally supposed that the "springing" mechanism was contained in that hoof. He wore a very small black cap on his head, in which was fastened one bright crimson feather. The upper part of his face was covered with black domino. When not in action the whole was concealed by an enormous black cloak, with one hood, and which literally covered him from head to foot.

He did not always confine himself to this dress though, for sometimes he would place the head of an animal, constructed out of paper and plaster, over his own, and make changes in his attire. Still, the above was his favorite costume, and our readers may imagine it was a most effective one for Jack's purpose.

These are almost all the published facts about this extraordinary man. But we have been favoured by the descendants of Spring-Heeled Jack with the perusal of his "Journal" or "Confessions," call it which you will. The only condition imposed upon us in return for this very great favor is that we shall conceal the real name of the hero of this truly extraordinary story.

The reason for this secresy [sic] is obvious.

The descendants of Spring-Heeled Jack are at the present time large landed proprietors in South of England, and although had it not been for our hero's exploits they would not at the present time be occupying that position, still one can hardly wonder at their not wishing the real name of Spring-Heeled Jack to become known.

As it will, however, be necessary for the proper unraveling of our story that some name should be used we will bestow upon our hero the name of Dacre.

Jack Dacre was the son of a baronet whose creation went back as far back as 1619. Jack's father had been a younger son, and, as was frequently the case in those days, he had been sent out to India to see what he could do for himself.

This was rendered necessary by the fact that although the Dacres possessed a considerable amount of land the whole of it was strictly entailed.

This fact was added to the perhaps more important one that each individual Dacre in possession of the title and estates seemed to consider that it was his duty to live close up to his income, and to give his younger sons nothing to start in life with, save a good education.

That is to say, the younger sons had the run of the house.

They were taught to shoot by the keepers; to ride by the grooms; to throw a fly, perhaps, by the gardener; and to pick up what little "book-learning" they could.

Not altogether a bad education, perhaps, in those days when fortunes could be made in India by any who had fair connections, plenty of pluck, and plenty of industry.

Jack's father was early told that he could expect no money out of the estate, and he was also informed that he could choose his own path in life. This did not take him long.

Sidney Dacre was a plucky young fellow, and thought that India would afford the widest scope for his talents, which were not of the most brilliant order, as may be expected from his early training. To India he therefore went, and managed to shake the "pagoda tree" to a pretty fair extent.

In 1837 he thought he was justified in taking to himself a wife, and of this union Jack, who was born in the year of Waterloo, was the only result.

Fifteen years later Sidney Dacre received the intelligence that his father and his two brothers had perished in a storm near Bantry Bay, where they had gone to assist as volunteers in repelling a supposed French invading party which it was anticipated would attempt to effect a landing there.

This untimely death of his three relatives left Sidney Dacre the heir to the baronetcy and estates; and although he had plantation after plantation in the Presidencies, he made up his mind that he would at once return to the old country. He therefore placed his Indian plantations in the hands of one Alfred Morgan, a clerk, in whom he had always placed implicit confidence.

This man, by the way, had been the sole witness to his marriage with Jack's mother.

A month later, and Sir Sidney and Lady Dacre, with their son, set sail in the good ship Hydaspes on their way to England.

Nothing of any importance occurred on the voyage, and the Hydaspes was within sight of the white cliffs of old Albion when a storm came on, and almost within gunshot of home the brave old ship which had weathered many a storm went to pieces.

All that were saved out of passengers and crew were two souls.

One, our hero Jack Dacre, afterward to become the notorious Spring-Heeled Jack; the other, a common sailor, Ned Chump, a man who is destined to play a not unimportant part in this history, even if the part he had already played did not entitle him to mention in our columns.

And when we tell our readers that had it not been for the friendly office of Ned Chump our hero must inevitably have perished with the rest, we think they will agree that they owe the jolly sailor a certain amount of gratitude.

Ned Chump had taken very great interest in our hero on the voyage home. Jack was such a handsome, bright-looking lad, that everyone seemed to take to him at first sight. Ned's devotion to him more resembled that of a faithful mastiff to his master than any other simile that we can call to mind.

When Ned saw that the fate of the Hydaspes was inevitable he made up his mind that Master Jack and he should be saved if there was any possibility of such a thing. The jolly tar bound Jack Dacre fast to a hencoop, and then attached his belt to it with a leather thong. This done Ned threw the lad, the coop, and himself into the sea, and beating out bravely managed to get clear of the ship as she went down headfirst. Had he not have done this they must inevitably have been drawn into the vortex caused by the sinking ship.

Fortunately for both of them Jack had become unconscious, or it is not likely that he would have deserted his father and mother, even at this critical juncture.

However, the Hydaspes and all on board, including Sir Sidney and Lady Dacre, had gone to the bottom of the sea ere Jack recovered consciousness and found himself on the shore of Kent, with his faithful companion in adversity bending over him with loving care.

As soon as Jack Dacre was sufficiently recovered, Ned proceeded to "take his bearings" as he expressed it, and knowing that Jack's ancestral home was somewhere in the county of Sussex, he suggested that they should move in a westerly direction until they should find some native of the soil who could inform them of the locality they were in.

They found upon inquiry that they had been cast ashore at a little village called Worth, in the neighbourhood of Sandwich, and that the good ship Hydaspes had fallen a victim to the insatiable voracity of the Goodwin Sands.

Shipwrecked mariners are always well treated in England, the old stories of wreckers and their doings notwithstanding, and Jack Dacre and the trusty Ned Chump had little difficulty in making their way to Dacre Hall in Sussex, though neither had sixpence in his pocket, so sudden had their departure from the wrecked ship been.

When Jack arrived at the home of his forefathers he found one Michael Dacre, who informed our hero that he was his father's first cousin, in possession.

"Yes, my lad," continued Michael Dacre, in a particularly unpleasant manner, "Sir Sidney's cousin; and failing his lawful issue I am the heir to Dacre Hall and the baronetcy."

"Failing his lawful issue!" cried Jack, with all the impetuosity of youth. "Am I not my father's only son, and therefore heir to the family honors and estates?"

"Softly, young man—softly," cringed Michael, "I do not want to anger you. Of course you have the proof with you that your father and mother were married, and that you are the issue of that union?"

"Proof!" cried Jack, fairly losing his temper. "Do you think one swims ashore from a doomed ship with his family archives tied round his waist?"

"There—there, my boy," said the wily Michael, "don't lose your temper; for you must see that it would have been better for you if you had have taken the precaution to have brought the papers with you."

"But," said Jack, quite non-plussed by his cousin's coolness, "Ned Chump, here, knows who I am, and that everything is straight and above board."

"Yes, yes, my boy," replied Michael; "and pray how long has Mr. Chump, as I think you call him, known you? Was he present at your father's marriage? I do not suppose he was present at your birth," and Michael Dacre concluded his speech with a quiet but diabolical chuckle.

"I have known him ever since the day we left India—" began the lad.

But Michael interrupted him by saying, in a somewhat harsher tone than he had used before—

"That is equal to not knowing you at all. I am an acknowledged Dacre, and until you can prove your right to that name I shall remain in possession of Dacre Hall; for the honour of my family I could not do otherwise."

"But what am I? Where am I to go? What am I to do?" stammered Jack.

Meanwhile, Ned Chump looked on with kindling eyes, and a fierce light in his face that boded ill for Michael Dacre should it come to blows between them.

Michael caught the look and felt that perhaps it would be better to temporize, he therefore said: "Oh! Dacre Hall is large enough for us all. While I am making the necessary enquiries in India, you and this common sailor here can knock about the place. It will, perhaps, be quite as well that I have you under my eye, so that if you turn out to be an impostor you may be punished as you deserve."

After a short consultation, Jack and Ned Chump made up their mind that it would be best to accept the churlish offer. "After all," said Ned, "you know that you are the rightful heir. And when the proofs come over from India you will easily be able to claim your own."

"Yes, Ned, I suppose we had better remain on the spot."

"Of course we had," said Ned. "There is only one thing against it, and that is that if I ever saw murder in anyone's eye it was in your cousin's just now. But never mind, lad, we'll stick together, and we shall circumvent the old villain, never you fear."

So it was arranged, and Ned Chump and Jack Dacre soon seemed to have become part and parcel of the establishment at Dacre Hall.

The sailor's ready ingenuity and willingness to oblige made him rapidly a great favourite among the servants and employees generally, while Jack's sunny face, and flow of anecdote about the strange places he had been in and the strange sights he had seen, rendered him a decided acquisition to what was, under the circumstances, a somewhat somber household.

So time passed on, and the first reply was received from India.

This reply came from Alfred Morgan, the late Sir Sidney's trusted representative. This letter destroyed in an instant any hope, if such ever existed, in Michael Dacre's breast that Jack might be an impostor.

But there was one gleam of hope in the cautiously worded postscript to the letter.

"Do not mention this to anyone. I am on my way to England, and I may identify the boy and produce the necessary papers—or I may not. It will depend a great deal upon the first interview I have with you; and that interview must take place before I see the boy."

"What did this mean?" thought Michael Dacre. "Did it mean that here was a tool ready to his hand, who would swear away his cousin's birthright?"

Time alone would show.

Then again the improbability of such a thing occurring would sweep over him with tenfold force, and he decided to take time by the forelock and remove Jack from his path.

Michael Dacre had not the pluck to do this fell deed himself, but he had more than one tool at hand that would fulfill his foul bidding for a price.

The man he chose on this occasion was one Black Ralph, a ruffian who had been everything by turns, but nothing long. He was strongly suspected of obtaining his living at the time of which we are writing by poaching, but nothing had ever been proved against him.

In the days when Jack's grandfather had been alive, Michael Dacre, who acted as steward and agent on the estate, always pooh-poohed any suggestion of the kind, and sent the complaining gamekeepers away, literally "with a flea in their ears."

The arrangement was soon made between Michael Dacre and Black Ralph.

The former was to admit the latter to the house, and he was to ransack the plate pantry, taking sufficient to repay him for his trouble. He was then to pass to Jack's bedroom, which Michael pointed out, and to settle him at once. He was then to proceed to Newhaven, where a lugger was to be in waiting, and so make his way with his booty over to France. This the cousin thought would make all secure.

But he had reckoned without his host. Or shall we say his guest, as it was in that light that he regarded the real Sir John Dacre?

The lad was a light sleeper, and on the night planned for the attack he became aware of the presence of Black Ralph in his chamber almost as soon as the would-be assassin had entered it.

Brave though Jack was, he felt a thrill of terror run through him as he thought of his utterly helpless condition, for Ned Chump had been sent on some cunningly contrived errand to keep him out of the way, and he had not yet returned.

That murder was the object of the midnight intruder Jack Dacre never doubted. There was but one way out of it, and that was to rush up into the bell tower which communicated with a staircase abutting on his chamber. Once here he could ring the bell, if he could only keep his assailant at bay. At the worst, he could but jump into the moat below, and stand a chance of saving his life. In an instant he had left his bed, and dashed for the door.

But the assassin was upon him.

Jack just managed to bound up the stairs, and enter the tower. Here he could seize the bell-rope he felt Black Ralph's hot breath upon his neck. In an instant the lad had sprang upon the parapet. Then an instant later he was speeding on his way to the moat below, having made the terrible leap with a grace and daring which he never afterward eclipsed, even when assisted by the mechanical appliances which he used in the adventures we are about to describe in his assumed character of Spring-Heeled Jack.

Our hero suffered nothing from his perilous jump worse than a ducking. And it is very probable that this did him more good than harm, as it served to restore his somewhat scattered thoughts.

By the time Jack Dacre had managed to clamber out of the moat, Black Ralph had put a considerable distance between himself and Dacre Hall. He had got his share of the booty, and whether Master Jack survived the fall or not mattered little to him.

He could rely upon Michael Dacre's promise that the lugger should be waiting for him at Newhaven, and once in France he could soon find a melting-pot for his treasure, and live, for a time at least, a life of riotous extravagance.

When Jack reached the house he found the hall door open, and without fear he entered; bent upon going straight to his cousin's room and informing him of what had happened.

Before he could reach the corridor which contained the state bedroom in which Michael Dacre had ensconced himself, Jack heard a low—

"Hist!"

He turned round and saw Ned Chump beckoning to him and pointing to the flight of stairs that led to their common chamber, and from thence to the bell tower. Our hero having perfect confidence in his sailor friend obeyed the signal. When the two were safely seated in their bedroom, Ned said, eagerly:

"Tell me, boy, what has happened?"

In a very few words Jack told him.

"My eye!" ejaculated Ned with a low whistle, "that was a jump indeed."

Then he continued: "But who was your assailant? Could you not see his face?"

"No; it was too dark," replied Jack; "but there was a something about his figure that seemed familiar to me."

"Yes, lad, there was," said honest Ned Chump. "I met the ruffian but now, making the best of his way to Newhaven, no doubt."

"Who was it?" asked the lad.

"Why that poaching scoundrel, Black Ralph," answered Ned; "and you may depend upon it that your worthy cousin has laid this plan to kill you, and so prevent any chance of a bother about the property."

"What had I better do?" asked Jack. "I will act entirely under your advice."

"Well, my boy," said Ned, "take no notice; let matters take their course. We are sure to find out something or other in the morning."

And the two firm friends carefully fastened their door and turned in to rest.

In the morning the alarm of the robbery was given, but neither Jack nor Ned uttered one word to indicate that they knew aught about it.

"How did you get in?" asked Michael Dacre, roughly, as he turned toward Chump.

The would-be baronet's rage at the appearance of Jack Dacre unharmed, although his plate-chest (as he chose to consider it) had been ransacked, knew no bounds. But Ned had his answer ready.

"I thought the door was left open for me, sir," he said, "so I simply entered and bolted the door behind me, and made my way up to bed."

"This is indeed a mysterious affair," said Michael Dacre, "but I have reasons of my own for not letting the officers of justice know about this affair. I have my suspicions as to who the guilty party is, and I think, if all is kept quiet, I can see my way to recovering my lost plate."

"Your lost plate!" said Jack, contemptuously. "Say, rather, my lost plate."

"I thought that subject was to be tabooed between us until Mr. Morgan arrives with the proofs of your identity, or imposture, as the case may be."

"Very well, sir," replied Jack; "so be it. But I cannot help thinking that Mr. Morgan ought to have arrived long before this."

However, in due course the long-looked for one arrived.

But instead of coming straight on to Dacre Hall, as one would have expected a trustworthy agent to have done, he took up his quarters at the Dacre Arms, and sent word to Michael Dacre that Mr. Alfred wanted to see him on important business.

The message, of course, was a written one, as the people belonging to the inn would have thought it strange had an unknown man sent such a message to one so powerful as Michael Dacre was now making himself out to be.

In an hour's time the two men were seated over a bottle of brandy, discussing the position of affairs.

"And if I prove to the law's satisfaction—never mind about yours, for you know the truth—that the boy is illegitimate, what is to be my share?"

"A thousand pounds," said Michael.

"A thousand fiddlesticks," replied Morgan, grinding his teeth. "Without my aid you are a penniless beggar, kicked out of Dacre Hall; and with no profession to turn your hands to. Make it worth my while, and what are you? Why Sir Michael Dacre, the owner of this fine estate, and one of the most powerful landowners in this part of the county of Sussex. A thousand pounds—bah!"

The would-be owner of Dacre Hall looked aghast at Morgan's vehemence, and with an imploring gesture he placed his finger on his lip and pointed at the door.

Then under his breath he muttered: "Five thousand, then?"

"No, not five thousand, nor yet ten thousand," said Morgan.

"Now look you here, Mr. Michael Dacre," he went on with a strong emphasis upon the prefix.

"Now look here—my only terms are these: you to take the Dacre estates in England, and I to have the Indian plantations. That's my ultimatum. Answer, 'yes' or 'no.'"

For an instant Michael Dacre hesitated, but he saw no hope in the cold grey eye of Alfred Morgan, and at last consented.

The two now separated, but met again the following day, when the necessary agreements were signed, and Mr. Alfred retired to Brighton to make his appearance two days later as Mr. Alfred Morgan, the Indian representative of the late Sir Sidney Dacre.

"My poor boy," he said sympathetically when he first met our hero. "My poor boy, this is a terrible blow for you."

"What do you mean?" asked Jack. "It was a terrible blow to me when my father and my mother went down in the Hydaspes—but Time, the great Healer, has softened that blow so that I should hardly feel it now, were it not for the doubts that my cousin here has cast upon my identity."

"Ah! Of your identity there can be no doubt, poor boy," sighed Alfred Morgan; "and that's where lies the pity of it."

"How do you mean?" cried Jack, an angry flush mantling his handsome features.

"How do mean, poor boy?" went on the merciless scoundrel. "Why, the pity of it is that, although I know so well that you are the son of your father and mother, the law refuses to recognise you as such."

"And why?" yelled Jack, with a sudden and overwhelming outburst of fury.

"Because," meekly replied the villain, "your father and mother were never married."

"But," cried Jack, thoroughly taken aback by this assertion, "you were the witness to the marriage. I have heard my father say so scores of times."

"Aye, my poor lad; but your mother had a husband living at the time," and Mr. Alfred handed a bundle of papers to the family solicitor, who had not yet spoken, the whole conversation having taken place between Jack and Mr. Alfred Morgan.

A silence like that of the tomb fell upon the occupants of the room as the lawyer examined the papers.

Ten minutes or a quarter of an hour passed, then, with a sigh, the kind-hearted solicitor turned to Jack and said, with tears in his eyes, "Alas, my lad; it is too true; you have no right to the name of Dacre."

Without a word Jack caught hold of Ned's hand, and, turning to his cousin, said, in a voice of thunder, "There is some villainy here, which, please Heaven, I will yet unravel. Once already you have tried to murder my body, now you are trying to murder my mother's reputation; but as I escaped from the first plot by a clean pair of heels and a good spring from the bell tower, so on occasion I feel that I shall eventually conquer. Come, Ned, we will leave this, and make our plans for the future."

"Aye, Master Spring-Heels, make yourself scarce, or I will have you lashed and kicked from the door, you wretched impostor!"

"Yes, cousin, I will go," answered Jack, impressively; "and I will accept the name you have given me, as you say I have no right to any other. But, beware! False Sir Michael Dacre, the time will come, and that ere long, when the tortures of the damned shall be implanted in your heart by me—the wretched, despised outcast whom you have christened Spring-Heeled-Jack!"

As our hero uttered these words Michael Dacre's cheek paled visibly.

And indeed there was good cause for his apparent fear.

Jack Dacre had thrown such an amount of expression into his words and gestures as seemed to render them truly prophetic.

At this moment Mr. Reece, the solicitor, advanced towards Jack and, holding out a well filled purse to him, said—

"Take this, my lad; it shall never be said that Sam Reece allowed the son of his old playmate, Sid Dacre, to be turned out of house and home without a penny in his pocket, legitimate or not."

Jack, responding to a nudge from Ned Chump, took the purse and said, "Thank you, sir, for your kindness. That there is some villainy afloat I am convinced, but whether I eventually succeed in proving my claim or not this money shall be faithfully returned. Once more, thank you, sir, and good-bye."

With this Jack and Ned left the room. As soon as they had taken their departure, the "baronet," as we must style him for a time, recovered his self-possession to a certain extent.

Turning to the solicitor, he said—

"How much was there in that purse, Mr. Reece? Of course I cannot allow you to lose your money over the unfortunate whelp."

The lawyer, who, although the documentary evidence was so plain, could not help thinking with Jack Dacre that some villainy was afloat, answered the baronet very shortly.

"What I gave the lad, I gave him out of pure good feeling, I want no repayment from anyone. And, mark my words, Sir Michael Dacre, that boy will return my loan sooner or later, and if there is anything wrong about these papers I feel assured that he will carry out his threat with regard to yourself."

"What do you mean, insolent—" cried the baronet.

But ere he could finish the sentence, Mr. Reece calmly said—

"You do not suppose that the matter will drop here? The poor lad has no friends, and I was stupid in not having detained him when he proposed to leave this house. However, I missed that opportunity of questioning him as to his life in India, and the relations that existed between his father and his mother. One thing is certain, however, and that is he will appear here again."

"Well, and if he does!" asked the angry baronet.

"Well, and if he does he will find a firm friend in Sam Reece," answered the lawyer. "I shall retain these papers—not by virtue of any legal right that I can claim to possess. So, if you want them, you have only to apply to the courts of law to recover possession of them."

"Then you shall do no more business for me," cried Michael Dacre.

"I should have thought," replied the solicitor, "that my few words had effectually severed all business relations between us. As it appears that you do not take this view, allow me to say that all the gold in the Indies would not tempt me to act as your legal adviser for another hour. A man who can behave to an unfortunate boy-cousin in the manner you have behaved to Jack Dacre, legitimate or not, can hold no business communications with Sam Reece."

"But how about my papers?" quoth the now half-frightened baronet.

"I will send you your bill, and on receipt of a cheque for my costs I will return you all the papers of yours that I hold—save and except, mark you, those relating to the marriage of the late baronet and the birth and baptism of his son."

The new baronet looked at his ally, Mr. Alfred Morgan, but saw very little that was consoling in that worthy man's face.

He therefore accepted the position, and with as haughty a bow as he could possibly make under the circumstances, he allowed Mr. Reece to take his departure.

By this time Jack Dacre and Ned Chump were more than a mile away from the hall. Ned, although far more experienced in the ways of the world than Jack Dacre, tacitly allowed the latter to take the lead of the "expedition," if such a word may be used.

Jack, boy as he was, was in no way deficient in common sense, so perhaps Ned was justified in accepting the youngster as his leader.

For some miles not a word escaped Jack Dacre's lips.

At last they arrived at the old-fashioned town of Arundel, and here Jack suddenly turned to his companion, and said—

"We'll stop here and rest, and think over what will be our best course to pursue."

"All serene, skipper," answered Ned, "I am quite content."

Jack gave a melancholy smile as he replied to the sailor's salutation—

"Oh! then you don't object to calling me your skipper, although you have heard that I am base born, and have no right to bear any name at all."

"Never fear, Master Jack—or Sir John, perhaps, I ought to say—there is some rascality at work, and I believe that that Mr. Alfred Morgan is at the bottom of it. But we shall circumvent the villains, I am sure, never fear."

"Yes," replied Jack, "I think we shall."

"Ah!" said Ned, "but how?"

"I have not been idle during our long walk," said Jack, as the two entered the hospitable portals of the Bridge House Hotel.

"I have not been idle, and if we can get a private room we will talk the matter over, and see how much money the good lawyer was kind enough to give us."

"To give you, you mean," said Chump, with a chuckle. "It's precious little he'd have given me, I reckon."

They managed to obtain a private room, and over a plain but substantial repast they counted the contents of the lawyer's purse.

To the intense surprise of both, and to the extreme delight of Ned Chump, it was found to contain very little short of fifty guineas.

The sailor had never in the whole of his life had a chance of sharing in such a prize as this.

With Jack, of course, the thing was different.

In India he had been accustomed to see money thrown about by lavish hands.

Between the ideas of Ned Chump, the common sailor, and those of the son of the rich planter, there could hardly be anything in common as far as regarded the appreciation of wealth.

But, nevertheless, the friendship that had sprung up between them in so short a time, never faded until death, the great divider, stepped in and made all human friendship impossible.

As soon as Jack had satisfied himself as to the actual strength of their available capital, he turned to Ned Chump and said, "This money will not last long, and I do not see how I can do anything in the way of working for a living, if I am ever to hope to prove my title to the Dacre baronetcy and estates."

"That's as it may be, skipper," said Ned, "but I don't quite see how we are to live without work when this here fifty pounds has gone."

"That's just the point I have been thinking over," said Jack. "I am not yet sixteen, but, thanks to my Oriental birth, I look more like twenty."

"That you do, skipper," chimed in Ned.

"Well, then, I'll tell you what I intend to do."

"Go on, sir," cried the anxious sailor.

"Some year or two ago I had for a tutor an old Moonshee, who had formerly been connected with a troop of conjurors—and you must have heard how clever the Indian conjurors are."

"Yes," replied Ned, "and I have seen for myself as well."

"Then," said Jack, "you will not be surprised at what I am going to tell you."

"Perhaps not, skipper—fire away," said Ned.

"Well, this Moonshee taught me the mechanism of a boot, which one member of his band had constructed, and which boot enabled him to spring fifteen or twenty feet up in the air, and from thirty to forty feet in a horizontal direction."

"Lor!" was the only exclamation that the open-mouthed and open-eared sailor could make use of.

"Yes," continued our hero, "and I intend to invest a portion of this money in making a boot like it."

"Yes, but," stammered the half-bewildered sailor: "but when you have made it, of what use will it be to us, or, rather, how will it enable you to regain your rights?"

"I have formed my plan," answered Jack, "and it is this. I'll make the boot, and then startle the world with a novel highwayman. My cousin twitted me about my spring into the moat and my nimble heels. I'll hunt him down and keep him in a perpetual state of deadly torment, under the style and title of Spring-Heeled Jack."

"But," asked the sailor, "you will not turn thief?"

"I shall not call myself a thief," said Jack, proudly. "The world may dub me so if it likes. I shall take little but what belongs to me, I shall confine my depredations as much as possible to assisting my cousin in collecting my rents."

"Oh! I see," said Ned, only half-convinced.

The faithful tar had the sailor's natural respect for honesty, and did not quite like his "skipper's" plan for securing a livelihood.

But Jack, who had been brought up under the shadow of the East India Company, had not many scruples as to the course of life he had resolved to adopt.

To him pillage and robbery seemed to be the right of the well-born.

He had seen so much of this sort of thing amongst his father's friends and acquaintances that his moral sense was entirely warped.

So speciously did he put forth his arguments that Ned at last yielded.

The sailor simply stipulated that he should take no active part in any robbery.

For the faithful salt could find no other term for the operation.

To this Jack readily consented, and a compact was entered into between them as to what each was expected to do.

Ned promised faithfully to do all he could to assist his master in escaping, should he at any time be in danger of arrest.

Jack, on his part, promising Ned Chump a fair share of the plunder gained by Spring-Heeled Jack.

This arrangement entered into, the next thing was to make the spring boot.

Jack, who was possessed with an intelligence as well as physique far beyond his years, suggested that they should make their way to Southampton.

There, he argued, they could procure all they wanted without exciting suspicion.

Ned, of course, had no hesitation in falling in with this proposal.

A fortnight later and the boot was completed.

Completed, that is, so far as the actual manufacture was concerned.

Whether it would act or not remained to be seen.

To have tried its power in any ordinary house would have been absurdly ridiculous.

There was no place where it would be safe to make the trial spring save in the open air.

Jack had manufactured the boot strictly according to the old Moonshee's directions, but he could not tell to what length the mechanism might hurl him, and he was a great deal too sensible to attempt to ascertain the extent of its power in any enclosed space.

So one morning, Ned and Jack started off from the inn where they were staying, for a ramble in the country, taking the magic boot with them.

Ned had by this time managed to allay his scruples and went into the affair with as much spirit as did Jack himself.

In due course they reached a spot which Jack pronounced to be a suitable one for the important trial.

The spot was an old quarry, or rather chalk pit, where at one spot the soil had only been removed for a depth of about twelve feet.

Descending this pit Jack placed the boot on his foot.

Ned looked on in the utmost wonderment.

He could hardly conceive that it was possible such a simple contrivance should possess such magical attributes.

To his astonishment, however, he saw his young master, for as such

Ned regarded Jack Dacre, suddenly rise in the air and settle down quietly on the upper land some twelve or fourteen feet above.

Ned, who, although a Protestant, if anything, had lived long enough amongst Catholics on board ship and elsewhere to have imbibed some of their customs, made the sign of the cross and ejaculated something that was meant for a prayer.

To his untutored mind the whole thing savored strongly of sorcery.

An instant later and Jack Dacre, who had thus easily earned the right to be called Spring-Heeled Jack, had sprung down into the quarry again, and stood by the side of his faithful henchman.

"Well, skipper," cried Ned, "I've heard of mermaids and sea-serpents, and whales that have swallowed men without killing them, but this boot of yours bangs anything I have ever heard of, though you must know, it isn't all gospel that is preached in the forecastle."

"It's all right, Ned," said Jack, "and with this simple contrivance you will see that I shall spring myself into what I feel convinced is my lawful inheritance."

"I'm with you," said Ned, as keen in the affair now as Jack Dacre himself.

"I'm with you, and where shall we go now."

"Well, old friend, I must purchase one or two articles of disguise, and then I think we will make our way toward Dorking."

"To Dorking?" queried Ned. "I thought you would have made your way toward Dacre Hall, especially as you said you wished to assist your cousin to collect his rents. Ha! ha! ha!" And the jolly tar finished his sentence by bursting into an uncontrollable fit of laughter.

"Well, you see," replied Jack, "that's just where it is. Although my poor father never dreamed that he would inherit the family estates, he had sufficient pride of birth to keep me, his own son, in spite of all that they say, well posted in the geography of the entailed estates of the Dacres. I consequently know that more than one goodly farm in the neighbourhood of Dorking belongs to me by right; and, therefore, to that place I mean to start to make my first rent collection, as I am determined to call my operations; for the terms robbery and thief are quite as repugnant to me as they are to you, Ned Chump."

"But, skipper, I never thought of you as a real thief," said Ned. "It was merely because I could not see how you could take that which belonged other people without robbery, that made me speak as I did. But if you are really only going to collect that which is your own, why there can be no harm in it, I am sure."

"That's right, Ned, and if I ever I do kick over the traces and make mistake, you may depend I'll do more good than harm with the money I capture, even if it should not be legally my own."

Four days later the two had arrived at Dorking.

Jack had provided himself with a most efficient disguise.

His tall and well-developed, although youthful, figure suited the tight-fitting garb of the theatrical Mephistopheles to a nicety.

Ned was perfectly enraptured at his appearance, and declared that he could not possibly fail to strike terror into the guilty breast of his cousin, the false baronet, should they ever meet again.

Jack merely laughed, and said that that was an event which would assuredly come to pass sooner or later.

It was an easy task, in a place like Dorking, to ascertain which were the lands that belonged to the Dacres.

The first farm that Jack chose as the one for his maiden rent collection was at a small place called Newdigate.

Jack chose this for his first attempt, partly because of the isolated situation of the farm, and partly because the tenant bore a very evil reputation in the neighbourhood.

Our hero, it must be remembered, was at that romantic period of life when youth is apt to consider it is its duty to become as far as possible the protector of virtue and the avenger of injustice.

It was currently reported that the tenant in question, whom we will call Farmer Brown (all names in this veracious chronicle it must be understood are assumed) had possessed himself of the lease in an unlawful manner.

It was also said that his niece, Selina Brown, who was the rightful owner of the farm, was kept a prisoner somewhere within the walls of the solitary farmhouse.

Rumour also added that she was a maniac.

To one of Jack's ardent and romantic temperament this story was, as our readers may easily conjecture, a great inducement for him to make his first venture a call at Brown's farm.

Ned received strict injunctions to remain at the inn where they had taken up their abode, and to be ready to admit our hero without a moment's delay upon his return.

The night was a truly splendid one.

As Jack set out on his errand, an errand which might as a result land him in goal, he felt not one tittle of fear.

"Thrice armed is he who has hit cause aright," runs the old saying, and Jack certainly believed that he was perfectly justified in the course he was pursuing.

Modern moralists would doubtless differ; but we must remember what his early training had been, and make excuses accordingly.

He arrived at Brown's Farm, Newdigate, in due course.

Now came the most critical point in the career of Spring-Heeled Jack.

This was his first venture.

Failure meant ruin—ruin pure and simple.

If his wonderful contrivance refused to act in the manner in which it had acted at the rehearsal, what would be the result?

There could be but one answer to that question.

Capture, ruin to all his plans, and the infinite shame of a public trial.

But our hero had well weighed the odds and was quite prepared to face them.

Arrived at the farm he had no difficulty in finding out the window of the room in which Mr. Brown usually slept.

This window had been so clearly described to him by the Dorking people that there was no fear of Jack making a mistake.

With one spring he alighted on the broad, old-fashioned window-sill, and an instant later he had opened the casement.

The farmer was seated in a comfortable armchair in front of a large old-fashioned bureau.

He had evidently been counting his money and appropriating it in special portions for the payment perhaps of his landlord, his seed merchant, and so on.

The noise that Jack made as he opened the window caused the farmer to turn swiftly round.

Judge, if you can, his dismay when he found what kind of a visitor had made a call upon him.

On this, his first adventure in the garb of Spring-Heeled Jack, our hero had not called the aid of phosphorus into requisition.

His appearance, however, was well calculated to strike terror into the breast of any one.

Still more so, therefore, into the heart of one, who, like the farmer, was depriving his orphan niece of her legal rights, as well as of her liberty.

With a yell like that of a man in an epileptic fit, Farmer Brown sprang to his feet.

In another instant, however, he had sunk back again into his chair—rendered for the time hopelessly insane.

Jack, without any consideration of the amount which might or might not be due to the owner of the Dacre estates, calmly took possession of all the cash that he could find in the bureau, and then thought it was time to turn his attention to the alleged prisoner, Selina Brown.

Satisfying himself that the bureau contained no money save that which he had already secured, Jack was overjoyed at finding a document, hidden away in a corner of a pigeonhole.

This document bore upon it the superscription, "The last will and testament of Richard Brown, farmer."

In an instant our hero pieced together the story he had heard in Dorking, and arrived at the conclusion that the present Farmer Brown, although he had usurped his niece's position and concealed his brother's will, had at the same time, actuated by some strange fear, such as does occasionally possess criminals, dared not destroy the important document.

And here it was in Jack's hands.

There seemed no chance of immediate recovery by the farmer of his lost senses, so our hero coolly opened the document and read it through.

"As I thought," he muttered to himself.

"As I thought, the whole farm belongs to this girl, and this rascally uncle, one of the same kidney as my precious cousin, has simply swindled her out of her inheritance."

"However, I will see if I cannot manage to find her, and if I do, I think it will go hard if she does not recover her own again."

Then, taking up a pen, he selected a sheet of paper, and wrote upon it in bold characters,

Received of the tenant of Brown's Farm, Surrey, the sum of £120. And I hereby acknowledge that the above sum has been so received by me in payment of any rent now due for the said farm, or which may afterward accrue until such sum is exhausted.

(Signed) SPRING-HEELED JACK

N. B.—If this receipt is shown to Sir Michael Dacre, as he calls himself, its validity will be accepted without question, otherwise let him beware.

With a quiet chuckle Jack read this over to himself, then he laid it down in front of the jabbering lunatic, Farmer Brown.

"Now for the girl." Jack said, as he carefully put the will in one of the pockets of his capacious cloak.

The search for the girl did not take long.

The farmhouse was not a large one, and our hero's ears soon discovered a low moaning sound that evidently came from a garret which could only be approached by a rickety ladder.

In an instant Jack was at the top of the frail structure.

There, right in front of him, lay the object of his search.

She was a young and lovely girl about his own age.

Jack's heart gave one bound as he looked at her, then with a grateful sigh he said, fervently—

"Thank Heaven! I have come here. I take this as an augury that even if there is any wrong in the life I have chosen, I shall gain absolution for the evil by the good that will come out of it."

This philosophy was undoubtedly rather Jesuitical, but allowance must be made for the manner and place in which he had been brought up.

The girl seemed perfectly dazed when she saw Jack, but she betrayed not the slightest sign of fear.

She advanced toward our hero as far as a chain which was passed round her waist and fastened with a staple to the floor, would allow her, and with a child-like innocence, said—

"Ah! I know you, but I am not frightened at you. You have come to take me away from this. I do so long to see the green fields again. Take me away. I am not afraid of you."

For an instant and an instant only Jack hesitated.

His hesitation was only caused by his self-inquiry as to what course he had better pursue under the circumstances.

He soon made up his mind, however.

With Jack to think was to act.

He had heard that one Squire Popham, a local justice of the peace, had expressed strong doubts as to the right of the present Farmer Brown to hold the farm.

To this worthy man's house our hero determined to convey the lovely child whom we have called by the unromantic name of Selina Brown.

To remove the chain from the girl's waist was work of no little difficulty, but perseverance, as it usually does, conquered in the end, and half an hour later Jack had carried the girl to Squire Popham's house, where, with a furious ring at the bell, he had left her, having first chalked on the door of the mansion the following words—

"This girl is the daughter of the late Farmer Brown, of Newdigate. Her father's will is in her pocket. Her wretched uncle is a jabbering idiot at the farm. See that the girl enjoys her rights, or dread the vengeance of 'SPRING-HEELED JACK.'"

In another instant, and before the hall-door had opened to admit the half-unconscious girl, Jack gave one bound and disappeared from sight, and so for the time ended the first adventure of Spring-Heeled Jack.

Before we follow our hero any further on his extraordinary career we may as well finish the story of Farmer Brown and his niece.

When Squire Popham's footman opened the hall door he at first failed to see the girl so strangely rescued by Spring-Heeled Jack.

He, however, saw the chalk marks on the door, but was unable to read them—no extraordinary circumstance with a man of his class in the early part of the present century.

Then, turning round, he saw the poor girl.

There was a vacant look on her face that told the footman, untutored as he was, that she was "a button short," as he expressed it to himself.

The mysterious chalk marks and the "daft" girl were a little too much for the footman, and he hastened to call the butler.

This worthy could read, and as soon as he made his appearance, and had deciphered Jack's message, he directed his subordinate to call the squire.

When Mr. Popham, a typical country gentleman of the period, made his appearance, and read the inscription and saw the girl, his sympathies were immediately enlisted on her behalf.

"Confound Mr. Spring-Heeled Jack, whoever he may be, and his impudence, too!" cried the irate squire.

"Does he think that it requires threats to make an English magistrate see justice done?"

Then bidding the butler to call all the men servants together, he instructed the housekeeper to see after the welfare of the poor girl.

As soon as the men had assembled Mr. Popham read Spring-Heeled Jack's message to them, and then for the first time recollected that he had not secured the will.

He told one of the men to go to the housekeeper's room, and ask for the document which was in the girl's pocket.

During the man's brief absence the squire told the men what he intended doing, and that was to go over to Brown's farm, and, of the wording of the will proved Jack's tale was correct, to seize the unworthy uncle there and then, and clap him in the Dorking watch-house.

A hasty glance at the will soon informed Mr. Popham that Jack had not exaggerated the facts of the case.

"Now, my men," he said, "we will get over to Newgate at once. It is as I suspected. The present holder of Brown's farm has no more title to it than I have. Let us go and seize him at once. You have all been sworn in as constables, so we have the law entirely on our side."

We may inform our readers that this was commonly the case in those days, when the guardians of the peace were few and far between, and immeasurably inferior to our present police, both in intelligence and physique.

The journey took some three-quarters of an hour—a much longer time than had been occupied by our hero, in spite of the burden which he had to bear.

The squire ordered the butler to knock loudly at the door, and his commands were instantly obeyed.

After a brief interval—so short, in fact, that it proved that the inmates of the house were up and dressed in spite of the lateness of the hour—the door was opened by a frightened-looking old woman.

"Who is it? What do you want?" she asked.

"I am James Popham, one of his Majesty's justices of the peace, and I want to see your master. Where is he?"

"Please, sir, he is in his bedroom," answered the old woman. "He has had a fit, and has only just recovered. Hadn't you better wait till the morning?"

"What ho!" thundered the angry squire. "We come in the name of the law. Lead us to your master's chamber at once."

At this juncture a querulous voice somewhere in the distance was heard to ask what was the matter.

Mr. Popham answered the query in person, for, pushing the woman on one side, he hastily ascended the stairs, two steps at a time, until he came to the door of the room from which the voice had apparently come.

Throwing open the door, Mr. Popham strode into the room, followed by his men servants.

"Mr. Brown," said the squire, "I arrest you in the name of the king, for suppressing your brother's will, and keeping his daughter, your own niece, in captivity since that brother's death."

Farmer Brown literally shook with fear.

Jack's sudden appearance had temporarily turned his brain, and he had hardly recovered his senses when this new and terrible surprise awaited him.

"It is false," he faltered. "My brother left the farm to me."

"Then what about the girl?" asked the squire. "Even if your brother did leave the farm to you where is his daughter now? Produce her at once, or you may be put upon your trial for murder instead of the lighter offence with which I have charged you."

Mumbling a few indistinct words, and still trembling violently, the farmer led the way to the foot of the ladder leading to the room where his niece had been for so long a time imprisoned.

Here he paused, as if he did not care to go up the ladder himself.

"Go on," said the squire, sternly, "and bring the girl down without any further delay."

Very unwillingly, but compelled by the force of circumstances, the farmer made the ascent.

As he entered the room a loud yell of terror and astonishment burst from his lips.

"She's gone!" he cried, "that must have been the foul fiend himself who called on me tonight, and he has spirited the girl away with him"

"What do you mean?" asked the squire.

In a few words the thoroughly cowed and frightened farmer explained the occurrences of the night to the squire, winding up by giving a description of Spring-Heeled Jack's personal appearance.

"This is indeed strange," said Mr. Popham. "But if it will be any satisfaction to you I may tell you that your poor niece is safe at my house, and I have her father's will in my pocket. You are my prisoner, and my men will at once take you to the lock-up at Dorking."

The crest-fallen farmer could not frame an inquiry as to how his crimes had been brought to light, and in silence he allowed himself to be carried off to the watch house.

Farmer Brown was tried at the next assizes, found guilty, and sentenced to fourteen years' transportation, from which he never returned.

His niece through kind treatment eventually recovered her senses, and subsequently married and became the mother of a large family of children in the very farmhouse where she had been imprisoned in solitude until the light of reason had fled.

When Sir Michael Dacre's agent called at the farm when the rent became due, he found Squire Popham's people in possession, for that worthy man was not one to do things by halves, and he had made up his mind that his own farm bailiff should look after the interests of the poor girl until such time as she might recover her reason.

The agent was shown the receipt that Jack had given for the money.

That worthy was immensely puzzled, but seeing that there was nothing to be done save to take a copy of the receipt and return with it to Dacre Hall for further instructions, at once adopted that course.

When the baronet saw the receipt, and heard his agent's description of our hero—somewhat exaggerated, as such things are apt to be by passing from mouth to mouth—his rage knew no bounds.

Of course he instantly recognized in the hero of the adventure his cousin, Jack Dacre.

Instantly summoning Mr. Morgan to his presence, for the unctuous agent had not yet returned to India, the two fellow-conspirators had a consultation as to what had better be done under the circumstances.

"My opinion," said Alfred Morgan, "is that you must grin and bear it. If you take any steps to secure the lad's apprehension and he is brought to trial, there is likely to be such a stir made over it as may bring witnesses over from the East, who may—mind you I do not say they will—but who may oust you from Dacre Hall, the title, and the other property which you possess.

"You must recollect that your late cousin was immensely popular in India, and his son would find a host of friends there to take up his cause."

The baronet had made many hasty exclamations during the delivery of this speech, but Mr. Morgan would not allow himself to be interrupted, and calmly continued to the end.

When he had finished, the baronet broke out rapidly, "What do you intend to do, then? If the case is as you state, how do you intend to obtain possession of the plantations?"

"Oh! That's all right," coolly replied Morgan. "I care nothing for the barren honour of being called the owner of the Dacre plantations. I shall go back to India just as if I was acting for the rightful owner of the property—but with this important difference that the rents and profits of the plantations will go into the pockets of Mr. Alfred Morgan."

"Then you won't help me to get rid of this spawn?"

"What time I am in England is entirely at your disposal," said Morgan; "but you must remember that my employer's interests require that I should return to India as soon as possible to look after his plantations."

And the wily villain concluded with a horrible chuckle.

"What course would you propose, then?" asked Sir Michael.

"Well, I think if I were in your place I would call on each tenant and warn him that someone is collecting your rents in a peculiar and perfectly unauthorized manner. Tell them the story of Spring-Heeled

Jack at Brown's farm, but without disclosing your suspicions as to the identity of the depredator."

"Suspicions! Certainty, man," cried Sir Michael.

"Well, certainty, then," went on Morgan. "This will put them on their guard, and in the meantime you must wait and hope. If the boy continues this career much longer he is tolerably certain to get a stray bullet through his brains one of these days."

"I will start to-morrow," the baronet promptly said.

"And I will accompany you," said Alfred Morgan, with equal promptitude.

"Thank you, Morgan," replied Sir Michael. "I'll tell my man to go over to Arundel at once, and book two seats to London. We will go there first, as I have considerable property in the neighborhood of Hammersmith."

"Have you?" sneered Morgan, with special emphasis on the pronoun.

The baronet coloured and bit his lip; but he dared not reply.

This was not the first time by many that his chains had galled him, and he heartily wished that Morgan were back again in India, although he knew that he should feel awfully lonely when the agent went away.

To return to our hero, whom we left as he was hurrying away from Squire Popham's house on the night of the rescue of Selina Brown.

Jack reached home in safety, and found the faithful Ned Chump waiting up for him.

The sailor's astonishment was as unbounded as his admiration when Jack gave him the history of the evening's adventures and showed him the money.

"£120!" said Ned. "My stars! and you haven't been away three hours altogether. Why, we shall make our fortunes fast!"

"Ah! Ned, Ned, where are your conscientious scruples now? But, never fear, I do not want to get rich in this fashion. I merely want to obtain my own—and this, my maiden adventure, has been so successful that I feel certain I shall do so."

Ned, recollecting what he had said to our hero regarding the morality of their proposed course of life, looked rather sheepish, but he made no reply, and a little while later the two separated, and made their way to their respective couches.

In the morning Ned asked Jack what their next step was to be.

"I think we will go back to Arundel, and take up our quarters there for the present. From that place I shall be able to reconnoiter and find out what my precious cousin is about. And the very first opportunity that offers I will show him a sight that will raise the hair on his head."

"All right, sir," cheerfully replied the sailor.

In the comparatively short time that the two had been together, Ned Chump had had ample opportunity of finding out that he had enlisted under a captain who was pretty well sure to lead him ultimately to victory, and the tar had therefore fully made up his mind that under no circumstances would he attempt to question Jack's plans or schemes.

Arrived at Arundel, they took up their quarters at the Bridge House Hotel, and passed some time in comparative quietude.

Jack managed to keep himself well posted up in all relating to Dacre Hall and its usurping tenant.

This he was enabled to do by reason of a disguise which he had assumed.

No one would have recognized in the dashing young buck, apparently four or five and twenty years of age, the lad who had so lately been turned out of Dacre Hall as an illegitimate scion of the ancient house.

Ned had contrived to give himself something of the appearance of a gentleman's body servant or valet, and the two represented themselves to be a Mr. Turnbull, a young gentleman who had recently come into a fine property, and his servant, who had come down into Sussex to rest after a course of dissipation into which Mr. Turnbull had plunged on having come into his inheritance.

Jack, however, did not find out anything of importance for some days, and then, quite by accident, he made a discovery which promised to make an interview between Spring-Heeled Jack and Sir Michael Dacre a very easy matter.

This discovery was made under the following circumstances.

Our hero was standing one evening in the entrance hall of the hotel, passing an occasional remark to the farmers and others who passed in and out, when he saw one of the gigs from the Hall drive up.

Jack was on the alert in a moment.

The man who had driven the gig was one of the servants at Dacre Hall, who had shown a special liking for our hero, and this accidental encounter would give Jack an excellent opportunity of proving the strength or weakness of his disguise, even if nothing else came of it.

As the man descended from the gig and threw the reins to an attendant ostler, Jack advanced to the door of the hotel and met the servant from the Hall face to face.

The man looked at him full in the face, but not the slightest sign of recognition passed over his features.

Jack gave a quiet chuckle.

If this man who had shown him so many tokens of friendly feeling during his short sojourn at Dacre Hall failed to recognize him, surely he was perfectly safe from detection!

Not that Jack had anything to fear even if he was identified, but he felt that with such an adversary as he had in the person of Sir Michael Dacre, his only chance of success was to meet his cousin with his own weapons, and so long as he could preserve his incognito the chances were greatly in his favor.

But this chance encounter led to much greater results than the mere testing of the strength of his disguise.

As the man entered the hotel Jack turned round and followed him to the bar.

"I want to book two seats to London by to-morrow's coach," said the man.

"All right," was the reply; "inside or out, the box seat is already taken."

"Oh, inside," replied the servant. "Sir Michael does not care about outside traveling at this time of the year."

"Oh, then, Sir Michael is going up to town, is he?" asked the attendant.

"Yes," was the answer, "and the gentleman from India is going with him."

"Rather a strange time for him to go to town, isn't it?" asked the hotel official, with the usual curiosity of his class.

"Well, yes, it is; but I fancy there is something wrong with his rent collector, and I think he is going up to take his London rents himself."

"Oh! I see," said the attendant as he handed over the receipt; "I suppose you'll take your usual pint of October?"

The man smacked his lips with an affirmative gesture, and the liquor having been drawn and consumed, remounted his gig and took his departure. As soon as the gig had been driven off Jack turned to the barman and said—

"If my man comes in, tell him I have gone along the river toward Pulborough, and ask him to follow me as I want him particularly."

"Yes, sir," said the obsequious attendant, and Jack strolled out of the hotel.

As soon as he had left the inn he turned into the park, and made his way to a secluded nook.

This was a spot which had been chosen as a meeting place for Ned Chump and our hero.

They were precluded from intercourse at the hotel, as it would have seemed singular for a gentleman and his servant—no matter how confidential the latter might be—to have held much private converse at a place like the Bridge House Hotel.

This spot had therefore been chosen, and it had been arranged that when Jack left word that he had gone toward Pulborough, Ned was to make the best of his way to the cozy corner of the park, where our hero awaited his advent.

When Ned made his appearance Jack plunged into the middle of the question at once.

"Which way does the London coach go?"

"Through Brighton, sir," said that worthy, "and then straight along the London-road."

"If we went post from here after she had started could we get to London before she did!"

"Lor, yes," said Ned; "why, we could give her three hours' good start, and then get to London first."

"That's what we'll do, Ned," went on Jack; 'but say nothing about this until the coach has started. There will be plenty of time then to order the post-chaise, and there are some people going by the coach who might be suspicious if they heard of an intended trip to town."

"Yes, sir," replied Ned.

"Why, Ned, old fellow, have you no curiosity? I should have thought you would have been in a burning fever to know the meaning of this sudden change in my plans."

"So I am, sir."

"Then why not have asked? Surely you know I have every confidence in you?"

"Yes. I know that, skipper; and that's the very reason why I did not ask. I knew you would tell me all in good time.'

"All right, Ned," said our hero.

And he proceeded to inform the sailor of what he had overheard in the bar of the hotel.

"So," he went on, "we'll get to London first, track them from the coach to whatever hotel or house they may put up at, then we will dodge their movements well."

"But what good will this do?" asked Ned, who did not quite see how his young master was to benefit by this.

"Why, don't you see? As soon as my unworthy cousin has collected the rents he is bound to take coach again, either for Arundel or to some other place where my property lies."

"Yes, sir?" queried Ned.

"Well, I intend to stop that coach, and make my rascally cousin hand over to me the proceeds of his rent audit, and I think that will prove a very good haul."

Ned, now thoroughly enlightened, grinned and wished our hero good luck in his enterprise.

The two now parted, and did not meet again until nightfall.

In the morning Sir Michael and Morgan made their appearance in due course, and Jack surveyed the departure of the coach from an upper window.

He met his cousin's eye more than once, but the latter utterly failed to recognize in the dashing young man about town the lad he had virtually kicked out of his ancestral hall.

Alfred Morgan, however, favoured Jack with a prolonged stare, and our hero more than once fancied he was recognized, but whatever suspicion might have existed in his mind was allayed when he asked the guard—

"Who is that young spark at yonder window?"

"He's a young fellow just come in for a lot of money, and mighty free he is with it too, sir, I can tell you," replied the guard.

"What's his name?" asked Morgan.

"Mr. Turnbull, sir," said the guard, as he proceeded to adjust his horn for the final blast.

This answer, so coolly given, speedily quenched any latent spark of suspicion that might have existed in the agent's subtle brain.

The coach started on her journey.

Two hours and a-half later Jack and his faithful henchman were bowling along at a rapid pace in the direction of London.

Arrived at Croydon, they inquired whether the Arundel coach had passed, and were informed that it had not.

The last stage of their journey was therefore performed at a slightly reduced pace, and the post-chaise arrived at the coaching-house fully half-an-hour before the arrival of Sir Michael and Morgan.

This enabled Jack to order a private room, which he desired might look out into the yard into which the coach would be driven.

The two were shown to a room which most admirably suited the purpose of our hero.

When the coach arrived there was Jack, snugly ensconced within a dozen feet of the top of the coach, but perfectly invisible to anyone outside, while himself able to see and hear everything. The coach arrived.

Jack had no difficulty in ascertaining his cousin's destination in London; for, in an imperious voice, Sir Michael shouted—

"Get me a private coach at once, and tell the coachman to drive me to the Hummum's, Covent Garden, and look sharp about it."

This was his first visit to London since he had usurped the title, and he meant to make the most of his importance.

Bidding Ned follow, Jack swiftly descended the stairs, paid the score, and passed out into the streets.

Here he hailed a passing hackney coach, and arrived at the Hummum's some time before Sir Michael.

Jack engaged a couple of rooms, and then proceeded to make some slight changes in his disguise, so that Morgan might not recognize him as the man who had watched the departure of the Arundel coach that morning.

For the best part of a week Jack tracked his cousin with the persistency of a sleuth hound, until he felt convinced that the last batch of London rents was collected.

It was during this period that the supposed unearthly visitant first made his appearance in Hammersmith.

Although the newspapers of the time inform us that Jack committed many robberies, there is no doubt that this is incorrect.

All that he did was to visit each successive tenant after his cousin's departure, and ascertain from the terrified people how much money they had paid to the landlord.

*

There is no doubt that Jack caused an immense amount of harm by frightening servant-girls and children, and even people who ought to have known better; but we are not writing to justify Jack's conduct, but merely to extract as much from the diary or confession of Spring-Heeled Jack as will enable our readers to form some idea of what manner of man our hero was.

By these nocturnal visits on the Dacre tenants Jack soon found out how much money his cousin was likely to be taking home with him.

This sum was approximately £250.

A nice little haul for our hero if he could only land it.

During Jack's nightly absences the faithful Ned kept watch over the baronet and his friend.

One night on Jack's return Ned informed him that the baronet had sent the hotel boots to book two seats for the morrow's coach to Arundel.

"Then he is going straight home," said Jack. "Well, perhaps, it is better so. If he had been going further afield he might have banked the money. As it is, I know he will have it with him, and I'll stick him and the mail up somewhere in the neighborhood of Horley, or I'll acknowledge that Michael is right, and my name is not Jack Dacre."

The following morning Jack ordered a post chaise to proceed to Horley.

From thence, after discharging one passenger, Jack, it was to take the other one on to Worth, and there to await until "Mr. Turnbull" made his appearance.

This programme was carried out to the letter.

Jack got out at Horley.

The carriage rattled on.

Jack took up his position at a fork in the roads, where he could see the stagecoach some time before it would reach him, and at the same time be himself unseen.

In due course the coach came in sight.

Jack's heart beat nervously, but not with fear.

This was his first highway adventure, and who can wonder at his excitement!

In another instant the coach was upon him, and with a spring and a yell that threw the horses back upon their haunches, he rose in the air right over the top of the coach, passengers and all, shouting: "Hand out your money and your jewelry—I am SPRING-HEELED JACK."

The coachman in his terror threw himself upon the ground, and hid his face in the dust, as if he thought he could insure his safety by that course.

The guard discharged his huge blunderbuss harmlessly in the air, thereby adding tenfold to the agony of fear from which the coach-load of passengers were without exception suffering.

Having performed this deed of bravery, the guard took to his heels and speedily disappeared from sight.

Jack's tall, well-built figure, dressed in its weird garb, was one that could not fail to strike terror into the breasts of the startled travelers.

One by one they threw their purses and other valuables at Jack's feet.

Our hero received the tribute as though he had been an emperor.

When the last passenger had deposited his valuables in front of Jack, that worthy youth said, with a sardonic laugh: "Now you can all pick your money and jewelry up again, and return them to your pockets—all save Michael Dacre and Alfred Morgan."

In an instant the passengers sprang from the coach and collected their valuables, too utterly surprised by the turn events had taken to utter a word.

Sir Dacre looked at his confederate, and Morgan returned the look, but neither of them could force their lips to articulate a sound.

Jack stared steadily at his cousin through the two holes in his mask, and to the guilty man's fevered imagination they seemed to emit flashes of supernatural fire.

Pointing a long, claw-like finger at the would-be baronet, Jack said, in the most sepulchral tone he could assume—

"Beware, Michael Dacre; your cousin's last words to you shall be brought home to you with full force. From this day forth until you render up possession of the title and estates you have usurped, you shall not know one hour's peace of mind by reason of the dread you will feel at the appearance of Spring-Heeled Jack."

"Who I am matters not to you. My powers are unlimited, I can appear and disappear when and where I will."

Then turning to Alfred Morgan, he said—

"Ungrateful servant of one of the kindest masters that ever lived, your fate shall be one of such nameless horror, that, could you but foresee what that fate would be, you would put an end to your wretched career of crime by your own hand."

Then gathering up the money and jewelry belonging to the two conspirators, Jack said—

"Good-day, friends. A pleasant journey to you. Just to prove to you that I can disappear when I like, look at me now."

In another second Jack had indeed disappeared, leaving behind him, as more than one of the bewildered passengers subsequently averred, a strong sulphurous odour.

The mystery of our hero's disappearance on this occasion is not difficult to explain.

While waiting for the coach he had discovered a convenient chalk pit—no rare occurrence in that part of the country—and into this he had sprung after uttering his parting words, which were of course intended for Sir Michael and Morgan.

After Jack's departure the panic-stricken passengers endeavoured to rouse the coachman from his prostrate position on the dusty road.

But for some time their efforts were vain, the man had fainted from sheer fright.

The guard, too, had totally disappeared. What were they to do?

At last one of the passengers volunteered to drive, and placing the still insensible driver inside, the coach proceeded on its way to its destination.

All the inmates of the coach looked askance at the baronet and his companion.

They looked upon these two as the Jonahs of the expedition, and it would probably have gone hard with both of them had anyone simply have suggested their expulsion.

Sir Michael was not slow to perceive this, and at the next halting place he resolved to leave the coach.

This resolution he communicated to Morgan.

"But," said the agent, "we have no money. How shall we get on so far away from home?"

"Oh! That's all right," replied Sir Michael. "I am well enough known about here—and even if I were not," he continued, in a whisper, "I'd risk everything to get rid of these cursed people who heard the fearful words that spectral-looking being uttered."

Morgan was about to reply, but a warning "Hush!" from the baronet stopped him in time, for more than one of the occupants of the coach seemed to be listening intently to the conversation between the confederates, although it was carried on in very low tones.

The guilty pair took their departure from the coach at Balcombe much to the satisfaction of their fellow travellers.

Sir Michael directed the landlord of the inn to show them into a private room.

The command was at once obeyed, for Sir Michael had not exaggerated when he informed Morgan that he was well known in that part of the country.

As Mr. Michael Dacre, the agent to the large and valuable Dacre estates, he had been well known.

As Sir Michael Dacre, the present owner of those said estates, he was of course much more widely known.

That is to say that people who would not have recognised the agent sought by every means in their power to scrape acquaintance with the baronet.

Once within the private room, and left alone with his companion in crime, the baronet breathed a sigh of relief.

"Phew!" he said, "I almost dreaded to enter this room, for fear that imp of darkness might have been here before me."

Morgan gave forth a nervous little laugh, as much as to say that he had no fears upon the subject, but he could not control his features, and if ever fright and cowardice were depicted on a human face, they might have been discerned on the not too prepossessing countenance of Mr. Alfred Morgan, the some-time agent to the Dacre Plantations in India.

"What is there to laugh at?" growled Sir Michael. "I have lost some £260, two rings, a gold repeater, and a bunch of seals."

Our readers will remember that gold watch chains were seldom worn in those days, the watch being usually attached to a piece of silk ribbon from which depended a bunch of seals. The time-keeper, a little smaller than one of the American clocks of the present day, was placed in a fob pocket, and the ribbon and seals depended on the outside of the waistcoat or breeches as the case may be.

"And I," answered the agent, "am in quite as sorry a plight, for I have lost £60, all the money I had left in England, besides my watch and chain."

This chain being a magnificent piece of oriental gold carving which Morgan had absolutely "stolen" from Jack's father, and consequently from Jack himself.

"Well," cried Sir Michael, testily, "it's no use crying over spilt milk; and still less use for us to quarrel. I will be your banker until you can draw upon your Indian property."

"None of your sneer, Sir Michael Dacre," began the agent, angrily.

"Tut, tut! man, let's make a truce of it, and if we cannot continue friends, let us at least avoid any resemblance to open hostilities."

"All right," sulkily assented Morgan.

"It is our only chance," went on Sir Michael. "I don't know who or what in the fiend's name this Spring-Heeled Jack may be, but I must confess that my nerves are terribly shaken by the events that have occurred since I turned my illegitimate cousin out of Dacre Hall."

"Illegitimate?" said Alfred Morgan with a sneer.

"That this so-called Spring-Heeled Jack," continued the baronet, ignoring the interruption, "is not an ordinary highwayman is self-evident, or he would not have returned some hundreds of pounds in money, and as much more in jewelry, to our fellow passengers by the Arundel coach."

"And it is also equally certain," said Morgan, "that this stalwart man who can spring over the top of a mail-coach, horses, driver, passengers and all, cannot be that puny lad who laid claim to the Dacre title and lands."

"Then who can it be?" cried Dacre, half in despair. "It cannot be that sailor, Clump, or whatever his name was."

"Chump, my dear Sir Michael, Ned Chump!" rejoined Morgan, who could hardly repress his sneering manner. "No, I do not see how it could possibly be the sailor; but one thing is certain—and that is that this individual is acting on behalf of your cousin, and although I have too much sense to believe in the supernatural, the whole thing passes all comprehension. First this Spring-Heeled Jack—and, recollect, your cousin adopted that name out of your own—appears at Dorking, puts a half-lunatic girl back in the possession of her property, collects more than the rent due to you from Brown's farm, but at the same time leaves a strangely worded receipt, which prevents you from doing anything but grin and bear it."

"True," broke in Sir Michael, angrily.

"Then we hear that a supernatural being has appeared to your Hammersmith tenants in turn, and has put to one and all the identical question . . ."

"How much rent have you paid to Michael Dacre?"

"True again," replied Dacre.

"You will notice," said Morgan, with what was meant to be cutting irony, "the absence of the 'Sir' in the formula."

"Yes, yes, proceed," snarled the unhappy wretch.

"Then we take the coach on our way to your ancestral halls—and what happens? Why this mysterious being about whom we have heard so much, and about whom we know so little, stopped our coach in a manner hitherto unheard of, half frightened the driver to death, takes all the money and valuables the coach contains, then calmly returns each of the other passengers their property, only retaining for his own use that which belongs to Sir Michael Dacre, the present head of that proud house, and that which belongs to Mr. Alfred Morgan, at your service, the agent for the Dacre plantations in the East Indies."

"Well, and what do you suggest, Morgan?" said the pseudo-baronet, growing pale as the agent went on with his cool and matter-of-fact statement.

"Well," answered Morgan; "I hardly know at present what to suggest. To one thing, however, I have made up my mind."

"And that is?" queried Dacre, anxiously.

"To remain in England till this ghost is laid," replied Morgan.

The baronet gave a sigh of relief.

"Yes," the agent continued, "I am not going to run the risk of losing my hard-earned Indian estates—and that is what I feel sure I must ensue if I leave you to cope single-handed with the trio who are in league against you—maybe against me."

"Trio!" cried the baronet, faintly.

"Yes, trio! Jack Dacre, Ned Chump, and last, but not least, Spring-Heeled Jack."

To carry on our extraordinary story in a perfectly intelligible form it is necessary that we should leave the conspirators at the inn at Balcombe, and look out for our hero and his faithful comrade.

Jack, thanks to his ample cloak, had no difficulty in reaching the appointed place of meeting at Worth.

Ned Chump, who had been worrying himself into a state of nervous anxiety almost bordering upon madness, received our hero literally with open arms.

"How did you get on, sir?" asked the tar.

"Don't 'sir' me," replied Jack, banteringly.

"Well, then, skipper, if that will suit you."

"Oh, I got on prime, Ned," replied our hero, and he broke out into such a peal of laughter as astonished even Ned, who had already had many experiences of his young master's gaiety and exuberance of spirits.

Ned, as was his wont, remained silent, and Jack, who by this time perfectly understood his henchman's manner, went on to explain the events that had occurred since they had parted at Harley.

"And now," said Jack, "I will change myself into Mr. Turnbull again for a short time."

"Yes, skipper," said Ned, as he laid Jack's private clothes out for him.

"And then we will make for the Fox, at Balcombe, where the Arundel coach must have stopped after I had left it."

"Yes, sir," said Ned, in a matter-of-fact tone, as if his interest in the affair was a very minute one.

"If my surmise is correct," went on Jack, "Michael Dacre and the rascal Morgan will be resting there."

"Why so, skipper?" asked Ned.

"Because, after my word of warning, the passengers by the Arundel coach would not look with very favorable eyes upon those two arch conspirators, and I take it that they will have been only too glad to leave the coach at the first opportunity, and that must most undoubtedly be the Fox Inn."

"All right, skipper," replied the sailor. "I'm on."

By this time our hero had changed his clothes, or rather had put those belonging to the supposed Mr. Turnbull on over his Mephistophelian garb.

Some refreshments which had been previously ordered were now brought in, and after discussing these and settling the bill, Jack and his attendant left the house, the former telling the host that he might be back that way later on, but he was not quite sure, as if he met a friend of his at the Fox he might pass the night there, but, under any circumstances, he should return to Worth the following day, as his one object in coming there was to inspect the famous old church, the only object of general interest which the village possessed.

Jack had made this explanation as he did not want to carry his and Ned's luggage about with him on this reconnoitering expedition.

The landlord, only too pleased at the thought of seeing his liberal guest and his servant once again, gladly took charge of the travelling trunks, and Jack and Ned were soon far on their way toward the Fox.

Entering the inn, Jack called for two flagons of ale, and in paying for the same took good care to expose the contents of his purse.

The host's eye caught a glimpse of the gold pieces it contained, and he instantly made up his mind that our hero should leave some if not all of them behind him.

"Fine day, sir," said mine host, by way of opening a conversation.

"Very," replied Jack, who wanted nothing better.

"Have you come down here to attend the coming of age of Squire Thornhill's eldest son?" asked the innkeeper.

"No," replied Jack. "My servant and myself are on a walking tour. We have left our luggage at Worth, and have merely strolled over here to see if my friend, Lord Amberly, is staying here or in the neighbourhood."

"No, sir," said the now obtrusively obsequious host, quite won over by "my friend, Lord Amberly," added to the sight of the gold in Jack's purse.

"Lord Amberly is not staying here; but we are not quite devoid of quality, for Sir Michael Dacre, one of our county magistrates, and a friend of his are at this moment inmates of my house."

"Sir Michael Dacre?" queried Jack, suppressing his excitement. "Why his hall is not more than twenty miles from here is it, how comes he to be staying at an inn so near his own home?"

"Twenty-five miles, sir," said the landlord, correctingly, "and the reason that he is staying here is that the Arundel coach was stuck up by a strange sort of highwayman."

"A strange sort of highwayman?" said Jack, in tones of well-assumed surprise.

"Yes, sir, a strange sort of highwayman," replied the landlord.

And the worthy host proceeded to give Jack a highly embellished account of the attack upon the mail coach, adding, "And as this strange joker, who calls himself Spring-Heeled Jack, only robbed the baronet and his friend, the other passengers seemed to think as how they weren't much good, and so were glad to get rid of them, when they decided to stop here."

"And how do you know that they are any good?" asked Jack.

"Oh!" replied the loquacious landlord, "I knowed Sir Michael when he was the late baronet's agent—he's all right as far as I am concerned, whatever he may be to others."

"What do you mean?" said Jack, who had noticed something peculiar in the host's utterance of the last words.

"Oh! Nothing, sir. Nothing!" replied the man, evidently discovering for the first time that his tongue had been wagging a little too fast.

Collecting his somewhat discomposed faculties as quickly as he could, the landlord put the question to Jack once more, "Then you have not come here to see the grand doings at Thornhill Hall?"

"No," replied our hero, "I did not come with that purpose, but as my friend Lord Amberly is not here, I may as well stop until I hear from him, and in the meantime the Thornhill festivities will serve to prevent my getting the vapors. That is if you can accommodate my servant and myself with a bed."

"Yes, sir," said the landlord, with a bright twinkle in his eye, as he thought of the contents of our hero's purse, to say nothing of the prestige that would attach to his house if only Lord Amberly should turn up to meet his young friend.

"Yes, sir," he said, "that is if you do not mind occupying a double-bedded room."

Then he continued in an apologetic manner, "Sir Michael and his friend particularly stipulated for a double-bedded room sir, and indeed we have only one other in the house."

"Ha! Afraid to sleep alone," said Jack to himself; "but I think I'll take a still further rise out of them to-night."

Then turning to the landlord, he said, "Oh! A double bedded-room will suit me. We've been through too many adventures together to mind that, haven't we, Ned?"

"Yes, sir," replied the sailor with a suppressed chuckle.

With a fulsome bow the host ushered Jack and Ned to their apartments, indicating as he did so the one already occupied by the baronet and his friend.

Our hero ordered dinner for seven o'clock, and leaving Ned in the bedroom, proceeded down into the bar again.

Finishing his ale he strode out of the door and rapidly took in the geography of the house.

He had no difficulty in fixing the position of the baronet's room, and to his intense delight saw that the windows were mere frail casements of lead and glass, that hardly served to keep out the elements.

It was rapidly getting dusk, and re-entering the house Jack said to the landlord: "I'm going for a little stroll, give my man all he wants, and put the charges down to me, and mind my dinner is ready at seven."

The host humbly bowed his acquiescence, and Jack again left the house.

He had about an hour in hand before dinner, and it was absolutely necessary for the success of his scheme that he should be back punctually to time, and he had a lot to do in that single hour.

To return to the would-be baronet and his fellow conspirator, who were still seated in the private room.

With Spring-Heeled Jack's name upon his lips—for that was the only topic of conversation between the guilty men—the baronet rose to ring the bell for lights.

Even as he did so a crash of glass was heard, and the object of their fears stood before them in the middle of the room.

"Strip yourselves, both of you," cried Jack in fearful accents. "Strip yourselves to the skin. I told you I was ubiquitous—and I am here. Strip at once, or dread the dire vengeance of Spring-Heeled Jack!"

Too thoroughly frightened to ring the bell for assistance, Sir Michael and Morgan stood as if turned to stone, looking at the weird intruder into the privacy of their room.

Our hero found it difficult to restrain a smile, so ludicrous was the terror exhibited by his unworthy cousin and the agent.

But the faint ripple of enjoyment which passed over his face was not noticed by either of the conspirators.

Jack knew that he could not afford to waste a moment, even though the prolongation of his cousin's fright would have afforded him exquisite enjoyment.

"Strip yourselves," he therefore repeated, in still louder tones, "and quickly, too, or it will fare badly with both of you."

Sir Michael looked at his fellow conspirator, but, seeing nothing of an encouraging nature in his face, he commenced to take off his coat.

Morgan, accepting the inevitable, proceeded to follow the baronet's example.

Jack watched them closely, and every time one or the other of them paused he threatened them with horrible penalties if they dared delay any longer.

At last the two worthies stood in front of our hero as naked as they were when they first entered this world.

Bidding them roll their garments into a bundle Jack prepared to take his departure.

He unfastened what remained of the casement through which he had so unceremoniously made his way into the apartment, and threw the broken frames wide open.

When the clothes had been made into a rather unwieldy-looking parcel, Jack caught hold of it, and, placing it on his shoulder, sprang literally head over heels out of the window.

For some five minutes after Jack's departure neither of the naked men could move to call for assistance, so utterly cowed were they by the suddenness of the weird apparition's appearance.

Morgan was the first to recover anything like self-possession, and with an unearthly yell he sprang toward the bell-rope, and gave such frantic tugs at it that it very soon broke under his vigorous hand.

But he had succeeded in making noise enough to rouse the whole house, and a minute later the room was half-filled by the landlord and his servants and many of his customers.

"What is the matter, gentlemen?" asked Boniface.

"Matter, indeed!" cried Sir Michael, who had by this time somewhat recovered his normal faculties. "Matter enough I should think. That scoundrel who robbed the coach we came down by, has been here and has taken away all our clothes."

The titters and smiles that had been heard and seen among the domestics suddenly stopped.

Dim rumours had already reached Balcombe of the existence of Spring-Heeled Jack, and now here he was, or had just been, right in their midst.

A great terror seemed to have crept into the hearts of all of them, and none seemed inclined to stir.

"Someone of you rush after him," cried Dacre, angrily. "The bundle is a heavy one, and he cannot have got far with it."

But no one offered to start in pursuit.

"Confound it!" cried Morgan; "if one of you had had the sense to start off directly I summoned you the thief would have been caught by this time, or, at least, our clothes would have been recovered," he added, as the thought flashed through his brain that, perhaps, it would be well for his employer and himself if Jack were not caught.

"I don't think we could have done much good," said the landlord, rather nettled at the tone affairs were taking. "If this Spring-Heeled Jack, as you call him, is good enough to stick up and rob a coach-load of people, and is clever enough to come here and take the very clothes from off your backs, I don't quite see what chance I or any of my people would have against him even if one of us had started off immediately in pursuit."

The two sufferers, who had by this time entirely come to their senses, both immediately acknowledged that the landlord of the Fox was right.

Sir Michael, therefore, putting the best face on the matter that he could, said, "True, landlord, true; and now, like a good fellow, see if you cannot get us some clothes, anything like a fit. Our present garb is not a pleasant one."

And indeed it was not, for Sir Michael was clothed toga-wise in a large tablecloth, which he had thrown over his shoulders in haste while Morgan was ringing the bell, and Morgan himself had only been able to secure the hearth-rug, with which he had enveloped his body, so as to preserve some semblance of decency.

Ordering the crowd of frightened servants and guests to leave the room, the landlord turned to Sir Michael, when they were alone, and said—

"I trust, Sir Michael, that you and your friend will leave my house as speedily as possible. I have my living to get, and this sort of thing is calculated to give a house a bad name."

"Insolent scoundrel," began Dacre.

"No names, Sir Michael," answered the landlord. "I pay my rent and my brewers regularly. There has been no complaint made against the Fox since I have had it, and I do not fear anything that you can do to me. As to you yourself, the case is different."

"What do you mean?" angrily asked Dacre.

"What do I mean? Well, it is strange that this mysterious Spring-Heeled Jack should be always on your track. I have heard that he collected rents in your name at Dorking. Then you tell me that he robs you on the Arundel coach; and, by-the-bye, all the passengers by that coach put you down as the cause of the stoppage, and now you tell me that this mysterious being has entered your room by your window, some twenty feet from the ground, and, though you were two and he only one, he managed to strip and leave you as naked as you were when you were born."

Morgan nudged Dacre, and Jack's cousin had sense enough to see that there was no good to come by continuing the argument.

"Very well," Dacre replied, in a gruff manner. "Let us have what clothes you have, and we will leave your house the first thing in the morning. It is too late to think of going on to Dacre Hall tonight."

The landlord acquiesced in a sullen manner, muttering, "If Master Spring-Heeled Jack takes it into his head to return here before the morning out you shall both turn, no matter what the time or the weather may be."

With this Boniface left the room.

"This is getting serious," said Morgan, as soon as he was left alone with the baronet.

"Serious, indeed," said Dacre, testily. "I fully believe, Morgan, that the foul thing's threats will come true, and that he will make our lives a curse to us."

"What can we do in the matter?" asked Morgan. "Can you not suggest something? Recollect what you have gained by denying your cousin's legitimacy, and pull yourself together and let us see what had better be done, under the circumstances."

"Better be done, forsooth," said Sir Michael. "How can we arrange to do anything when we do not know whether our adversary is mortal or not. If he is mortal we dare not lock him up, as he evidently knows the secret of the Dacre succession; and if he is not mortal, of what I avail our struggles against him?"

"Not mortal, pshaw!" replied Morgan.

"The man's mortal enough, though there is something mysterious about him, I'll allow. We'll provide ourselves with a pair of pistols, and when next we are favored by a visit we will test with half an ounce of lead whether Spring-Heeled Jack is mortal or not."

As the agent concluded, a wild, wailing shriek, ending in a peal of demoniacal laughter, struck upon their ears, and, rushing to the window, they beheld, standing on the top of the pump in front of the Inn, the awful figure of their hated foe.

With another unearthly scream Jack turned a somersault from the top of the pump, and long ere any of the inmates of the inn who had heard the taunting laugh had time to pass out of doors, Spring-Heeled Jack had disappeared, the gathering gloom leaving no trace behind.

Ten minutes later, and "Mr. Turnbull," looking as cool and calm as it is possible for a young English gentleman to look, returned to the Fox, and as he called for a glass of sherry and bitters he asked if his dinner was ready.

With a thousand apologies the landlord explained to him that, owing to the state of excitement into which the whole house had been thrown by the appearance of Spring-Heeled Jack, the dinner was not quite ready.

Jack, of course, asked for particulars, and the garrulous host gave the chief actor such a highly embellished narrative of what had actually occurred, that our hero absolutely suffered in his endeavor to keep from laughing.

He succeeded, however, and bidding the landlord hasten the dinner as much as possible, he entered the room reserved for himself and Ned Chump.

Here he found his faithful follower, and that jolly salt broke into a peal of uncontrollable laughter as Jack narrated the story of the last hour's adventure, winding up the tale by explaining that he had quietly dropped the bundle of clothes down a neighboring disused well.

In the meantime a very dissimilar scene was being enacted in the room occupied by Sir Michael Dacre and Alfred Morgan.

Both of the conspirators felt dissatisfied.

Morgan inwardly accused Dacre of cowardice, and felt certain that eventually John Dacre would gain his own.

The usurping baronet, on the other hand, blamed Morgan for all the ills and evils that had arisen.

The two passed the night somehow, but it is comparatively certain that neither of them enjoyed even one half-hour's sleep.

Our hero and his henchman, on the contrary, partook of a capital dinner, smoked and drank and enjoyed themselves, and then slept the sleep of the just.

In the morning, much to the delight of the landlord of the Fox, Sir Michael Dacre and Alfred Morgan took their departure from the inn.

Our hero and Ned Chump, who had been informed that they were about to leave, had secured a position from which they could obtain a good view of the two disconsolate men.

And a pretty pair of beauties they looked.

Sir Michael was attired in a suit of clothes belonging to the landlord, and which was almost large enough to have accommodated his companion in crime as well as himself.

Morgan's borrowed suit fitted him a little better, but as the original owner occupied the position of ostler, gardener, and general factotum, it may easily be imagined that the garments were not particularly becoming.

"Well, skipper," cried Ned, as the post-chaise drove off, "no disrespect to you, but a more ugly, hang-dog fellow than your cousin I never. saw; he looks well enough when he is dressed spick and span, but now he looks what he really is."

And Jack could not dissent, for it would have been difficult to find a more despicable-looking man than the mock baronet decked in the innkeeper's clothes.

Jack thought it advisable to stop at the Fox for another night, and then sent over to Worth for the luggage.

"Not the slightest suspicion had been aroused in anyone's mind that this sedate Mr. Turnbull had had anything to do with the stoppage of the Arundel coach or the robbery of the clothes of the two guests at the Fox Inn."

Jack and Ned left a very pleasant impression behind them when they took their departure for Arundel.

Our hero had resolved to make the Bridge House his headquarters, as he had had such a remarkable piece of luck there already.

For was it not owing to what he had heard while staying there that he was enabled to relieve his cousin and Mr. Alfred Morgan of their superfluous cash?

If our hero had known what important results his resolve to go back to the hotel at Arundel would have, he would have literally danced for joy.

This visit to Arundel led to an adventure which introduced him to his future wife, and we may safely say that hardly ever was man blessed with such a helpmate as was the wife of Spring-Heeled Jack.

The manner of our hero's introduction to his future wife was as follows.

The day after the arrival of Jack Dacre and Ned at the hotel a carriage drawn by four horses drove up to the inn door.

The occupants were an old gentleman and lady, apparently his wife; in addition there were two younger women, one might have been a servant or companion, the other was evidently the daughter of the old gentleman, so great was the likeness between the two.

Jack was lounging about in front of the hotel when the carriage drove up, and a strange but almost indescribable thrill passed through his whole body at the sight of the girl we have just alluded to.

People may laugh at love at first sight, but in the case of Jack Dacre it was an undoubted fact.

Our hero pressed forward to get a better view of the young lady who had made such a strange impression upon his ardent imagination, and as he did so he had the satisfaction of hearing the old gentleman say to the host that he intended to pass the night in the house if beds were available.

Mine host informed the traveller that there was plenty of room, and to Jack's intense delight the party entered the hotel.

"Hang it!" said Jack to himself. "She's a stunner, and no mistake. Now, how can I contrive to get an introduction to her? I wonder whether the old gentleman will go to sleep after dinner, and if she will go for a walk? I must keep my eyes open, and chance may befriend me."

And chance did indeed befriend Jack, for after the old gentleman and his family had dined, the young lady and her companion (for such the third female of the party turned out to be) started off for a walk.

Jack, affecting a nonchalance which he was far from feeling, sauntered out after them, keeping, however, at a respectful distance.

The two girls made their way down to the side of the river Arun, and choosing a quiet spot looked about for a seat.

A few yards further on they spied a tree, a large branch of which stretched right across the towing-path till it reached nearly half way across the river.

Surely no more delightful seat could have been devised.

The two girls at once proceeded to take advantage of this charming resting-place.

Jack ensconced himself close by, just out of hearing, but where he could see every movement they made.

Once the two girls had made themselves comfortable a very animated conversation seemed to commence between them; then suddenly, whether by accident or design Jack did not at the time know, the companion placed her hand on the young lady's shoulder, and an instant later the only girl who had ever found her way to Jack's heart was being rapidly carried toward the sea in the swirling waters of the Arun.

Without waiting to see what became of the girl who had caused the catastrophe, Jack threw off his coat and sprang into the water.

Strong and steady was his stroke, and the girl had only just come to the surface for the first time when our hero was beside her.

One minute later and she was on shore, and Jack had the supreme satisfaction of seeing the rich glowing tint of life return to her pallid cheeks.

She opened her eyes and stared at Jack in wonder.

"Where is my maid, Ellen Clarke?" she asked, as she glanced hastily around.

"I don't know," answered Jack. "I was so anxious to be of service to you that I did not see what became of her. And, what is more, I don't think you need care much, for it certainly seemed to me that but for her you would not have been subjected to such a ducking. But come, let me carry you to the hotel. The sooner you get out of those wet clothes the better."

And without waiting for a reply Jack caught her in his arms and started off toward the hotel with her at a gentle trot.

To his sturdy young frame such a burden counted next to nothing.

Jack could see by the look half of terror and half of curiosity in her face that there was something to be accounted for in the manner in which she had fallen into the river; but he wisely refrained from worrying her with any questions at the moment.

Before Jack reached the hotel with his fair burden they met the maid, accompanied by three or four of the hotel attendants, making their way toward the river.

The maid's face flushed crimson, and then as suddenly paled, as she caught sight of Jack and her young mistress.

Our hero's quick, shrewd glance marked her manner, and he had no need to ask any question.

Whatever might have been her motive, beyond all doubt the companion had pushed her mistress into the river.

Young Dacre had gone through so much since his inopportune arrival in England that he had acquired an amount of worldly wisdom far beyond his years.

He, therefore, wisely held his tongue, and did not tell the girl that he had seen the "accident" and its cause.

The companion recovered her self-composure in a moment when she found that Jack did not accuse her of attempting to murder her mistress.

"Oh! Miss Lucy," she cried. "Thank Heaven you are saved. I should never have forgiven myself had you been drowned. It was my fault that you fell in. I must have leant too heavily on your shoulder, and caused you to lose your balance."

These last few words were accompanied by a swift, sly glance at our hero.

Although Jack caught the look he took no notice of it, but simply strode on towards the Bridge House.

Surrendering his charge to her father, he proceeded upstairs to change his clothes.

While so engaged a knock was heard at the door, and a waiter handed in a card on which was written, "Major-General Sir Charles Grahame will be pleased to see the savior of his child at the earliest opportunity."

Our hero with a bright smile told the man that he would wait upon the general immediately, and he was vain enough to take a little extra care over brushing his hair, and so on, in case he should have the felicity of seeing the lovely girl whom he had just rescued from a watery grave.

Finding his way to the general's room, Jack's courage nearly deserted him.

He who had shown so much daring in endeavoring to checkmate his rascally cousin, felt as nervous as a young girl at her first ball, at the idea of meeting the lovely creature who had made such an impression upon him.

But his nervousness was entirely unnecessary, for on entering the room he found it tenanted by the general and a lady who was certainly some dozen years older than the charming girl he hoped and yet feared to see.

"Permit me to present to you my wife, Lady Grahame, Mr.—," said the general with a pause.

"Turnbull, sir, Jack Turnbull, at your service," replied our hero with a guilty blush, for he absolutely hated himself at that moment for the deception, innocent as it was, that he was practicing on the father of the girl with whom he had so madly and so unaccountably fallen in love.

The formality of introduction having been gone through, the general, who had noticed the flush on Jack's cheek, but who had attributed it to a far different cause, endeavoured to place Jack entirely at his ease.

Thanking our hero cordially, but not fulsomely, for having saved his daughter's life, the general wound up by saying, "But Lucy shall thank you herself in the morning."

"Then she is in no danger?" asked Jack.

"Oh! dear no," replied the general. "The doctor has seen her, and he says that it wants nothing but a good night's rest to put her right."

The lady had not spoken until now, having merely curtseyed when Jack was presented to her, but now she seemed compelled to say something, and, smiling in a manner that caused our hero to shudder, she said, "Oh! Yes, my dear daughter shall thank you herself in the morning, Mr. Turnbull."

"Your daughter?" said Jack, in accents of surprise, for the general's wife could not, by any possibility, have been the mother of the fair girl he had saved.

"Well, my stepdaughter," she said, with a self-satisfied smirk, for she took Jack's exclamation of surprise as a compliment.

After a few more words our hero returned to his own room, and gave Ned an account of his adventure, winding up the story by saying, "And I cannot help thinking that Lady Grahame and the companion have leagued together to destroy that lovely girl's life."

"Monstrous!" cried Ned.

"Yes, monstrous, indeed. But I will spoil their little game. I shall keep close watch upon them, and if I find them in conversation together tonight I will treat them to a view of Spring-Heeled Jack, and in their terror find an opportunity of extracting a confession from one or both of them."

Our hero speedily changed his attire for his demoniacal garb, and, wrapping himself in his huge cloak, he passed down the stairs, and left the hotel without attracting any undue attention.

It was now quite dark, and, making his way round to the back of the house, where the general's suite of rooms was situated, Jack with one spring landed in the balcony which ran round that side of the house.

He looked in at the first window he came to, and the only occupant of the room was the old general, who was taking an after-dinner nap.

The next room he passed he did not look through the window. Something subtle seemed to tell him that this was where his loved one lay at rest.

But at the next window he paused and listened.

The words that fell upon his ears literally burnt themselves into his brain.

"Heavens!" he cried; "I am only just in time."

Another instant, and the occupants of the room, Lady Grahame and Ellen Clarke, beheld standing before them the terrible figure of Spring-Heeled Jack.

"Ha! ha!" cried Jack. "Your intended crime is such a monstrous one, that even I, Spring-Heeled Jack, fiend though I may be, am bound to prevent its consummation."

Only one of the two women heard these words, for Ellen Clarke had fainted at the appearance of the fearful apparition.

Lady Grahame was possessed of stronger nerves, or she would never have been able to plan the death of her lovely and innocent stepdaughter.

For that was the purport of the conversation which Jack had overheard whilst standing outside the window.

It appeared that the whole of General Grahame's private fortune must pass, by the provisions of his father's will, to Lucy Grahame, but if she died before the general, then he would have absolute control over the property and could leave it to whomsoever he pleased.

Lady Grahame had argued to herself that if she could but remove Lucy from her path she could easily work upon the general to make a will in her sole favor.

This once accomplished how easy it would be to rid herself of her elderly husband, and with the wealth that would then be at her disposal she would easily be able to marry a younger and handsomer man, and spend the rest of her days in riotous luxury and dissipation—for such was the bent of her mind, and the general's quiet mode of life did not at all meet her views.

All this Jack had been able to gather whilst standing in the balcony before the window of Lady Grahame's chamber.

No wonder, then, that the sudden appearance of Jack in the midst of such a conversation should have sent the lady's maid into a fainting fit.

Upon the hardened Lady Grahame, however, his appearance produced no outward appearance of fear.

What amount of trepidation was at her heart Heaven alone could tell.

She stood erect and looked Jack dauntlessly in the face.

"I fear not fiend nor man," she cried; "the former I doubt the existence of, therefore you must be the latter. So name your price, Spring-Heeled Jack, I will pay it whatever it is, and trust to your honour to hold your tongue when you have received it."

Jack gave a demoniacal grin.

"Not that you could do me any harm by repeating the words that you have doubtless overheard," she went on.

Again Jack smiled his fearful smile.

"Who would take the word of a highwayman and midnight thief against that of Lady Grahame?" she cried, defiantly, now thoroughly convinced that she did stand in some amount of danger at the hands of this extraordinary being.

Jack made no reply, but seizing her by the wrist drew her toward the chamber door.

Vainly she struggled, Jack's powerful grasp bound her too fast for any chance of escape.

Surely but slowly she felt herself approaching the door that would lead her straight into the presence of her husband.

She was about to offer Jack money once more, though she felt certain from his manner that it would be of no avail, when the door suddenly opened and the general stood in the doorway.

With a startled look he took in the whole scene.

Ere he had time to inquire the meaning of the strange drama being enacted before his very eyes Jack had released his hold upon Lady Grahame's wrist, and bowing gravely to the general, said, "Pardon this intrusion, Sir Charles Grahame."

The baronet started slightly as he heard his name mentioned, but said nothing.

"Pardon this intrusion; but I am here on a very serious mission, and I must kindly ask you to answer any questions which I may put to you."

Again the baronet bowed, for he was strangely impressed by Jack's manner, and felt that our hero's presence in that room was caused by no sinister motive.

"Go on, mysterious being; whatever you may be, go on, and anything consistent with honour I will tell you."

"You have a daughter, Lucy?" said Jack.

"I have," answered Sir Charles.

"By the terms of your father's will she is entitled to the whole of your estates at your death, and you cannot alter it?"

"By the terms of the entail of the Grahame estate, which are bound to descend to the eldest daughter in the absence of male issue, Lucy is irrevocably entitled to my estates at my death; all that I have power over is any money which I may have saved."

The baronet answered freely and fully, for he was more than ever confident now that Jack was here for the good of himself and his daughter.

"If she died before you it would be in your power to dispose of the property as you chose?" asked Jack.

"Yes, for the entail would cease then. We two, my daughter and I, are the only living representatives of our branch of the Grahames, and the time-honored baronetcy must die with me."

"Then let me tell you," cried Jack, rising to his full height and pointing his long claw-like finger at the still defiant, although silent, Lady Grahame. "Let me tell you that I have heard this night a plot—a plot so fiend-like that I cannot doubt but that you will feel incredulous at first, but a plot the existence of which you are bound eventually to believe."

"Go on, for Heaven's sake!" cried the baronet, hoarsely.

"At any rate," said Jack, "whether you believe my words or not I shall have the satisfaction of knowing that I have saved your lovely daughter's life; for after hearing what I am going to tell you, doubt it as you may, you will be put upon your guard, and that will be quite sufficient."

At the mention of his daughter's name the baronet gave a gasp, but he could not articulate the words he desired to.

Briefly but impressively Jack told the baronet how he had witnessed the attempted murder on the Arun, of course concealing his identity with Jack Turnbull.

Lady Grahame now for the first time spoke.

"Why listen to this midnight thief?" cried she.

"Silence!" thundered Jack.

Then turning to the baronet he explained that his suspicions being aroused he had listened outside the window, and he repeated word by word the conversation he had overheard between Lady Grahame and Ellen Clarke.

Horror, doubt, and uncertainty were expressed on the baronet's face as Lady Grahame vehemently denied the charge, showering every kind of vituperation upon the head of Spring-Heeled Jack.

Our hero stood motionless, the satanic grin on his face.

He knew full well that whether the old soldier believed his story or not, Lucy's life was at least safe from the machinations of her murderous stepmother.

Before the baronet had time to open his lips to reply to his wife, a fresh voice broke upon his ear.

The girl Ellen Clarke had recovered her senses, and had thrown herself upon her knees at the feet of the general.

"Oh! Forgive me, Sir Charles," cried the girl, as she groveled on the ground in front of the astonished baronet. "It is all true; but I was sorely tempted by Lady Grahame, who had me in her power, as I had once stolen a diamond ring belonging to her, and she threatened me with imprisonment if I did not comply with her request, or rather commands. Pray—pray forgive me."

The poor old man, who had faced the enemy on many a well-fought field, thoroughly broke down at this, and agonizing sobs thrilled his manly chest.

Lady Grahame stood pale and silent.

She knew the game was up.

She had played her last card, and had lost.

Well, she must accept the inevitable.

She had not much fear of any earthly punishment for her meditated crime.

She knew full well that Sir Charles's keen sense of honour would never permit him to blazon his shame abroad.

For shame it would be for one who bore the honoured name of Grahame to stand at a criminal bar, charged with conspiracy and attempt to murder a step-daughter.

Jack surveyed the scene for a moment in silence.

Then he moved toward the window.

Turning to the baronet, he said, "My work is done; I have saved your daughter's life; with the punishment you may mete out to these two wretched women I have nothing to do. Farewell!"

"Stay!" cried the baronet, recovering his self-possession, after a struggle. "Who are you, mysterious man? At least let me thank you for my child's life."

"I want no thanks," said Jack; "and as to who I am that I cannot at present tell, for there are reasons why my identity should be concealed. Someday, perhaps, I may present myself to you in proper person."

"But how shall I know that whoever presents himself to me is really yourself?" asked Sir Charles.

"Give me your signet ring," said Jack; "and rest assured that whoever hands it back to you will be Spring-Heeled Jack in person."

The general at once complied, and endeavored to shake Jack by the hand, but our hero dexterously contrived to wrench it away just as he received the ring.

"No, Sir Charles," said he; "I cannot shake you or any honest man by the hand just now. A time may come—nay, it shall come—when I can do so. Till then, farewell!"

Another instant and Jack had left the room as suddenly as he had entered it.

We will leave the two guilty women and the baronet together for the present, and follow Jack.

Taking his cloak from the balcony, where he had placed it, our hero pulled it closely round him, and, with a spring, alighted on Mother Earth once more.

Hastening round to the front of the hotel, he ordered some brandy to be sent to his room, and calling to Ned, who was in one of the side bars, used as a tap, Jack proceeded to his own room.

Ned Chump followed immediately afterwards, and our hero soon put him in possession of the extraordinary event of the last hour.

"Well, Ned," said he, "I shall commence direct and final operations at once. I have just about time to reach Dacre Hall a couple of hours before daylight."

"Dacre Hall!" cried the astounded salt. "Why, does your honour recollect how far it is?"

"Yes, perfectly," was the reply.

Ned, seeing that his master had made up his mind thoroughly for the adventure, did not further attempt to dissuade him from it.

"I have reckoned the distance," then went on Jack, "and I have ample time to perform all that I intend to do long before the sun peeps above the horizon. Meanwhile give me a glass of that brandy which the waiter has just brought in, and put the rest in my flask. I shall probably have need of it ere my return. In case I am not back till late in the day, which might make my absence noticed, you had better tell the landlord in the morning that I am slightly indisposed, and you can order my meals to be brought to my room just as if I really was confined to my bed."

"But how about your return? How will you get in?"

"Ha! ha!" laughed Jack. "Why, Ned, you have only to leave the casement of the bedroom wide open, and when I come back surely I can vault on the sill, and so make my entry without being seen."

"Well, you are a wonder, skipper, you are a wonder. Talk about what's his name, Baron—Baron—"

"Munchausen," put in our hero.

"Yes, skipper, that's the name, but I cannot pronounce it. But talk about he, why, nothing that he wrote about is half so wonderful as what you have already done, let alone what you are going to do."

"Well, good-bye for the present, Ned, I must be off now."

And shaking Ned warmly by the hand the sailor said—

"And may all good luck follow you."

Jack sprang lightly from the casement window, and a quarter of an hour later was considerably over a mile on his way to Dacre Hall, so rapid was the pace at which he was proceeding.

Ned's wondering admiration at his master's powers and good generalship was in no way misplaced, for even while the conversation just narrated was taking place, Jack had packed the garments usually worn by Mr. Turnbull into a compact parcel which he attached by a hook to the lining of his capacious cloak.

This he had done because he knew that after his mission at Dacre Hall was performed some hours must elapse before he could regain his quarters at the Bridge House Hotel, Arundel.

By taking the plain clothes with him he could make everything safe.

All he had to do was to deposit the bundle in some convenient nook, and then, when his mission was accomplished, he could regain possession of the clothes, and, by placing them over his tight-fitting disguise, and removing his mask and other facial disfigurements, he could speedily transform himself from Spring-Heeled Jack into Jack Turnbull.

In the garb of that young gentleman, and with the cloak slung over his arm, he could go anywhere he pleased during the time which must elapse ere he could return to his hotel.

About a mile from Dacre Hall he met with the only adventure which befell him on his midnight journey.

He heard, apparently some little way in front of him, the sound of a horse's hoofs quietly ambling along the road.

Jack thought to himself, "That's a farmer going to Lewes market, I'll be bound. Shall I give him a fright, or not?"

Our readers must recollect that Jack was young, and blessed with health and excellent spirits (or he could never have fought against fate as he did), so they will, undoubtedly, excuse the temptation which passed through his mind to frighten the approaching traveller, be he farmer or be he squire.

But ere he had made up his mind whether he should play one of his practical jokes or not, he heard a loud voice cry—

"Stand and deliver!"

This was by no means an uncommon cry in those days, but it was the first time that our hero had had the pleasure of beholding a real live highwayman, so he pushed rapidly along the road until a bend in it revealed a strange spectacle.

An apparently well-to-do farmer, on a smart and sleek-looking cob, was in the middle of the road.

At the side, where a retired lane branched off, stood what seemed to Jack one of the grandest sights he had ever beheld.

The sight in question was worthy of the pencil of Frith, whose picture of Claude Duval, the highwayman, dancing a coranto with a lady in Hounslow Heath, is doubtless well known to most of our readers.

One of the grandest thoroughbreds Jack had ever seen stood motionless at the mouth of the lane, from the ambuscade of which it had evidently just emerged.

Mounted on the back of this magnificent charger was a man who might have stood as model for the greatest sculptor the world ever produced.

His whole form, save his lips, was as motionless as that of the noble animal he bestrode.

His dress was picturesque in the extreme.

He had eschewed the orthodox scarlet, save that in his three-cornered hat he wore the bright red feather of a flamingo.

His tunic, however, was of a beautiful blue, relieved here and there with silver.

His white buckskin breeches, and his well-blacked boots, rising far above his knees, stood out sharply and well-defined in the cold glare of the moon.

His right arm was pointed straight at the head of the unhappy-looking farmer, and that right arm ended in a hand containing a handsomely mounted pistol.

"Good Mr. Highwayman, spare me! I have but little money about me, and that I am going to take over to my landlord's agent, who threatens to turn me out of my farm unless I pay him something by eight o'clock in the morning, and I have now only just got time to get to his house by that hour."

"Liar!" thundered the highwayman. "I know you are loaded with money, for you are off to Lewes market to buy cattle. Hand over your money, or you are a dead man."

Here was an opportunity for our hero's practical joke, too good to be resisted.

He grasped the situation in an instant, and ere the highwayman had time to fire his pistol, or the farmer to produce his cash, Spring-Heeled Jack, with an awful cry, sprang in the air clean over the heads of the highwayman and his destined victim.

It would be utterly impossible to find words to describe Jack's appearance as he went over the heads of the two horsemen.

The rapidity of his flight in the air distended the flaps of his coat, until they resembled a pair of wings.

His peculiar costume, fitting so tightly to his skin, made him look like a huge bat, with a body of brilliant scarlet.

With a yell of fear from the farmer, and a screech of unearthly sound from the animal he bestrode, horse and rider disappeared along the road to Lewes.

The highwayman on the other hand did not stir, and as well trained was his beautiful steed, that although it trembled with fear for an instant, it did not attempt to bolt as the farmer's horse had done.

As Jack touched the ground again the highwayman took aim at our hero and fired.

The part which he had intended to hit was Jack's forehead, and had the forehead have been where it was apparently situated, the bullet must have gone crashing straight through our hero's skull.

As it was, however, Jack's mask was so constructed as to make his face look about two inches longer than it really was.

This two inches of added matter formed the supposed cranium through which the highwayman's bullet had sped.

With another shriek more supernatural than the first Jack wheeled round, and sprang once more over his adversary's head.

This was too much even for the highwayman, who up till now had not known what fear was.

He had watched the track of his bullet clean through the uncanny-looking being's brain, and felt that it would be impossible to cope with an enemy possessing such extraordinary if not unearthly attributes.

Digging his spurs right up to the hilt in his steed's sides, he lifted the reins, and just as our hero gave a loud mocking laugh of defiance, and waved his plumed cap in the air, the highwayman gave his horse a cut, and leaping the hedge at the roadside, the noble steed and its rider were soon lost to view.

"Well, that was a lark," said Jack to himself as he rapidly strode on in the direction of Dacre Hall; "but it was a close shave, though, for I felt that bullet graze the top of my scalp in a most decidedly unpleasant manner."

Half an hour later, and he was at the lodge-gates of his ancestral home.

Everything now depended upon his caution, and Jack was resolved that no fault of his should mar the performance of his plans.

He knew the room which had been allotted to Morgan when he first took up his abode at the Hall, but still that room might have been changed, and it would have been fatal to our hero's scheme to have made a mistake on that score.

The only thing, therefore, was to rouse up the lodge-keeper, and find from him in his certain fright the position of the room occupied by Mr. Alfred Morgan.

The lodge consisted of only two rooms—one up and one downstairs.

In the former Jack knew that the lodge-keeper slept.

There was a stone balustrade outside the window of the bedroom, and on to this Jack lightly sprang.

To open the casement was an easy task.

This done, Jack cried out, in sepulchral tones, "Awake, awake, awake! Old man, awake!"

The lodge-keeper woke with a start, but he was not so frightened as Jack had expected him to be.

The fact of the matter was, Michael Dacre was not at all popular with the servants, and they had heard with some amount of delight of the various adventures he and Morgan had had with Jack.

"Good Mr. Spring-Heeled Jack," cried the lodge-keeper, "what do you want? If it is anything I can do for you tell me, and consider it done."

"I merely want to know in which room Mr. Morgan sleeps," replied Jack, highly delighted at the turn things had taken.

"In the blue room, sir," answered the lodge-keeper.

"Can I trust you not to raise an alarm for an hour or so? I have important business with Mr. Alfred Morgan, but shall not trouble your master."

"Aye, Mr. Spring-Heeled Jack, that you can," he said; "and if you can only frighten him out of this place you will earn the thanks of the whole household."

The man's tone was so self-evidently sincere that Jack, with a farewell warning, sprang to the ground, and hastened toward the window of the blue room.

To his surprise and momentary annoyance, he found that there was no vestige of a sill to the window.

The diamond-paned leaden casement was flush with the outer wall.

After a brief consideration, Jack made up his mind.

"I'll risk it," he said. "I have been successful so far, and surely I shall not fail now."

In another instant he had sprang harlequin-like clean through the window, carrying before him glass, frame, and all.

As he dashed like a stone from a catapult into the room his head struck against a human form, and when our hero had recovered his lost balance he discovered in the full light of the moon Morgan lying prone on the floor.

"Rise, and give me all the papers you have, or stay—you can lay where you are. I can see your valise there, and there, I know, you carry your private journal, and so on. I'll take it, and save you the trouble of rising. Lay where you are, and don't attempt to leave this house for three hours, or fear the hangman, for yours is a hanging offence."

Without another word Jack flung the valise out of the window, and speedily followed it himself.

As Jack left the room Morgan rose from the floor, and, trembling with fear, said, "Fear the hangman! Fear the hangman, indeed! I fear nothing but this cursed Spring-Heeled Jack, who seems to haunt every moment of my life. I'll end it at once."

And end it he did, for half-an-hour later the dead body of Alfred Morgan was swinging from a hook in a rafter above his bed.

He had cheated the hangman, but he had hanged himself.

Jack did not reach the Bridge House until late the next night, when all was quiet in the hotel.

He had no difficulty in effecting an entrance into the bedroom, but he found he could not carry the valise up with him, so he secreted it in an outhouse.

He rapidly made Ned acquainted with the events which had occurred, and wound up by saying, "And I really believe that the valise contains the proofs of my cousin's and his accomplice's villainy."

And so it proved in the morning, when Ned, who had risen very early, had contrived to smuggle the bag in unseen.

There lay every link in the chain of fraud, including a paper signed by the baronet and witnessed by two of the hall servants, stating that he was well aware that Jack was legitimate and the rightful heir to the Dacre baronetcy and estates.

"I must see Sir Charles Grahame about this," said Jack.

"He has enquired for you several times during your absence, Sir John," replied the faithful fellow.

A glow of pride passed over Jack's face as he stretched forth his hand to Ned.

"Thanks, old fellow; it is only fitting that you, who have stuck to me in adversity, should be the first to congratulate me in my prosperity. Go and ask the general if he can favor me with an interview."

Ned immediately obeyed, and a quarter of an hour later our hero was closeted with Sir Charles Grahame. Little more remains to be told.

The general was delighted when he found that the man who had twice saved his daughter's life, first in the guise of Jack Turnbull, and secondly in that of Spring-Heeled Jack, should turn out to be no less a personage than Sir John Dacre, of Dacre Hall, Surrey.

In answer to an inquiry made by Jack, Sir Charles informed our hero that Lady Graham had consented, to avoid scandal, to become the inmate of a private lunatic asylum for not less than two years; if she behaved herself during that time Sir Charles intended to take steps for her liberation, and to provide her with an income which would enable her to live in comparative obscurity abroad.

Jack and the general ordered a chaise, and started at once for Dacre Hall, armed with Mr. Morgan's documents.

The task before them was an easier one than they had anticipated. Michael Dacre had been so shocked by the suicide of Morgan that he at once caved in, and agreed to quit the country, Jack, of course, having no wish to prosecute any one of his own kith and kin, no matter how treacherous his conduct might have been.

In due course, as our readers must have guessed, Jack and Lucy were married. Ned was appointed to a post of trust at the hall, and as children grew up around them few mortals enjoyed so much earthly happiness as the family and household of Sir John Dacre.

Our story is ended. After Jack's resumption of his title many scamps and ruffians played the part of Spring-Heeled Jack in various garbs in and around London, but the story which we have told of brave Jack Dacre, is the only authentic history of SPRING-HEELED JACK.

APPENDIX 2

Principal Sightings of Spring-Heeled Jack

This is based in part on Mike Dash's exhaustive listings, which can be consulted in his extensive essay in *Fortean Studies,* volume 3, edited by Steve Moore (London: John Brown Publishing, 1996). There may be more that have yet to be uncovered, but these constitute the main appearances of the leaping terror. Excluded are the earlier, unconfirmed sightings that were only mentioned following the first outbreak of attacks. Where possible the dates are those of the actual dates of the attacks; otherwise, of the newspaper reports. Not all are confirmed as real, but I have included them as indicators of the continuing fascination and identification of leaping figures with Spring-Heeled Jack.

1838

January 9, Peckham, Lewisham, and Blackheath. The *Times* reports numerous sightings of a ghostly figure.

January 14, Brentford. Attack on a clergyman's daughter.

January 22, Dulwich. A Miss Dickson attacked.

February 13, Upminster. Attack on a butcher.

February 20, Old Ford. Attack on Jane Alsop.

February 25, Commercial Road. Knocked at door of a Mr. Ashworth.

February 28, Limehouse. Lucy Scales encountered Jack in Green Dragon Alley.

February 28, Vere Street, London. Jack goes into the White Lion Pub.

February 29, Islington. Young women attacked by James Priest copying Jack.

March 17, Kentish Town. Daniel Granville dresses as Jack and is arrested and later discharged with a caution.

March 31, Kilburn. James Painter dresses as Jack and is fined.

April 1, Southend. Woman attacked in cliffs.

[n.d.], Lavender Hill. Mary Stevens attacked.

[n.d.], Clapham High Street. Elderly lady sees leaping figure.

1839

[n.d.], Hounslow. Schoolboys find footprints attributed to Spring-Heeled Jack.

1845

November 12, Jacobs Island, London. Murder of Maria Davies reported by Peter Haining but almost certainly false.

1847

January–April, Teignmouth. Louisa Herd attacked. Edward Finch convicted.

1872

October–November, Peckham. Various sightings of a ghost.

December. Copycat attacks in Brixton, Peckham, and Islington.

1873

April–May, Sheffield. Various appearances of the "Park Ghost."

1877

March–April, Aldershot. Jack attacks the army barracks.

September, Aldershot. Jack appears again.

October, Newport, Lincoln. Sightings of Jack including the Newport Arch.

1879

Winter, Colchester. Jack attacks guards; a man named Alfrey is suspected.

1904

September, Everton. Jack appears several times in William Henry Street.

1940–1945

[n.d.], Prague. Various sightings of the Spring Man.

1945

October–December, Provincetown, Cape Cod, Massachusetts. The phantom sighted leaping over buildings.

1951

July, Baltimore, Maryland. The phantom sighted leaping at O'Donnell Heights.

1953

June 18, Houston, Texas. Houston bat-man sighted.

1986

Summer, South Herefordshire. Traveling salesman is buzzed by Jack.

2012

February 14. Family sees leaping man on their way home to Ewell near Epsom.

Notes

CHAPTER 1.
BIRTH OF A LEGEND

1. *Morning Chronicle,* January 10, 1838.
2. Ibid.
3. *Times* (London), January 11, 1838.
4. *Observer,* January 14, 1838.
5. *Sun,* January 20, 1838.
6. *Morning Herald,* February 23, 1838.
7. Ibid.
8. *Chelmsford Chronicle,* February 27, 1838.
9. *Morning Chronicle,* February 28, 1838.
10. Ibid.
11. Ibid.
12. *Times* (London), March 2, 1838.
13. *Times* (London), March 3, 1838.
14. Ibid.
15. Ibid.
16. Ibid.
17. Ibid.
18. Ibid.
19. Ibid.
20. Ibid.
21. Ibid.

CHAPTER 2. THE LEGEND SPREADS

1. *Morning Post,* March 7, 1838.
2. Ibid.
3. Ibid.
4. Ibid.
5. Ibid.
6. Ibid.
7. *Morning Post,* March 13, 1838.
8. *Examiner,* "Police—Marylebone," March 25, 1838.
9. Ibid.
10. Villiers (Isobel Mary Thorne), *Stand and Deliver,* 1928.
11. Ibid., 241–42.
12. Ibid., 243.
13. Ibid.
14. Ibid.
15. Ibid.
16. Ibid., 247–48.
17. Ibid.
18. Ibid.
19. Ibid.
20. Ibid.
21. Dash, *Fortean Times,* 26.
22. Haining, *The Legend and Bizarre Crimes of Spring-Heeled Jack,* 1997.
23. Ibid., 7–9.
24. Dickens, *Oliver Twist.*
25. Haining, *The Legend and Bizarre Crimes of Spring-Heeled Jack,* 84.
26. Ibid.
27. Ibid.
28. Ibid., 44–45.
29. *Hampshire Advertiser,* March, 10, 1838.
30. Quoted by Bell in *Penny Satirist,* March 10, 1838, 82.

CHAPTER 3. JACK TAKES A HOLIDAY

1. *County Herald and Weekly Advertiser,* April 24, 1838.
2. *Illustrated London News,* September 27, 1845.

3. Ibid.

4. *Woolmer's Exeter and Plymouth Gazette,* March 27, 1847.

5. Ibid., March 27, 1847.

6. Ibid.

7. *Woolmer's Exeter and Plymouth Gazette,* April 3, 1847.

8. Session case brought before the magistrates at Bicester, Oxfordshire, October 4, 1861.

9. *Times* (London), May 15, 1877.

10. Dash, *Fortean Times.*

11. *Notes and Queries,* June 2, 1907.

CHAPTER 4. THE URBAN GHOST

1. *Camberwell and Peckham Times,* November 3, 1872.

2. Card from "the Ghost" himself.

3. Response from the editor.

4. Letter from H. E.

5. Ibid.

6. Quoted in della Porta, *Natural Magick,* 2003.

7. *Camberwell and Peckham Times,* November 9, 1872.

8. Ibid.

9. *News of the World,* November 17, 1872.

10. *Camberwell and Peckham Times,* November 23, 1872.

11. Letter from Mr. F. S.

12. Letter from "well known resident."

13. *Camberwell and Peckham Times,* November 30, 1872.

14. Ibid.

15. Ibid.

16. Ibid.

17. Ibid.

18. Ibid.

19. Ibid.

20. Ibid.

21. Ibid.

22. *Sheffield Times,* May 31, 1873.

23. "Observer," *Rotherham and Masbrough Advertiser,* November 8, 1873.

24. Henry Tatton, unpublished manuscript, 1936.

25. Bishop Nicholas Ridley, in Foxe, *The Actes and Monuments,* 1563.
26. Anonymous, *The Infernal Wanderer, or The Devil Ranging upon Earth,* 1702.

CHAPTER 5.
ROOTS IN MYTH AND FOLKLORE

1. Mayhew, *London Labour and the London Poor,* 1861.
2. Jack Valentine, www.information-britain.co.uk/. (Accessed 5-25-16.)
3. "Jack is Backm," www.norwichlanes.co.uk. (Accessed 5-25-16.)
4. Limbird, ed., "Manners and Customs," in *The Mirror of Literature, Amusement, and Instruction,* 280.
5. Raine, *Fairwell Happy Fields,* 1973, 67.

CHAPTER 6. WHO WAS JACK?

1. Neville, *Sporting Days and Sporting Ways,* 1910.
2. Ibid.
3. Ibid.
4. Ibid.
5. Ibid.
6. *Times,* April 6, 1837.
7. Police report.
8. Doctor's report filed with the British Consul.
9. *Bergen Morgenavisen,* quoted in: Haining, *The Legend and Bizarre Crimes of Spring-Heeled Jack.*
10. *London Gazette,* October 11, 1837.
11. Haining, *The Legend and Bizarre Crimes of Spring-Heeled Jack.*
12. Ibid.
13. Ibid.

CHAPTER 7. JACK'S BACK

1. Kuhn, to Ulrich Magin, *Fortean Times.*
2. Dyall, "Spring-Heeled Jack—The Leaping Terror," *Everybody's Magazine,* 1954.
3. Ibid.
4. Ibid.

5. Ibid.
6. Vyner, "The Mystery of Spring-Heeled Jack," *Flying Saucer Review,* 1961.
7. Ibid.
8. Ibid.
9. Ibid.
10. Sandell, *Flying Saucer Review,* 1971.
11. *Baltimore Sun,* July 25, 1951.
12. *Baltimore News-Post,* July 27, 1951.
13. Vyner, "The Mystery of Spring-Heeled Jack," *Flying Saucer Review,* 1961.
14. *Haunted Scotland,* July 1996.
15. Ibid.
16. Ibid.
17. Greenwood, cited in Haining, *The Legend and Bizarre Crimes of Spring-Heeled Jack.*
18. Ibid.
19. Greenwood, "A Short Way to Newgate," 1854.
20. Pullman, *Spring-Heeled Jack, a Story of Bravery and Evil,* 1989.
21. Matthews, Matthews, and Kinghan, *The Steampunk Tarot: Wisdom from the Gods of the Machine.*

Bibliography

SOURCE TEXTS

Anonymous. *The Apprehension and Examination of Spring-Heel'd Jack, who has appeared as a Ghost, Demon, Bear Baboon etc.* London: N.p., ca. 1838.

Anonymous. *Authentic Particulars of the Awful Appearance of Spring-Heeled Jack.* London: N.p., ca. 1838.

Anonymous. *Spring-Heeled Jack—The Terror of London.* London: Newsagents, 1867.

Anonymous. *The Surprising Exploits of Spring-Heeled Jack in the Vicinity of London.* London: N.p., ca. 1838.

Dash, Mike. "Spring-Heeled Jack: To Victorian Bugaboo from Suburban Ghost." In *Fortean Studies.* Vol 3. Edited by Steve Moore. London: John Brown, 1996, 7–125.

Limbird, John, ed. "Manners and Customs." In *The Mirror of Literature, Amusement, and Instruction*, Vol. 29. (London: J. Limbird, 1837), 280.

Monstery, Thomas Hoyer. "Spring-Heel Jack; or, The Masked Mystery of the Tower." *Beadle's New York Dime Library*, no. 332 (March 4, 1885).

STUDIES

Ackroyd, Peter. *London: The Biography.* London: Albion, 2000.

Asma, Stephen T. *On Monsters: An Unnatural History of Our Worst Fears.* New York: Oxford University Press, 2009.

Barker, Gray. *The Silver Bridge*. Clarksburg, W.Va.: Saucerian Books, 1970. Reprinted as *The Silver Bridge: The Classic Mothman Tale*. North Charleston, N.C.: BookSurge Publishing, 2008.

Bell, Karl. *The Legend of Spring-Heeled Jack: Victorian Urban Folklore and Popular Cultures*. Woodbridge, UK: Boydell Press, 2011.

Brunvand, Jan Harold. *The Vanishing Hitchhiker: American Urban Legends and Their Meanings*. New York: W. W. Norton, 1983.

Chess, Shira, and Eric Newsom. *Folklore, Horror Stories, and the Slender Man: The Development of an Internet Mythology*. New York: Palgrave Pivot, 2014.

Clarke, David. "Bogeyman or Spaceman? The Legend of Spring-Heeled Jack." *Paranormal Magazine*, no. 45. (March 2010): 20–25.

———. "Unmasking Spring Heeled Jack: A Case Study of a 19th Century Ghost Panic." *Contemporary Legend* 22, no 9. (2006): 28–52.

Clarke, David, and Andy Roberts. *Flying Saucerers: A Social History of UFOlogy*. Avebury, UK: Alternative Albion, 2007.

Dyall, Valentine. "Spring Heeled Jack—the Leaping Terror." *Everybody's Magazine*. February 20, 1954, 12–13.

Fitzgerald, David. "Robin Goodfellow and Tom Thumb." *Time*, March, 1885, 304–14.

Golicz, Roman. *Spring-Heeled Jack: A Victorian Visitation at Aldershot*. Farnham, UK: Don Namor Press, 2006.

Goss, Patrick. *UFOS at Close Sight*. http://ufologie.patrickgross.org/ce3/1877-04-uk-aldershot.htm. (Accessed 5-25-16.)

Green, Thomas. "Jack & Arthur: An Introduction to Jack the Giant-Killer." 2012. www.arthuriana.co.uk/arthuriad/Arthuriad_VolOne.pdf. (Accessed 5-25-16.)

Greenwood, James. *The Wilds of London*. London: Chatto and Windus, 1874.

Haining, Peter. *The Legend and Bizarre Crimes of Spring Heeled Jack*. London: Frederick Muller, 1977.

Hamilton, Lord Ernest. *Forty Years On*. London: George H. Doran, 1922.

Kuhn, Dietrich. *Sagen und Legenden aus Sachsenn*. Wartburg, Germany: Verlag GmbH, 1994 .

Keel, John A. *The Mothman Prophecies*. London: Hodder & Stoughton, 2002.

Kennedy, Douglas. *England's Dances*. London: G. Bell & Sons, 1950.

Leslie, Desmond, and George Adamski. *Flying Saucers Have Landed*. London: Werner Laurie, 1953.

Matthews, John. *Robin Hood, Green Lord of the Wildwood.* Glastonbury, UK: Gothic Image, 2000.

Matthews, John, Caitlín Matthews, and Wil Kinghan. *The Steampunk Tarot: Wisdom from the Gods of the Machine.* North Clarendon, Vt.: Tuttle, 2012.

McDonald, Callum, and Jan Kaplan. *Prague in the Shadow of the Swastika: A History of the German Occupation 1939–1945.* London: Quartet Books, 1995.

O'Donnell, Elliot. *Haunted Britain.* London: Rider, 1948.

Porta, John Baptist. *Natural Magick.* Sioux Falls, S.D.: NuVision, 2003.

Raine, Kathleen. *Farewell Happy Fields.* London: Hamish Hamilton, 1983.

Sandell, Roger. "Spring Heel Jack: Victorian Humanoid?" *Flying Saucer Review* 17, no. 1 (1971): 22–24.

Simpson, Jacqueline. "Research Note: Spring-Heeled Jack." *Foaftale News,* no. 48 (January 2001).

Simpson, Jacqueline, and Steve Roud. *Oxford Dictionary of English Folklore.* Oxford, UK: Oxford University Press, 2000.

Smith, Alan. "Jack Valentine in Norfolk." *Folk Lore Society News,* no. 45 (November 2004): 8.

Vallee, Jacques. *Passport to Magonia: From Folklore to Flying Saucers.* London: Neville Spearman, 1970.

Villiers, Elizabeth. *Stand and Deliver.* London: Stanly Paul, 1928.

Vyner, J. "The Mystery of Springheel Jack." *Flying Saucer Review* 7, no. 3 (1961): 3.

AUDIO DRAMAS

Bowman, Jack, and Robert Valentine. *The Strange Affair of Springheel'd Jack,* series 1–3.

www.wirelesstheatrecompany.co.uk/product-category/the-springheel-saga/. (Accessed 5-25-16.)

Index

Tanaka, Wayne, 228
Terror of London, The. See Spring-Heeled Jack—The Terror of London
Trnka, Jiri, 189
Turpin, Dick, 170
twentieth- and twenty-first century appearances, 188–242
  in Baltimore (1951), 204–9
  in Cape Cod (1938–1945), 204
  in comics, 227–30, plate 15
  earliest U.S. appearance (1880), 203
  in fiction, 230–31
  in films, 226–27
  ghost with weakness for ladies, 196–97
  man in white (September 1926), 197–202
  Monkey Man, 211–12
  Mothman, 209–11, plate 13
  Pérák, 188–89
  principal sightings, 324
  Saxony jumping men, 189–90
  Slender Man, 212–16
  in *The Springheel Saga* (audio play), 232–42, plate 14
  UFO connections, 190–97

UFO connection
  Dyall's account and, 190–92
  Great Moon Hoax of 1835, 194–96
  Jack as a spaceman, plate 12
  Sandell on, 194
  Vyner's speculation about, 192–94, 208–9
Uldenhoft, Anne, 176

United States appearances
  Baltimore Phantom (1951), 204–9
  Cape Cod (1938–1945), 204
  earliest, in Kentucky (1880), 203
  Mothman, 209–11, plate 13
  Slender Man, 212–16

Valentine, Robert, 232
Vanishing Hitchhiker, The, 210–11
Villiers, A. C. H., 244
Villiers, Elizabeth
  Mary Stephens "leaping menace" story by, 51–53
  Stand and Deliver by, 50
Vyner, John, 192–94, 208–9, 229

Walker, Hilda, 209
Walker, Mrs., 201
Waterford, Marquis of. *See* Marquis of Waterford
Welby, Alfred C. E., 88
Wellesley, Arthur, 62
Wellington, Duke of, 62
Westbury Street prowler, 131–33
white bull, 167–68
Whitechapel Murderer, 1, 2
Williams, Rhynwick, 185–87
Wills, W. G., 226
Winch, Mr., 201–2
women
  ghost with weakness for, 196–97
  stereotypical view of, 64–66

Yarmouth bull-man, 72–73

Zenaty, George, 188

BOOKS OF RELATED INTEREST

Taliesin
The Last Celtic Shaman
by John Matthews
with Caitlín Matthews

Walkers Between the Worlds
The Western Mysteries from Shaman to Magus
by Caitlín Matthews and John Matthews

The Secret History of Vampires
Their Multiple Forms and Hidden Purposes
by Claude Lecouteux

Witches, Werewolves, and Fairies
Shapeshifters and Astral Doubles in the Middle Ages
by Claude Lecouteux

The Lost Tomb of King Arthur
The Search for Camelot and the Isle of Avalon
by Graham Phillips

**Encyclopedia of Norse and Germanic Folklore,
Mythology, and Magic**
by Claude Lecouteux

Monsters
A Bestiary of Devils, Demons, Vampires, Werewolves,
and Other Magical Creatures
by Christopher Dell

Barbarian Rites
The Spiritual World of the Vikings and the Germanic Tribes
by Hans-Peter Hasenfratz, Ph.D.

INNER TRADITIONS • BEAR & COMPANY
P.O. Box 388
Rochester, VT 05767
1-800-246-8648
www.InnerTraditions.com

Or contact your local bookseller